THE DISINHERITED MIND

THE

DISINHERITED MIND

ESSAYS IN MODERN GERMAN
LITERATURE AND THOUGHT

ERICH HELLER

Jede dumpfe Umkehr der Welt hat solche Enterbte,
denen das Frühere nicht und noch nicht das Nächste gehört.

RILKE

Philadelphia
DUFOUR AND SAIFER
1952

Copyright
1952

Printed in Great Britain for DUFOUR & SAIFER, Philadelphia, U.S.A.
by METCALFE & COMPANY, LIMITED in the City of Cambridge.

To
R. B. H.

v

PREFACE

ANYONE engaged in the study, teaching and criticism of literature as a University discipline is likely to become at some time or other aware of one fundamental problem raised by his own pursuits, or a difficulty that is all his own and is not, or at least not to the same extent, shared by his colleagues in other subjects. For however sincerely he may struggle against bias and prejudice in his own approach and appreciation, his work will still be very intimately related to his experiences in wider fields. It is true that his devotion to literature is capable of purging his affections of too narrowly subjective and emotional elements; yet his comprehension will remain largely determined by his own character, his spontaneous sympathies or antipathies, the happiness he has enjoyed or the disasters that have befallen him. And this, he will see, is no shortcoming of his own discipline, to be conquered in scientific campaigns or disguised by scientific masquerades, but is in fact its distinctive virtue. For the ultimate concern of his subject is neither facts nor classifications, neither patterns of cause and effect nor technical complexities. Of course, strict honesty in the face of facts and a certain mastery in dealing with their manifold interconnections are the indispensable qualifications of the literary scholar. In the end, however, he is concerned with the communication of a sense of quality rather than measurable quantity, and of meaning rather than explanation.

Thus he would be ill-advised to concentrate exclusively on those aspects of his discipline which allow the calm neutrality of what is indisputably factual and 'objective'. His business is, I think, not the avoidance of subjectivity, but its purification; not the shunning of what is disputable, but the cleansing and deepening of the dispute. As a teacher he is involved in a task which would appear impossible by the standards of the scientific laboratory: to teach what, strictly speaking, cannot be taught, but only 'caught', like a passion, a vice or a virtue. This 'impossibility' is the inspiration of his work. There are no methods that comprehend his subject; only methods, perhaps, that produce the intellectual pressure and temperature in which perception crystallizes into conviction and learning into a sense of value. Goethe tells of a Greek nobleman who was asked about the education of his children. 'Let them be instructed,' he said, 'in that which they will never be able to learn.'

The unifying theme of this book, then, is the sense of values as shown or embodied in the works of some modern German poets, writers and thinkers from Goethe to Kafka. Perhaps it would be more correct to say: the sense of the value of life. For I have stressed what appears to be one of the distinctive symptoms of modern literature and thought: the consciousness of life's increasing depreciation. If Thomas Aquinas saw the link between poets and philosophers in their preoccupation with the marvellous, their modern successors seem united in the reverse; either they try systematically to strengthen, or desperately to ward off, the predominance of the prosaic. I deal with this problem in its most direct form in the essay 'Rilke and Nietzsche' (particularly in the discourses on the relation between thought, belief and poetry) and in the second section of the essay 'The World of Franz Kafka'.

I do not wish to suggest that the selections of this book can be justified on any other but personal grounds. Yet its choices are, I believe, representative enough to avoid the charge of arbitrariness. Arbitrary are merely its omissions. For I could have included, without losing sight of the central theme, many more names. In fact, I can hardly think of one major writer or thinker within this period of German literature, whose works would not reflect the situation of mind and spirit which I have tried to describe within the limits of my choice. In a way it is even true to say that the silent centre of this book is Hölderlin; its theme and its hesitant hope are certainly contained in Hölderlin's lines:

Und nun denkt er zu ehren in Ernst die seeligen Götter,
    Wirklich und wahrhaft muss alles verkünden ihr Lob.

Aber wo sind sie? wo blühn die Bekannten, die Kronen des Festes?

Warum zeichnet, wie sonst, die Stirne des Mannes ein Gott nicht,
    Drückt den Stempel, wie sonst, nicht dem Getroffenen auf?
Oder er kam auch selbst und nahm des Menschen Gestalt an
    Und vollendet und schloss tröstend das himmlische Fest.

Aber Freund! wir kommen zu spät. Zwar leben die Götter,
    Aber über dem Haupt droben in anderer Welt.
Endlos wirken sie da und scheinens wenig zu achten,
    Ob wir leben, so sehr schonen die Himmlischen uns.

Denn nicht immer vermag ein schwaches Gefäss sie zu fassen,
  Nur zu Zeiten erträgt göttliche Fülle der Mensch.
Traum von ihnen ist drauf das Leben. Aber das Irrsal
  Hilft, wie Schlummer und stark machet die Noth und die
    Nacht.

                    Indessen dünket mir öfters
  Besser zu schlafen, wie so ohne Genossen zu seyn,
So zu harren und was zu thun indess und zu sagen,
  Weiss ich nicht und wozu Dichter in dürftiger Zeit?

[Now will he strive in earnest to honour the dwellers in Heaven,
  Everything living must utter their praise, in word and in deed.

Where, though, where are they, the famous, those crowns of the
    banquet?

Why does a god no more inscribe the brow of a mortal,
  Setting his seal, as of old, on the victim chosen above?
Or he would come himself, assuming the shape of a mortal,
  Thus with solace and peace to crown the celestial feast.

But we, my friend, are too late. The gods, it is true, are living,
  Yet far above ourselves, away in a different world.
There they are endlessly active and seem but little regardful
  Whether we live or no, such is their tender concern,
Knowing that fragile vessels like us cannot always contain them,
  Only at times can man endure the abundance of gods.
Life thereafter is but to dream of them. Yet our wanderings
  Help, like sleep, and anguish and night give strength.

                    Meanwhile, it seems to me often
  Better to slumber than live without companions, like this,
So to linger, and know not what to begin or to utter,
  Or, in such spiritless times, why to be poet at all?]

ACKNOWLEDGMENTS

My thanks for permission to reprint previously published material are due to *The Cambridge Journal*, *The Listener* and *The Times Literary Supplement*. *The Hogarth Press* and Messrs. *Secker & Warburg Ltd.* have kindly allowed me to quote from English translations published by them; the former, from Rilke's *Duino Elegies*, translated by J. B. Leishman and Stephen Spender, from Rilke's *Sonnets to Orpheus* and Hölderlin's *Selected Poems*, both translated by J. B. Leishman; the latter, from Willa and Edwin Muir's renderings of Franz Kafka's *The Castle* and *The Great Wall of China*. In all these cases the use of mere fragments of translations has made it necessary for me to introduce occasional changes in order to get the precise emphasis required by my context.

The number of friends, colleagues and pupils who, through conversations, questions and criticisms, have helped me in writing this book is too large for individual acknowledgments. They will easily recognize their share and, I hope, be sure of my gratitude. The debt, however, acknowledged by the dedication is truly immeasurable.

The essay 'Rilke and Nietzsche' owes much to Professor Eudo C. Mason. Indeed, it was his book *Der Zopf des Münchhausen* and the ensuing correspondence with its author that have given the essay its direction. The knowledge that my conclusions would be different from his has not deterred this pre-eminent scholar and interpreter of Rilke from generously supplying me with much information and material. Even if he cannot accept all I have done with it, I would like him to accept the expression of my profound gratitude and of my respect for his convictions, which is unimpaired by disagreement.

Finally, I would like to thank my friends and colleagues, E. K. Bennett, of Gonville and Caius College, Cambridge, and R. J. Taylor, of University College, Swansea, for the great help they have given me at the proof-reading stage.

E. H.

June, 1952

For the convenience of the reader I have separated footnotes
(marked by asterisks) which have some bearing on the text from
mere references to sources of quotations (marked by numbers).
The latter, much more frequent than the first, are relegated to the
Appendix and need not interrupt the reader's attention.

CONTENTS

I

GOETHE AND THE IDEA OF SCIENTIFIC TRUTH

GOETHE AND THE IDEA OF SCIENTIFIC TRUTH

I

'1794—here at last was a year which I felt was going to compensate me by some diverting activities, some inspiration, some pleasure, for much that I had missed and suffered in the preceding years; and goodness knows I was badly in need of it.' This is how Goethe, in his *Annals*, begins his report on the year 1794. The modern reader can hardly fail to respond to Goethe's catalogue of grievances: the agitated restlessness of Europe; rumours of the approach of the enemy and of fussy aunts evacuated from more directly disturbed areas; the hasty selling of houses, the loss of friends through political partisanship; the clandestine distribution of French revolutionary manifestoes—'they even found their way to me,' Goethe exclaims, 'and this through people whom one would never have suspected'; and above all the rule of Robespierre, 'the terrors of which had so deprived the world of any sense of joy that nobody felt like rejoicing even at the downfall of the tyrant'. And in addition, the distressing chaos, the obstreperous hollowness of the German literary scene! Goethe had returned from Italy with that vision of serenity and equipoise with which he hoped he would conquer the national imagination which he had previously done so much to fill with unruly enthusiasm for suicidal lovers and rebellious knights with fists of iron. But, alas, while the Master recuperated in the sun of the South, the infection, the cold and the fever, were spread by his disciples in the unregenerate nordic climate. There was, for instance, that man Schiller, this 'vigorous but immature talent', as Goethe calls him, whose drama *Die Räuber* 'disgusted me in the extreme', 'because he poured out over the country, in a gushing, irresistible torrent, precisely those moral and theatrical paradoxes which I had striven to eradicate from my own work'. And there were more such offenders: Heinse, for instance, whose *Ardinghello* was hateful to Goethe because its author used his art for the purpose of 'giving affected glamour to crass sensuality and abstruse modes of thought'. 'I was terrified,' Goethe continues, 'by the hubbub they caused in the country, and by the applause with which the monstrous creations of their fancy were received by wild undergraduates and genteel ladies of the court alike.' 'Imagine the state I was in! I had

B   3

hoped to cultivate and to communicate the purest ideas; and now I found myself squeezed tight between Ardinghello and Franz Moor.' 'It seemed as though all my labours would be lost, all the things towards which, and all the ways in which, I had educated myself would be abolished and frustrated.' Goethe's intense dissatisfaction, his conviction of futility, culminates in the wish to abandon 'the contemplation of the arts and the practice of poetry altogether'— and we know that this was more than the fleeting whim of a disgruntled Olympian—'for there appeared to be no chance whatsoever to compete with those wild productions of disorganized genius'.

Yet Goethe's desolation was caused not merely by the unseemly behaviour of the world around him; there was an inner uncertainty too—an uncertainty which, in one form or another, was to provide the rest of his life with a deep dilemma, a source of inspiration as well as confusion, now raising his poetry and thought to those heights to which only the force of tension could carry them, now again trapping his genius in a tangle of insoluble contradictions. His doubts about the worth-whileness, indeed the possibility, of continuing his work as a poet will recur, and the blame will not always fall on the Robespierres of this world and other poets' successful *Robbers*. Now, in the year 1794, the dilemma took this form: 'The conflict which my scientific efforts had brought into my life was as yet by no means resolved; for my dealings with nature began to make claims on *all* my inner faculties'.

Thus, for the time being, Goethe was divided within himself, and out of harmony with nature; for his goddess Nature did not take the slightest notice of the afflictions of this year: 'The crops of the fields prospered magnificently, everything ripened a month too early, the fruit of the trees grew to perfection; apricots and peaches, melons and even chestnuts offered themselves in choice profusion, and also among the years of exquisite vintage 1794 has its place'.

The exquisite vintage is reassuring; Goethe's anger at Schiller's success in the theatre had nothing to do with sour grapes; moreover, it seems certain that this year, in which nature was in so exuberant a mood, could not possibly end for Goethe on a note of unrelieved gloom. But it is a coincidence as neatly ironical as the sweetest apricots ripening in that summer of acrimonious discontent, that the light fell into Goethe's darkness through the arrival in his life of the author of the repulsive *Robbers*: Friedrich Schiller. This is what

Goethe's diary says: 'In the midst of all these oppressions and conflicts the suddenly developing friendship with Schiller gave more to me than I could have dared hope for; it ranks among the most precious gifts of fortune which my later years held in store for me'. The irony of fate is indeed profound, and deeper still than appears at first glance. For, as we have seen, Goethe's depression was partly due to his fear that his absorbing interest in scientific studies was feeding on his poetic resources; and now it is in a meeting of a society of natural scientists that the friendship begins with the man to whom four years later he was to express his gratitude for having cured the paralysis of his poetic genius. 'And this happy occasion came about through my work concerning the Metamorphosis of Plants.' After that meeting—it took place in Jena and some scientist lectured— Goethe and Schiller, leaving the room, happened to reach the door at the same time. 'A conversation ensued; he, Schiller, appeared to have taken an interest in the lecture, and remarked, very intelligently, perspicaciously and to me most agreeably, that such a dissecting manner of dealing with nature could not possibly attract the layman. I replied that this manner may be uncanny even to the initiates, and that perhaps there was still the possibility of another method, one which would not tackle nature by merely dissecting and particularizing, but show her at work and alive, *manifesting herself in her wholeness in every single part of her being*. He said he would like to learn more about this, though he did not conceal his doubts. He would not admit that all this emerged, as I insisted, *from experience itself.*'

In no time at all, it seems, their conversation had reached the crucial point. This is a dramatic climax in the history of German thought and letters: Goethe and Schiller, whose names will for ever mark the summit of literary achievement to which the genius of their nation, and probably of Europe, could rise in the second half of the eighteenth century, wandering through the streets of Jena, really in contact with each other for the first time. That it had not happened before—in spite of some previous chance meetings—was the outcome of strategy on the part of Goethe who was determined to avoid the man from whom he was separated 'by more than the earth's diameter', and whom he found guilty not only of theatrical excess, but also of philosophical wrongheadedness. Schiller's essay *Anmut und Würde* (The Graceful and the Exalted) had displeased him by its Kantian abstractness, but above all by its antagonism to Nature in which Goethe, significantly enough, saw hostility towards himself; 'and if it was *not* aimed at me, so much the worse !' But there they go, engrossed in what seems merely a discussion about the growth of vegetables, but is, in fact, about the human mind in its search after truth.

They arrive at Schiller's house and, still talking, Goethe enters. This is Goethe's account of the occasion: 'I explained to him with great vivacity the Metamorphosis of Plants and, with a few characteristic strokes of the pen, conjured up before his eyes a symbolical plant.· He listened, and looked at it all with great interest and intelligence; but when I had ended, he shook his head saying: This has nothing to do with *experience*, it is an *idea*. I raised my eye-brows, somewhat annoyed. For he had put his finger on precisely the point which separated us. His argument from *Anmut und Würde* came to my mind; the old anger began to stir, but I constrained myself and replied: Well, so much the better; it means that I have ideas without knowing it, and can even *see them with my eyes*.' They carried on their discussion, with great polemical obstinacy on each side. Goethe reports that some of Schiller's sentences made him 'quite unhappy'; for instance, the following: 'How can one ever equate experience with ideas? For an idea is characterized precisely by the fact that experience can never be fully congruous to it.' And Goethe, in his account of the discussion, reflects that 'if he takes for an idea what to me is experience, then there must, after all, prevail some mediation, some relationship between the two'.[1]

At this point Goethe's account of his first conversation with Schiller breaks off. Owing to his new friendship, this year of troubles and tribulations ends, as he says, with a foretaste of spring. And, indeed, there will be flowers and colours; but also a theory of colours and much speculation about the objects of nature. In the period to come Goethe was to write, if not his most popular, yet his profoundest poetry. The danger of inspiration drying up in later years, the fate of Wordsworth, is averted. The dilemma of which we have heard appears to be solved. There will be poetry *and* science—a science, it is true, radically at odds with the scientific temper of the age; a science doubtful and often unambiguously wrong in its results, but of immense importance for our understanding of the intellectual and spiritual situation of the age, and of the nature of poetic and scientific truth. Goethe's science has contributed nothing substantial to the scientific progress between his time and ours, and nothing whatsoever to the advancement of techniques for the mastery and exploitation of nature; but he has, by his opposition to contemporary science, laid bare in his time, with remarkable precision, the very roots of that crisis and revolution in scientific method in which the twentieth-century scientist finds himself involved. In the history of science from Newton to Einstein, Goethe, the scientist, plays a Cinderella part, showing up the success and splendour of his rich relations, but also the potential *hubris* inherent in their pursuits. There may come a day when this Cinderella story will find the conclusion proper to such tales—but perhaps not before the new ecclesia of technology has had its consummate triumph by bringing to their explosive fusion the iciest mathematical abstractions and the hot appetite for power.

We had left the first disputation between Goethe and Schiller where Goethe himself chose to leave it. Perhaps it was a wise break, for the next step would lead still deeper into the region of metaphysics, an area which is strictly out of bounds for the brave soldiers of the positivist age, and full of the unspeakable dreads and bogies which inhabit the nursery-tales told to the children of science. But it is, at the same time, the very workshop where the invisible mould is cast and re-cast, from which all our organized intellectual activities take their shape. It may be rewarding to ignore the warnings and enter it for a while. First, however, it is advisable to look at that symbolical plant which Goethe had sketched out for Schiller, and which, in spite of Goethe's 'characteristic strokes of the pen', remained an 'idea' for that disciple of Immanuel Kant, even in the face of Goethe's assurance that he could see it with his eyes.

2

Palermo, April 17th, 1787—seven years before Goethe's first meeting with Schiller. This is what the chronicle of the *Italian Journey* says under that date:

'It is a real disaster if a man is tempted by a host of conflicting demons. This morning I went to the Public Gardens, calmly and firmly determined to carry on with my poetic designs; yet in no time another ghost which had secretly pursued me all these days, had caught hold of me. The many plants which elsewhere I used to see only in pots, and mostly under glass, grow here cheerfully under the open sky, and, living as they are really meant to live, reveal themselves to us with greater clarity. Confronted with so many new shapes, I was once more overcome by my old whimsical fascination: might I not discover among this crowd the *Urpflanze* (that original plant from which all others are derived)? After all, it must exist; how could I otherwise know that this shape *and* that are both plants if they were not all organized according to one principle?' And even then the cry of the distracted poet: 'My poetic intention had come to nothing. . . . Why are we modern people so open to distraction, why so easily provoked into pursuits which are bound to lead nowhere?'[2] Yet this particular diversion did seem to lead somewhere. Exactly a month later, on May 17th, 1787, he wrote from Naples to Herder: 'And then I must confide to you that I am very close to discovering the secret of the creation and organization of plants. Under this sky one is able to make the most beautiful observations. The crucial point from which everything else must needs spring, I have already established beyond doubt; the rest too I can see in outline; only a few points have still to be ascertained. The *Urpflanze* is to be the strangest creature in the world; Nature herself shall be jealous of it. After this model it will be possible to *invent* plants *ad infinitum*, which will all be consistent, that is, they *could* exist even if they have no actual existence; they would not be mere picturesque or poetic shadows or dreams, but would possess an *inner truth and necessity. And the same law will be applicable to everything alive.*'[3]

These enthusiastic outbursts seem to bode ill for the scientific work that was to be based on the discovery made in Italy. Yet, when three years later, in 1790, Goethe's *Metamorphosis of Plants* appeared, it was as quiet in tone, as systematic in approach, as painstaking in minute observation, as any classical scientific composition. Its central idea is that all the single parts which constitute a plant are derived from one original formation, and that all varieties of plants, beginning with those of the simplest organization and ascending to the most complex structures, are the result of a gradual metamorphosis or transformation, brought about by the *responsiveness* of the organism to the restrictions put upon it, or the advantages offered to it by the surrounding world, the soil, the weather, the insects. This responsiveness, however, is not a mere giving-in to external influences, it is rather like a creative conversation between within and without, a kind of dialectical education through which the individual form becomes in actuality what from the very beginning it had been potentially. For what is within and what is without are for Goethe mere poles of one and the same thing:

> Natur hat weder Kern
> Noch Schale,
> Alles ist sie mit einemmale.[4]

[Nature has neither kernel nor shell; she is everything at once.]

Classifying the various types of metamorphosis as progressive, retrogressive and arbitrary, he starts with investigations into the manifold forms of the cotyledon, the seed-leaf of plants, and seeks to establish its development from shapelessness to shape, from something that looks, as it were, like nothing, to something that distinctly looks like a leaf; he observes a gradual increase of this embryonic leaf in the direction of 'leafishness', an ever clearer articulation, in which the slow emergence of greenness plays its part, until it becomes the full-grown leaf of the plant. It is this very leaf which in its turn is modified and diversified into sepal, petal, pistil and stamen; he shows us how, for instance in the carnation, sepals merge with petals, and how they can be met, in an effort to produce a full corolla, by an identical transformation of filament, anther and stigma. Everything is leaf, is Goethe's final finding, but he is perfectly aware of the *verbal* embarrassments and misunderstandings that such a theory must needs produce; he himself anticipated the objections which Helmholtz was later to raise to this monistic simplification, showing the tautological character of Goethe's theory. Any definition of that unique vegetable organ, Goethe's 'leaf', Helmholtz says, which is to comprehend all other aspects of the plant, would have to end up by stating that it is 'a lateral appendix of the plant axle'—in fact, the same as the flower itself. 'And in order to see that no Goethe was needed.'[5]

Even if one grants that Goethe's theory is untenable, Helmholtz's criticism makes no sense either, but only shows how unbridgeable is the gulf between Goethe's vision and what can be comprehended through the mental operations of modern science. The two never meet, and polemic becomes an intellectual fidgeting-about in strictly separated and closed compartments. It is obvious that, if Goethe says 'leaf', he does not mean a 'lateral appendix of the plant axle'; he means, or rather sees before his eyes, what is the Platonic idea of a plant in its simplest and, in its perfect simplicity, most perfect form. Goethe himself felt over and over again with naïve dismay and painful poignancy how ill-served *his* science was by the established methods of scientific exposition. His inquisitive gaze was focused on a sphere of experience which defies that logical analysis proper to the sphere of modern science, and whose language is fundamentally untranslatable into the logically respectable medium of polite abstractions. This will be still more obvious when we come to Goethe's campaigns in physics and to his Thirty Years' War against Newton.

For the time being we can see Goethe desperately trying to straighten out the vicious circle of tautologies in which, very much later, Helmholtz showed the 'scientific fallacy' of his omnipresent leaf to move. In one of the concluding paragraphs of his *Metamorphosis of Plants* Goethe says: 'It is evident that we would need a general word with which to denote that organism which is capable of transforming itself into such a variety of shapes, and against which we could set up all the phenomena into which it unfolds. For we can say just as well that a stamen is a contracted petal as we can say of the petal that it is a stamen in the state of expansion. . . .'[6] And among his posthumous notes there was found the following jotting: 'Leaf as a definite organism in the empirical sense, as a determinable organism in a higher sense'.[7] Add to this what he says about the *Urpflanze* in the *History of my Botanical Studies*, written during the last years of his life: 'As all these manifold forms of plants can be subsumed under one idea, it became increasingly clear to me that my intuition could be aided by a yet higher means—a possibility which hovered before my mind's eye in the concrete shape of an ideal *Urpflanze*. I followed up all the changing forms as they appeared to me, and at last, at the end of my journey, in Sicily, the *original identity* of all parts of the plant stood revealed before me's[8]—and Goethe's struggle to convey in scientific terms the intuitive nature of his vision emerges in all its pathetic beauty.

His difficulty is, in reverse, the same as that which obstructs the way of the modern physicist when he sets out to translate the findings of his science into the language of concrete images; then we are in no time in a Walt Disney world of colourful absurdities, watching the voids of infinitely finite space heaving and waving with nothing to heave and wave with, but providing in this odd manner the ideal medium for insubstantial substance to travel through with unimpeded speed; or we applaud the surprisingly clever devices by which our universe expands, where nobody would have expected anything to expand into; or we are entertained by the merry-go-rounds of tiny nonentities, performing from time to time the most unpredictable antics, for no obvious reason but just to exercise their own free will.

If one takes into account the underlying incongruity between Goethe's vision and the medium in which modern science operates, and, resulting from it, Goethe's own indecision as to the nature of the *Urpflanze*, now treated as though it were the pragmatical ancestor of all plants, and now again like their Platonic idea, then it is still more surprising to see how fruitful Goethe's biology was. He is one of the first to be fully conscious of the morphological problem in biological studies. It is the unsolved problem and the inspiration of all theories of evolution, concerned, as it is, with the living *form*, its genesis and transformation. 'To recognize living forms *as such*, to see in context their visible and tangible parts, to perceive them as manifestations of *something within*, and thus to master them, to a certain extent, in their *wholeness* through a concrete vision (*Anschauung*),'⁹ this is how he introduces the purpose of his morphological studies. Their pursuit clearly presupposes more than an analysis of sensory preceptions. Goethe's morphology, with its insistence on the relevance of 'something within', was incommensurable with the scientific methods of his age; and Goethe knew it. 'How few,' he exclaims, 'draw their inspiration from what is visible to the mind alone!' 'He who concentrates his powers of understanding entirely on the particular and on those exact observations which can be analysed, tends to regard as a nuisance everything that, emerging from an idea, leads back to an idea.'¹⁰ His biological interest is centred in that *inner* principle which determines the organization of living forms. Indeed, he is aware, as we have seen, of the perpetually modifying forces working from without, but remains fascinated by what he calls 'the self-revealed mystery' (*das offenbare Geheimnis*) which maintains the fundamental unity of the created shape, its idea, through all its variations and modifications.

Thus Goethe's biology has its somewhat puzzling place in as close a neighbourhood to Plato and Aristotle on the one hand, and to Darwin on the other—as through his literary output he divides the camps of critics by his mystifying kinship to both Homer and Stendhal. Hold beside one another the two following biological statements of his: 'What determines the living form, is its innermost nucleus; the external elements modify its appearances'[11] and, at the other end of the scale, 'The more highly organized beings advance a few evolutionary stages, leaving behind their fellow-creatures,'[12] and you see his mind most busily occupied in a splendidly equipped half-way house of which, however, you cannot be quite sure whether it looks like the Academy of ancient Greece or the Cavendish Laboratory at Cambridge. It would be unwise to see the first utterance, with its emphasis on the decisive power of the inner-most nucleus of an organism, as an ingenious anticipation of genes and chromosomes; it is, in fact, far nearer to Aristotle's *entelechy* than to modern genetics. And concerning the second quotation with its Darwinian ring (and it is only one out of many that could be quoted), the interpreters of Goethe's science are by no means united; those who see in Goethe's works nothing but the second coming of the spirit of antiquity suggest that he would have rejected *in toto* Darwin's theory; others for whom Goethe is the first-born of modernity claim him as one of the direct ancestors of the *Origin of Species*. It is more likely that Darwin's work would have attracted as well as repelled Goethe; attracted, because it supplied powerful evidence for Goethe's fondest belief in the fundamental oneness of all that lives, and above all in the uniformity prevailing within each type of living creature. It was with rhapsodic enthusiasm that in 1784 he had reported to Herder his first scientific triumph: the discovery of the *os intermaxillare* (the intermaxillary bone) in the human skull which finally showed the complete structural identity of all vertebrates, including human beings. The assumed absence in the human skeleton of this peculiar bone of contention had, in a generation of scientists afflicted by an unbelievable feebleness of spiritual convictions, been the last shred of proof that they had been created by God according to a very special anatomical design.

And yet, Goethe would also have been repelled by Darwin's theory. He would have seen in it yet another, and very decisive, step along that road which, he believed, would lead to spiritual perdition. No, Goethe was not afraid of the first chapter of Genesis being discredited as a set book by the Honours schools of geology, biology and anthropology; but he was terrified that experimental science in alliance with a mechanistic philosophy of nature, so successful in posing and answering questions about the 'How' of things, so prolific in establishing expected and unexpected *relation-ships between* this, that or the other, might finally abolish in the world all creative interest in *what* this, that or the other *are* and *mean*. For Darwin's theory was bound to feed the body of superstitious beliefs that had grown rampant ever since medieval scholasticism suffered its final defeat at the hands of Francis Bacon.

Willingly or unwillingly, Darwin had to give still greater force to that system of unsystematized, inarticulate metaphysical fallacies which one might term the Creed of the Ontological Invalidity; both in the sense that it dismisses *a priori* as invalid all ontological assertions, i.e. assertions about the nature and meaning of Being (as different from the laws governing the processes, connections and interconnections of the phenomenal world, of all that becomes, develops, evolves), as well as in the sense that it has made an incurable invalid of that faculty of the human intelligence which, grasping their relevance, is capable of responding positively to questions asked about *what* the world is. To such questions the modern intelligence is prone to respond with that mixture of shame, embarrassment, revulsion and arrogance which is the characteristic reaction of impotence to unfortunately unmanageable demands. This invalid has been left ever since in the nursing care of unhappy poets, dreamers or religious eccentrics if he was not satisfied with the treatment he received as an outpatient of the Church. Once man's ability to respond creatively to the ontological mystery had been stunted into something that produces merely an irritated state of mystification, he was left to the spiritual destructiveness of that battle raging within himself: between the conviction of being nothing in the vastness of the universe, and the natural urge which, prompted by the ungrace of self-assertion, persuades him of his all-importance. To be nothing and yet everything—this seeming paradox is the pride and the humility of the creature before a God of infinite power and infinite love; but it is the spiritual death suffered by man in the incessant struggle between arrogance and humiliation, in his exposure to the mighty lovelessness of a chance constellation of energy. It is this gloomy story that is told by modern literature from Nietzsche to Kafka, from Proust to Sartre, from Yeats to T. S. Eliot, from Dostoevsky—to his being banned by a government which has decreed that the ontological mystery is to be abolished.

This state of spiritual affairs accounts for Goethe's strange position in the history of modern science. He had appointed himself a kind of emissary of Being in a territory of the human mind which had given itself up to the alluring mechanics of becoming, progressing,

evolving and revolving. He too realized—and more profoundly
than the world around him—that growth, transformation, metamorphosis, was the element of life. One of his greatest poems,
Selige Sehnsucht, ends with the verse:

> Und solang du das nicht hast,
> Dieses: Stirb und Werde!
> Bist du nur ein trüber Gast
> Auf der dunklen Erde[13]

meaning that we remain but dim shadows on a dark planet as long
as we have not experienced within ourselves, not consummated
through our being, many a death and many a resurrection. 'Die and
rise again!' But this sequence of dying and becoming, of systole and
diastole, of breathing in and breathing out, this polarity of life
within man and outside him, is for Goethe not the rhythm of
a motion prompted by external, and spiritually neutral forces,
directed towards an unknown destination in an as yet empty future,
but is held together at every moving point and at every fleeting
moment by a centre of stillness:

> Und alles Drängen, alles Ringen
> Ist ewige Ruh in Gott dem Herrn.[14]

[And all this struggle, whirl and stir is infinite peace in God.]

That man is related to the animal world (and to all that is alive)
Goethe knew before Darwin; the theory that he has descended (if
anything, *ascended*, Goethe would have said) from some sort of ape-
like creature, would have roused in him a technical interest, the same
that he took in the colours with which the painter painted and the
material in which the sculptor hewed. But beyond that he would,
I think, have regarded it as the kind of knowledge not worth having.
If it were not preposterous to add to the unmanageable quantity of
things that Goethe has said, a few guesses about what he might have
said, it would be very tempting to let one's imagination play on the
possible responses which Darwin would have evoked in Goethe. It
might bring out very clearly one of the most important aspects of
Goethe's idea of truth. And as I have already been unguarded
enough to say that he would have dismissed a great deal of the
knowledge supplied by Darwin, not as incorrect, but as worthless,
let me dwell a little on this apparently outrageous paradox. Paradox

or not, there *is* a sense in which Darwin's theory, though it be perfectly correct, may yet be blatantly *untrue*. There is a very simple mystery behind this assertion, shocking to common sense only because common sense in each epoch consists in an astonishingly complex agglomeration of highly sophisticated half-truths. One such half-truth in which our common sense indulges (and much in our higher education is based on it, including its 'crisis') is the doctrine that any kind of knowledge, as long as it supplies us with correctly ascertained facts, is worth teaching and learning, and that the more such correct facts we accumulate, the nearer we come to Truth. We have become so democratic in our habits of thought that we are convinced that Truth is determined through a plebiscite of facts.

To all this Goethe's idea of Truth, including, to his own bewilderment and ours, 'scientific' truth, is in radical opposition. Nobody familiar with Goethe's writings can possibly overlook the deep-rooted antagonism of his genius to the mental habits predominant in his age; but neither must one ignore his occasional strains, embarrassments and confusions, caused by the simultaneous desire to realize to the full his citizenship in the contemporary world. Very often in Goethe's works—with the exception of his lyrical poetry—there comes a point where the innate tendency of his genius and his mundane wisdom get into each other's way, producing artistic discords. Take, for instance, his *Tasso*: here the emotional defeat of the poet is meant to carry the message that even poetical souls should heed the ways of the world; yet this defeat gives birth to such exquisite poetry, and the executive organs of the victorious world appear at times so unconvincing and even petty, that often, instead of being spontaneously persuaded by the instruction of wisdom, one longs to have a soul as sensitive, as alive and as innocently uncompromising as Tasso's. To be Tasso, the poet, *and* Antonio, the worldling, was Goethe's consciously accepted programme. But how is the poet to remain in the world if the world becomes more unpoetic every day? How is one to keep spiritual communion with the Earth Spirit, and at the same time outphysic Newton? Only if Tasso was as much prepared to learn his lesson from Antonio as the Newtonians in their turn were prepared to listen to the poet. Undoubtedly, the world is made of harder stuff than the poetic imagination, and is altogether too dark a place to suit to perfection a soul asking from beginning to end, and with its very last words, for 'more light'; therefore leave the light alone in its unsynthetic whiteness, and the colours, the offspring of light and darkness.

Behind Goethe's scientific experiments and results, presented in a detached, sober and even laboriously pedantic fashion, one can discern clearly the strategic plan of a man engaged in a campaign for restoring the balance of power between analytical reason and creative imagination, between the 'merely concrete' and the 'idea'. For 'the better part of human nature' will always try 'to bestow upon the concrete the honour of the idea', as he wrote to Schiller (February 10th, 1798), and 'pursue its inalienable right . . . to penetrate to the point where idea and object are as much at one as they can possibly be' (February 14th, 1798). For him all things had an ideal character, not merely within an actual work of art, but also as potential subjects for a work of art. The anxiety that the world, in the course of its increasing analytical disruption, may approach the point where it would become poetically useless and a barren place for the human affections to dwell in, informs Goethe's scientific motives and makes him persist in an activity which, for long periods, to the detriment of his poetic creativeness and to his own dismay, 'absorbs all my inner faculties'. William Blake, unknown to Goethe, but his brother-in-arms against Newton, found things easier. He was a medieval peasant compared with Goethe, who had so big a share in mundane sophistication. For Blake the inventor of modern physics was simply party to a conspiracy of spiritual sin, a mythological ambassador, the second person in the Trinity of Evil, flanked by Bacon and Locke. But then, Blake saw angels in pear-trees, Goethe only 'ideas'. For him it could not be enough to say that modern physics was wicked; it had to be proven wrong by experimental methods. Yet somewhere, behind all the scientific paraphernalia, he too denounces sin where he appears to expose, by sinning himself in a slightly modified fashion, the faultiness of a scientific theory.

But there is a dimension of experience where, on the other side of tricky philosophical speculation and rational argumentation, it becomes self-evident that what is not right, cannot be true. It is the moment of comprehending what the indefinable good life is. Then there is no doubt that a man, given up to fascinations which exercise only those of his faculties which have the least bearing on what he is as a person, namely on his affections, his passions, his beliefs, his imagination—the least bearing, in fact, on the truth in which and by which he is a person—is merely digging away in the gulf between him and the good life. For Goethe all knowledge which cannot be assimilated in a concord of all the human faculties of understanding, heightening and cleansing them all in their mutual interplay, man's 'senses and reason, his imagination and his critical intelligence', as he puts it; all knowledge which will only cause a man 'to fret away his days in the narrowest and most joyless limitation',[15] is fundamentally worthless and undeserving of the name of truth. Can man, in this sense, assimilate, 'realize', his descent from the apes? Does he know better—not how he came to be, but what he *is*? Has the mathematical waving of a nondescript medium anything to do with the light and colour as man experiences them and as they affect him? These simple-minded questions carry the flavour of that simple mystery which I have said was at the bottom of Goethe's conviction that there was neither grace nor truth in that type of science which he took so much unrewarded trouble to oppose.

3

Goethe's *Theory of Colours* which appeared in 1810 and of which he said one year before his death that it was as old as the world, is based—as all his scientific theories—on what he calls an *Urphänomen*, an idea so fundamental to the *quality* of a group of phenomena that the human mind is ill-advised to penetrate beyond it. It is that idea which, manifesting itself through the phenomena themselves, Goethe can, as he said to Schiller, see 'with his own eyes'. One step further, and we have lost sight of the world in which man *actually* lives, of everything that matters to him as a human being, of the sights, sounds, touches, smells, tastes, loves and hatreds—finding ourselves instead in an unrealizable infinity of potential abstractions. Thus the *Urphänomen* marks for Goethe the point where the observer is still in contact with what he observes, and beyond which the *real* relationship between a human being and an object of nature ceases, with the object no longer being what it is and the human mind establishing itself as a subjective tyrant: the physicist becomes the task-master of nature, collects experiences, hammers and screws them together and thus, by 'insulating the experiment from man, and attempting to get to know nature merely through artifices and instruments', engineers what Goethe calls 'the greatest disaster of modern physics'.[16] Goethe regards it as his own scientific mission to 'liberate the phenomena once and for all from the gloom of the empirico-mechanico-dogmatic torture chamber'.[17] After him, he hopes, scholars will refer to the Newtonian interlude in science as 'the pathology of experimental physics'.[18]

The *Urphänomen* underlying Goethe's *Theory of Colours* is the polarity between light and darkness. Light for him is the bright, white radiance of a sunny day, not that ray distilled by Newton, forced through the tiniest holes and tortured by complicated mechanisms. That white light should be a concoction of various colours is to Goethe 'a manifest absurdity'. It is not the colours which produce the white light, but the white light which produces the colours. 'Colours are the actions and sufferings of light',[19] he says, the result of its meeting with darkness. Thus darkness is not merely defined as the absence of light, it is a creative force in its own right. Darkness interferes with light through all the shades of opaqueness provided by various media. When Goethe, having studied for the first time, and misunderstood, Newton, looked through a prism he was taken aback by the fact that the white wall still appeared white. Colours appeared only where the whiteness of the wall came to an end at the frontier of something darker; the window-frame. Thus a demarcation line is necessary for colours to emerge, the frontier between light and darkness. There are only two fundamental colours, yellow and blue, yellow emerging at the point where light has to yield some of its territory to darkness, and blue where light makes its first tentative inroad into blackness. By intensification and mixing one obtains all the other colours; allow more and more darkness to intrude into yellow and you get orange and red, and give light a better chance in its combat with black, and violet and a bluish red appear. Mix the two elemental colours, yellow and blue, and you have green. Thus Goethe arrives at his colour-cycle where yellow and blue, red and violet, green and what he calls purple, face one another; they are complementary colours. It is all very delightful and very obvious: you need only look at the sun, setting behind the vapours of the evening; it turns yellow, orange, red as the opaqueness of the atmosphere increases; look at the smoke rising from the chimney of your neighbour's house; now it is a light bluish-grey colour, and now again almost black, according to the density of the opaque particles which it carries.

Though it is delightful and obvious, it is yet quite useless to the mathematical physicist. Less useless were Goethe's theories to the physiologist; for he was the first to treat seriously of the *active* role which the eye assumes in the creation of light- and colour-effects. The opening section of his work is devoted to what he calls 'physiological colours', as distinct from physical and chemical colours, and it is this section which inspired the work of Johannes Müller, the founder of the theory of specific sense-energies. Through him Goethe, ignored by the physicist, still plays his part in modern physiopsychology (and, of course, in aesthetics, an aspect of the problem of colours to which the last section of Goethe's work is devoted and which abounds, as one would expect, in the most penetrating observations about the emotional value of colour and colour-compositions—very similar in approach and results to the theorizing on the subject by Leonardo da Vinci, whose writings on colour seem to have been unknown to Goethe).

It may have become clear by now that Goethe's physics, though anti-Newtonian in motivation, is, in fact, not anti-mathematical, but, as it were, a-mathematical, which is as much as to say that it is not physics at all—at least, not in the now accepted sense of the word. Newton's and Goethe's theories never meet, except at some points of confusion on the part of Goethe. I have attempted to say something about the nature and motive of Goethe's opposition, his method and approach. Yet there is more to it, and it is this 'more' which is at the very centre of Goethe's idea of truth of which we have already seen some facets. In order to approach that centre more closely, we have to risk that long postponed plunge into metaphysics which loomed darkly before us when we left Goethe and Schiller debating the question whether the *Urpflanze* was an 'idea' or something 'real'.

The preface to Goethe's *Theory of Colours* contains the following key-passage: 'It is the strangest claim in the world—raised sometimes, but never lived up to even by those who raise it—that one should present experiences without any theoretical link between them, and leave it to the reader, or the pupil, to form his own convictions. But the mere looking at a thing is of no use whatsoever. Looking at a thing gradually merges into contemplation, contemplation into thinking, thinking is establishing connections, and thus it is possible to say that every attentive glance which we cast on the world is an act of theorizing. This, however, ought to be done with consciousness, self-criticism, freedom, and, to use a daring word, with *irony*—yes, all these faculties are necessary if abstraction, which

C

we dread, is to be rendered innocuous, and the result which we hope
for is to emerge with as much liveliness as possible.'[20]

Goethe, with all his insistence on objectivity, concreteness of
thought (*Gegenständlichkeit*), with his un-Kantian confusion—so
exasperating to Schiller—of transcendence and immanence, idea
and experience, with his repeated protestations that 'philosophy is
not my métier', in this passage gives himself away as a profound
philosopher. 'Theorizing' is inherent in all human experience,
and the highest intellectual achievement, he says elsewhere, 'would
be to comprehend that everything factual is already theory'.[21]

Now Goethe had no distinct historical interests, but his *History of
the Theory of Colours* may well be the first history of scientific
method. It is, though the student of Goethe is apt to avoid it carefully, in parts an astonishingly interesting book. Read with one's
attention focused on certain problems, it exposes the naïve fallacy
of the still predominant absolute belief in the pragmatic test. One
knows, of course, how many scientific theories have, for very long
periods of time, stood the test of experience until they had to be
discarded owing to man's decision, not merely to make other
experiments, but *to have different experiences*; one also knows how
often, after having lain for whole epochs in the cosmic dustbin of
untruth, a theory, in one form or another, has been fetched back in
triumph. For more unsophisticated aesthetic demands the game of
musical chairs in which, ever since Newton and Huygens, the
corpuscles and waves of light have found themselves involved—
until, by a blatant breach of the rules of the game, they simply sat
down together on one seat—may be as entertaining as the out-dated
but certainly loftier delight of musical spheres. And has not Einstein
shown that the whole quarrel between Rome and Galileo had been
merely the outcome of a scientific misunderstanding?

But it is not only this exuberant dance of scientific hypotheses
which is revealed by Goethe's history of science. What, above all,
emerges most clearly is the fact that every scientific theory is merely
the surface rationalization of a metaphysical substratum of beliefs,
conscious or unconscious, about the nature of the world. And it is
these beliefs too, these models of reality constructed in human
minds and souls, which live and prosper for vast stretches of history
in perfect pragmatic integrity, and, to a remarkable extent, *create*,
not find and accept, the shape of the external world. The totems and
taboos of savages, the pyramids of Egypt, the acropolis of Athens,

the cathedral of Chartres *pragmatically* prove as much, or as l
the ultimate nature of reality as any modern scientific experin
It is indeed amazing how malleable the world is and how easil
models and remodels itself according to the inner vision of ma
how readily it responds to his 'theorizing'! Thus the most important advice which an educator can give to his pupils, may easily be:
Be careful how you interpret the world; it *is* like that. One usually
assumes that the beliefs or unbeliefs of modern man originate in the
scientific discoveries made in the seventeenth century; it may be
equally correct to say that the scientific discoveries of the seventeenth century could not have been made without the vision of
reality, held by man, having previously undergone a radical change.
There is perhaps a direct line linking the minds of the Reformers of
the sixteenth century, invoking the authority of the Bible against
the tradition of the Church, to the mind of Francis Bacon claiming
the authority of nature against the tenets of scholastic philosophy;
from Luther's biblical pragmatism to Bacon's natural pragmatism,
and from Rome being discredited as the focus of Christendom to
the earth being dislodged from its central position in the universe.

Goethe's *History of the Theory of Colours* gives us a few chapters of
this Odyssey of the human mind. 'The history of the world must
be rewritten from time to time,' he says, 'not because many events
of the past are being rediscovered, but because new vistas are
opening up, new ways of looking at things, which show the past in
a different light.'[22] Of Bacon he says: 'In the second half of the
sixteenth century the emancipation of the individual progresses.
Everyone comfortably enjoys what has been gained, and rushes
through the liberated spaces; the disinclination to acknowledge
authority becomes more and more marked, and as one has protested
in religion, so one will protest, at all costs, in science, and at last
Bacon of Verulam dares to wipe out, as if with a sponge, everything
that had been inscribed upon the tables of mankind.'[23] And in one
of his diary jottings he anticipates with remarkable precision what
in our century Whitehead has called the Fallacy of Misplaced Concreteness, the fatal illusion of an age which accepts the sketch of the
model of reality that it has drawn itself, its own theoretical pre-
suppositions, as the concrete nature of reality. Goethe says: 'Have
thought about fiction and science. The disaster they cause comes
from the need of reflective reason which creates, for its own use, a
sort of image, but will afterwards set it up as true and concrete.'[24]

Or again: 'However fully developed our nomenclature is, we must remember that it is only a nomenclature; that a word is merely a sign of syllables attached to a certain phenomenon. Thus it can never express nature completely and ought to be regarded as mere equipment for our comfort.'[25]

But all this profound insight into the follies and fallacies of man thinking his way through the ages, does not with Goethe, as it so easily could, lead to any historical relativization of the idea of truth. What saves him is what would save the authentically great artist and what would be shatteringly naïve on any other level but his: the faith in the intuitive, indeed visionary faculty of his genius. Of course, this faith never becomes pompously articulate. When Goethe speaks of it, he speaks with that irony which with him is a prerequisite of intellectual honesty—perhaps it hardly ever becomes conscious. But there is one occasion where, again with some irony, he seems to reach a final, and for him indeed very satisfactory, conclusion to that argument with Schiller, and through Schiller with Kant, which I quoted at the beginning. That Kant had absolutely denied to human intelligence the possibility of 'seeing ideas', of reaching the absolute lucidity of Plato's ἐπιστήμη, that the human understanding should be for ever imprisoned within the confines of that unhappy hunting ground where the physical scientist is after his phenomenal game, had been a secret vexation for Goethe ever since he came into contact with that philosophy which satisfied the philosophical need of the modern mind, as Thomas Aquinas had satisfied that of the Middle Ages.

On the occasion of which I am speaking, he had once more struggled with Kant and underlined the following sentence in which the philosopher deals with the rational possibility of conceiving of a divine mind: 'We are able to think of an understanding which, not being discursive as ours, but intuitive, starts with a universal vision and descends from there to the particular, that is, from the One to the Many'. And Goethe notes: 'I suppose the author hints here at divine intuition; yet if it is possible for us [as Kant admits] to lift ourselves up to a higher region in the moral sphere, through faith in God, virtue and immortality, and draw nearer towards the supreme Being, then, perhaps, it may be the same in the intellectual sphere and we may, by our contemplation of incessantly creative Nature, become worthy of some intellectual participation in her creativeness. If, to begin with, I strove, unconsciously and merely prompted by an inner motive, to reach the *Urphänomen* and the secret of the type, and if I even succeeded in erecting on this basis a theory in accordance with Nature, then nothing shall prevent me from braving now what the old man of Königsberg himself calls the *Adventure of Reason*.'[26]

And so he braves it. To the end of his life he will fail, or refuse, to grasp completely what Schiller and Kant were about. The unfathomable before which he too resigns himself, is yet revealed to him in the world of phenomena; not the Absolute itself, but the mirrored reflection of its majestic remoteness: 'Im farbigen Abglanz haben wir das Leben'. Absolute Truth and the Goethean Scientific Truth are not different in kind, merely in degrees of, as it were, absoluteness. Therefore by scientific truth Goethe never means the results, correct or incorrect, produced by what he denounces, implicitly and explicitly, as a strange aberration of the human mind, a rather perverse marriage between the crudest empiricism and the most abstruse mathematical abstractness. His science, like his poetry, is founded on the conviction—self-evident to him—that man, if only he exercises *all* his faculties of understanding, is, as he says, 'adequately equipped'[27] to know what he is meant to know about life without having to put 'nature on the rack'; for there, he says, she remains silent.[28]

Truth is what man is meant to know—this is the centre of Goethe's intellectual existence. It is rather perturbing for the modern intelligence; where are the measures, it will ask, by which we can assess what is 'meant'? Goethe himself cannot define them. He merely feels that 'in natural sciences as much as in ethics we need a categorical imperative'.[29]

We have seen that his opposition to Newton springs from a moral impulse expressing itself in scientific language; yet it can, despite the strains imposed upon it by the incongruous situation, express itself in such language because both Goethe's ethical and scientific convictions are mere aspects of that faith which forms the core of his spiritual existence: the faith in a perfect correspondence between the inner nature of man and the structure of external reality, between the soul and the world. Hence there is for Goethe neither tragedy—for tragedy results from a fundamental misunderstanding between the human heart and the order of the world—nor modern physical science, which he sees but as the mind's strategy in its self-assertive campaign against nature. It is in this sense that Goethe

calls modern physics, rather startlingly, 'subjective'. To him it
seems the outcome of an excessive emancipation of the subject from
a totality of which it is a mere part, and therefore involved at every
point in a manoeuvre of cosmic impiety. He resigns himself, as he
says, on reaching the *Urphänomen*, that is, 'at the boundaries of
humanity'; the mathematico-analytical scientist, on the other hand,
appears to him imprisoned 'within the hypothetical limitations of
an obstinately self-willed and narrow-minded individuality'.[30]

Goethe deems his own science 'objective' because it has its source
in his belief in a pre-established equation between subject and object.
In his *Theory of Colours* he praises the Ionian school for 'repeating
again and again, with so much emphasis, that knowledge is only
through the response of equal to equal', and he translates Plotinus'
Neque vero oculus unquam videret solem nisi factus solaris esset into
German verse:

> Wär nicht das Auge sonnenhaft,
> Wie könnten wir das Licht erblicken?
> Lebt' nicht in uns des Gottes eigne Kraft,
> Wie könnt uns Göttliches entzücken?[31]

[If the eye were not sun-like, how could we ever see light? And
if God's own power did not dwell within us, how could we delight
in things divine?]

To Eckermann he says (February 26th, 1824): 'If I had not
carried, through anticipation, the world within myself, I would
have remained blind with my eyes wide open, and all search and
experience would have been nothing but a dead and vain effort'.
Therefore, he says, Truth is 'a revelation emerging at the point
where the inner world of man meets external reality. . . . It is a
synthesis of world and mind, yielding the happiest assurance of the
eternal harmony of existence'[32]; and again, 'there resides, in the
objective world, an unknown law which corresponds to the unknown law within subjective experience',[33] and—though he used
them himself—'when it comes to it, microscopes and telescopes
merely confuse the pure human vision'.[34] Unknown and yet
revealed—this is the nature of truth which Goethe seeks to make
more and more his own by exercising his intuition, imagination *and*
discursive intelligence, with freedom and irony.

It is only on those very few occasions when he seems to be persuaded that Kant is right after all and that Schiller may have justly

denied him the privilege of direct intercourse with the ideas, that he seems to be prepared to leave science alone and resign himself to his poetry. This he expresses in a little meditation (*Bedenken und Ergebung*—Reflection and Resignation) in which he gives a most exact précis of Kant's philosophy, stating in conclusion that 'understanding cannot think together what the senses convey to it in separation, and so the conflict between perception and idea remains for ever unresolved. Therefore we shall escape into the sphere of poetry where we may hope to find some satisfaction.'[35]

It is this impulse (which Goethe hardly ever allows to get the better of him), this emphasis on the superiority of the inner vision as against a spiritually barren external world, that ever since has dominated European poetry. This trend became more and more conspicuous with time, so that the Romantics whom Goethe rejected seem almost Realists compared with the later excesses of inwardness perpetrated by the Symbolists. The great significance of Goethe in the history of the European mind lies in the fact that he is the last great poet who lived and worked in a continual effort to save the life of poetry *and* the poetry of life. All his fundamental scientific ideas are capable of expansion into pure poetic vision. *The Metamorphosis of Plants* is the title not only of a biological treatise, but also of a poem, and the *Theory of Colours* extends into some of the best verses of his later years. It is the same principle that informs his poetry as well as his science, his *Faust* and his *Theory of Colours*: that 'all that is transient is but a symbol', and 'everything that exists is an analogy of existence itself'.[36] Thus Goethe is not merely against Newton, but also against the Romantics and against Beethoven; for it is no more the artist's business to melt away the solid reality of symbolic living forms in the hot paroxysms of the inner life, than it is the scientist's to tyrannize these symbols of eternity which surround our temporal existence into the subjective abstractions of mathematical reasoning, for, Goethe asks, 'what is there exact in mathematics except its own exactitude?'[37]

At times he is convinced that his science is of far greater historical importance than his poetry. 'Two things are necessary for a man to make an epoch in the world,' he once said to Eckermann (May 2nd, 1824), 'first to have a good brain, and then to come into a big fortune. Napoleon inherited the French Revolution, Frederick the Great the Silesian War, Luther the obscurantism of the monks, and to my lot have fallen the errors of Newtonian physics. The present generation has, of course, no idea what I have achieved in this field; but future ages will confess that in my time I had come into no small fortune.' Perhaps he was not quite so wrong after all. Can one not discern a very marked echo of Goethe's voice in the following sentence of the physicist Heisenberg: 'The dangers threatening modern science cannot be averted by more and more experimenting, for our complicated experiments have no longer anything to do with nature in her own right, but with nature changed and transformed by our own cognitive activity'.[38]

It was Goethe's ambition to play in the history of thought the role of another Francis Bacon, insisting on not merely pragmatic, but what he understood to be objective dealings with nature; or that of an Immanuel Kant of the Objective Reason. He said in a review of a scientific work: 'A man, born and bred in the so-called exact sciences will, on the height of his analytical reason, not easily comprehend that there is also something like an exact concrete imagination.'[39] This exact concrete imagination is the glory of Goethe's poetry, and he knew that it was the great instrument of truth. 'Beauty,' he says, 'is the manifestation of secret laws of nature which, were it not for their being revealed through beauty, would have remained unknown for ever.'[40] All searches, discoveries and inventions, thrust on a world which is through these very activities and achievements progressively alienated from that truth which resides in the imagination and in a precise vision rather than in abstract formulae of the fittingness, beauty and significance of things, would ultimately spend themselves, Goethe feared, in the vain and desperate fidgetings of the good intention to make hell a better place to live in.

II

GOETHE AND THE AVOIDANCE OF TRAGEDY

GOETHE AND THE AVOIDANCE OF TRAGEDY

Wenn ein moderner Mensch ... an einem so grossen Alten Fehler zu rügen hätte,
so sollte es billig nicht anders geschehen als auf den Knien.—Goethe to Eckermann,
March 28th, 1827

I

IN 1797, after a lapse of seven years following the publication of
the *Fragment: Faust*, and more than twenty years after the com-
pletion of the first draft of the dramatic poem, the *Urfaust*, Goethe
announced in a letter to Schiller (June 22nd) that, finding himself in
a state of acute unrest, he was preparing, as a kind of spiritual
sedative, to take up *Faust* once more and to retreat 'into that world
of symbols, ideas and mists' (June 24th). He begged his friend 'to
think it over in a sleepless night', and to tell him what he would
expect of the whole work and, as it were, 'interpret, as a true
prophet, his [Goethe's] own dreams' (June 22nd). Goethe must
have known that he would arouse some uneasiness in Schiller's
methodical mind when he added: 'As the various parts of the poem
can be treated in different modes if only they fall in with the spirit
and the tone of the whole, and as, moreover, this creation is subjective in kind, I shall be able to work at it in odd free moments now
and then'. Schiller's reply was as prompt as it was suggestive of
misgivings. 'With all its poetic individualism,' he said, 'this play
cannot escape the demand for symbolic significance.... The
duality of human nature and the unsuccessful striving for a
reconciliation in man between what is divine and what is physical—
this is something one cannot lose sight of; and just because the story
tends towards shrillness and formlessness one does not wish to be
arrested within the subject itself, but to be guided by it towards
ideas. In brief, the claims made upon *Faust* are, at the same time,
philosophical and poetical, and in whatever direction you may
turn, the very nature of the subject will impose upon you a philosophical treatment, and the imagination will have to put up with a
period of employment in the service of an idea' (June 23rd).

It is, once again, the issue raised by *Naive und sentimentalische
Dichtung*. In that essay, which had appeared in the preceding year,
Schiller defended the workings of his own reflective genius against
the overpowering spontaneity of Goethe's. This time, Schiller

seems to imply, Goethe will have to leave behind the state of innocence, submitting himself to a more complex, more philosophically disciplined inspiration. If it appeared to Schiller that in *Werther*, in *Tasso*, a miraculously preserved innocence, a poetic imagination of almost terrifying integrity had told the story of a world divided and coming to grief—as though the genius of the tree in paradise had opened its mouth to announce to the world the news of the Fall—then the continuation of that record could only come from the creature that had eaten the apple. For the hero of *Faust* was no longer the kind of person that Werther was, or Egmont, or Tasso, or Iphigenie, who are all profoundly 'naïve'—the word to be understood with its German connotations. One might be tempted to apply to them Pascal's reflection that 'the heart has reasons of which the reason knows nothing', were it not for the fact that Pascal meant *reasons* of the heart (Hölderlin had them), tools of the highest *understanding* of the world, whereas Werther, Egmont, Tasso and even Iphigenie, live, with regard to the world, in a state of fundamental incomprehension, varying between the raptures of bliss ('himmelhoch jauchzend') when the heart, wholly immaculate, to use Iphigenie's phrase, enjoys itself, and the agonies of woe ('zu Tode betrübt') when the uncomprehended world interferes. *They do not know*—in the sense in which knowledge means the knowledge of good and evil; they live, not beyond, but before that fatal rift, and thus reflect an essential characteristic of their creator's genius and sensibility. Here is at least one of the roots of Goethe's uniqueness within the European tradition, a uniqueness revealed in achievement as well as in failure. This also accounts for the extremes of Goethe worship (mostly inside Germany) and Goethe rejection (mostly outside Germany, and by critics of the stature of, for instance, Irving Babbitt, Ortega y Gasset, George Santayana, T. S. Eliot).

Any criticism of Goethe requires the utmost tact. Not only is the man so immense—and nothing is more difficult in criticism than to keep alive at every moment that sense of proportion which the very difference in level between creativeness and critical judgment demands; criticism is, alas, an unaristocratic habit, easily tempted into a false intimacy, in praise and negation alike—but also so much of the perennial discussion about Goethe is so massively wrongheaded, and so passionate that it has filled the atmosphere around him with an abundance of electrical charges, making it all too easy to produce short circuits. I am saying this because I wish to speak of a limitation in Goethe's range of awareness and of a defect in his sensibility, and because I believe, paradoxically enough, that this limitation lies in the very boundlessness of his genius, and the defect in the inexhaustible richness of his sensitivity. It would be preposterous to derive the standards for an assessment of Goethe's achievements from anywhere else but the great classics of European civilization. Yet it would be futile to seek a place for him in a pattern determined by Homer, or Sophocles, or Virgil, or Dante, or Shakespeare. His range is too wide, and his gifts too universal ever to find full realization in one type of work alone, and his genius too diffused ever to concentrate on a single exemplary, classical achievement; and while in scope he is too vast ever to represent the character of an age, the mode of his imagination, its susceptibilities and idiosyncracies partake, at the same time, too definitely of the unresolved problems of the late eighteenth century, for him easily to be acknowledged as being for all times and all places. With regard to Goethe's position within his own nation, it is very revealing that it could be said with some justice—as it was said immediately after the Second World War by Karl Jaspers—'that we came face to face with experiences in which we had no inclination to read Goethe, but took up Shakespeare, or the Bible, or Aeschylus, if it was possible to read at all'.[1]

What was the nature of the experience in the face of which Goethe seemed to offer no help? It was the very kind of experience before which Goethe himself has always proved helpless: the exposure to the manifestations of evil and sin. 'The mere attempt to write tragedy might be my undoing,'[2] he once said, and it was the truth —at least for the greatest part of his life. Among his dramas there are three dramatic poems which, more than any other dramas he wrote, established his fame: *Iphigenie*, *Tasso*, *Faust*. All of them are potential tragedies, indeed so much so, that one may feel that the tragic conclusion could only be avoided at the price of complete artistic conclusiveness. They show a moving and yet unsatisfactory reluctance of mind and imagination to accept the rule of the road leading to the very centre of human destiny. This is not to imply that in that very centre there dwells, inescapably, tragedy. But once a man is compelled to penetrate to that central point in all seriousness, then there is only one region left that stretches, for the European,

beyond tragedy. Beyond Hamlet and the rest that is silence, there
stands only Prospero:

> And my ending is despair,
> Unless I be reliev'd by prayer,
> Which pierces so that it assaults
> Mercy itself, and frees all faults.

And frees all faults; the German translation of this is: *Alle
menschliche Gebrechen*, which, we are told by Goethe, are redeemed
by 'pure humanity', of which Iphigenie is the embodiment.

Anyone who has ever come under the spell of Goethe's *Iphigenie*
knows its power to persuade, to convince and to move. There
seems to be no doubt that it is poetically true. But which aspect of
poetic truth do we mean? The same that applies to *Antigone* or *King
Lear*? No, certainly not. *Iphigenie* is lyrically, but not dramatically,
true, which is as much as to say that it has the truth of a vision of
what life and the world could be if they corresponded to what is
best in a great and good soul. It is dramatically not true because
the objective world which is the scene of the play is not real enough
to offer serious resistance to the realization of that vision. In other
words, there is no real evil in that world. All the evil inherent in
the mythological pattern taken over from the Greeks, is considerably
reduced in stature so as to lose an essential degree of reality. The
reality of evil asserts itself poetically on only three occasions which
are scattered about the play like three erratic blocks in the gentle
groves of human kindness: Iphigenie's story of the horrible deeds
perpetrated in her family, Orestes' account of the murder of his
mother with the rage of madness that follows, and the *Parzenlied*
(the song of the goddesses of Fate). For the rest—and it is all but the
whole play—the inexorable hardness of the Greek myth is dissolved
into the softer substance of the goodness of human nature.

From the opening monologue of the first act onwards we are sure
that, unless the poem were to become grossly incongruous, Iphigenie
cannot seriously be asked to perform, or indeed seriously consider,
human sacrifices, let alone the sacrifice of her own brother. And the
much-discussed question of the 'cure' of Orestes reveals, through the
very wording of the question as suggested by the play, the surprising
shift of emphasis from what was once, and is again, the centre of the
problem, to a more humane periphery. Cure? Of what? Of a temporary fit of madness? For surely there is no 'cure' for the murder

of a mother. There is, for the Greeks, only the supreme sacrifice to atone for it, or else the direct intervention of the gods to lift the curse—which is, in spite of all the fundamental differences, nearer the Christian repentance and the forgiving grace than the administering of pure humanity. If the curse on the house of Tantalus and the deed of Orestes are to be taken as real—as real, say, as the murder committed by Macbeth—then Goethe's solution is not dramatically true. We simply have to discard the reality of curse and murder—and, indeed, this oblivion is granted to us by the lyrically soothing climate of Arcadian Tauris itself—we have to accept curse and murder as mythological names for a less spectacular kind of guilt, and finally allow a more vaguely general state of spiritual restlessness to assume the place of any articulate guilt if we are to remain convinced of the effectiveness of a purely human redemption.

Schiller's dramatic instinct sensed this defect of Goethe's Orestes; by criticizing him in terms of purely dramatic considerations, he yet pointed to the profounder issue when he wrote to Goethe (January 22nd, 1802): 'Orestes is the most doubtful figure of the drama. There is no Orestes without Furies; and when the cause of his condition does not strike the senses but lies hidden in his mind and emotions, his is too long and monotonous an agony—without an object. Here we are up against one of the limitations of modern drama as compared with ancient tragedy. I wish you could think of a remedy; but bearing in mind the economy of the play, I do not think it likely that you will; for you have indeed done everything that is possible without gods and spirits.'

I have said that the theme of *Iphigenie* would lend itself to, indeed invite, a tragic treatment. The reply that the play of Euripides from whom the story is borrowed is not a tragedy either, would be beside the point, for it is too obvious that Goethe's heroine is a person totally different from Euripides' Iphigenia. Yet there is one Greek tragedy which, in situation and aspects of the main character, is related to Goethe's *Iphigenie*: the *Antigone* of Sophocles. In both plays it is a loving sister who has determined in her soul to abide by the divine law as it is given to her, and to remain, as Antigone says, 'imprisoned in the fear of the gods', and thus to defy all worldly power and the rules of common sense. In both plays the conflict involves death—or, at least, potentially death—not merely for the one who is so madly resolved, but for those whom she loves as well:

in *Antigone* for Ismene, perhaps, the sister, and for Haemon, the lover, and in *Iphigenie* for Orestes, the brother, and Pylades, the friend. In the one play as much as in the other, the heroine is bound by bonds of gratitude to him whom she has decided to disobey; in both plays the king has provided a home for the child of a cursed race after her great tribulations. For Antigone as well as for Iphigenie it is not merely the wish for full moral realization of her own character that inspires her deed, but the hope of redeeming the guilt of ancestors. Moreover, in both plays the king is finally moved to revoke his own law and to yield to an overriding commandment. Thus it is through the contrast between Sophocles' *Antigone* and Goethe's *Iphigenie* (and not in comparison with the play of Euripides, where such problems never enter) that one can see most clearly the limitations of the Iphigenie faith.

These limitations might be artistically irrelevant were the play not such that its subject could not be dealt with on the level which Goethe set himself, without implicitly giving a comprehensive vision (a vision, not a discussion) of the ultimate nature of the moral problem involved. Also one cannot state these limitations by simply drawing attention to the tragic ending of *Antigone*, and the happy solution of *Iphigenie*. But perhaps one can bring home the point that matters by saying that Iphigenie would not do what she does—or rather, would not be what she is—if her vision of life really comprehended the possibility of her having to put her brother to death; whereas Antigone, whether or not she is to die herself and bring death to others, *is* the realization of the truth that the triumph of divine law may involve at every point disaster in terms of human aspirations. In other words, there is in Goethe's *Iphigenie* an incongruity between the radicalism with which the moral problem is posed, and the certainly lovable gentleness of the spiritual nature that has to carry it. The *dramatic* flaw of Goethe's other great poetic drama, *Torquato Tasso*—lyrically as supremely successful as *Iphigenie* —is that the spiritual excitement of the hero is in excess of the moral facts of his situation, while in *Iphigenie* the moral situation outweighs the spiritual stature of the protagonist. It is because in the dramatic order of things natures like Iphigenie must not be made to encounter such situations (which could only crush them without affording them even the semblance of spiritual triumph) that, in this case, the moral problem is identical with the problem of dramatic integrity.

At the root of this problem there is not merely the time-honoured and, in this form, interminable antithesis between the belief in the fundamental goodness and the dogma of the essential corruption of the human heart. Not one of the characters of *Antigone* is 'bad'. If Creon were a wicked man there would still be catastrophe, but no tragedy. For both Greeks and Christians it is not in terms of morality that the moral problem can be solved. Once more, it is not the belief in man's readiness to be persuaded and moved into goodness that limits the spiritual scope of Goethe's *Iphigenie*. The uneasiness springs from a different question which is, I think, implicitly answered by Goethe; the question: what would happen to the human spirit if all human goodness were of no avail on this earth, as happens to be the case in *Antigone*? Would the ending be despair then, or a faith beyond despair? The light and the beauty which emanate from *Iphigenie* have their source in her (or Goethe's) conviction that in the final reckoning such questions will not be asked. Yet as it happens, Iphigenie actually does ask the question. From the depth of her conflict she implores the gods that good should prevail on the shores of Tauris, that they should save her and thus *'save their image in her soul'*.[3] In other words, the image of the gods in Iphigenie's soul is such that it would be undone by catastrophe and her faith would crumble. But this is an extraneous and somewhat illegitimate consideration; it would be better to say that *Iphigenie* simply embodies the belief that the gods cannot fail her by contradicting her own convictions of what is good and necessary. Thus she stands for the impossibility of tragedy. Antigone, on the other hand, knowing that she is to die and lamenting her fate, asks on which right of the gods she might have trespassed. Why should she in her wretchedness still raise her eyes to the heavenly powers? 'My lot was godlessness received in exchange for piety. But if this is good before the gods then I shall suffer, and in suffering come to know my sin.'

If it can be said that Goethe's limitations have their origin in the apparently limitless scope of his genius, then what is meant is his *genius*, not his talents; on the contrary, he always used his talents to defend himself against his genius. In the deployment of his extra-poetic talents he often seems to insist stubbornly on a playfully cultivated mediocrity. This we can see at work in his unsophisticated taste for rather dull drawings, in his 'classical' preoccupation with the most uninspired examples of Roman sculpture, in his preferring Zelter's innocuous music to Beethoven's and, above all, in the

D

all but philistine pedantry betrayed by his endless collecting,
cataloguing, describing and displaying of all manner of objects,
documents and instruments. People lacking in a sense of humour
have often blamed Goethe for so irresponsibly scattering his interests
and wasting his time. Their insatiable desire for still more and still
greater poetry is sadly frustrated by the Herr Geheimrat's habits of
painstaking theatrical management and time-squandering minera-
logical meticulousness.

Yet there is, of course, in all seriousness something puzzling in
those radical defensive manoeuvres of Goethe, and I think that only
by understanding them as necessary defences can one hope to arrive
at some comprehension of Goethe's genius. Only then may one see
a little more clearly why his lyrical achievements should have been
so truly incomparable, his embarrassment in the face of tragedy so
conspicuous, the moral solutions offered by some of his works such
anti-climaxes that Irving Babbitt could speak of them as 'sham
solutions', and, incidentally, his science so aggressively anti-
Newtonian. It may also help to explain why his greatest work,
Faust, had to remain so ambiguous (and I mean an ambiguity
falling short of the essential ambiguity of all great art, an ambiguity
not in terms of unresolvable paradox, but of plain contradiction)—
so ambiguous that throughout the message-ridden German nineteenth century it could, with the support of what were quite un-
ambiguous quotations, be interpreted as the high-poetical celebration
of restlessly active striving and of a freedom that resides in conquest;
whereas now, with the ethos of action and aggrandisement deflated,
and again with quite unequivocal support from the text, it can be
shown to proclaim the hope in the inscrutable workings of divine
grace which may descend upon the greatest sinner.

2

Critics have always tried to account in various ways for Goethe's
more baffling waverings and uncertainties. Some say that at times
he jeopardized his genius by occupying himself with the wrong
things; others, that he allowed himself too easily to get entangled in
the wrong emotions. Yet it is difficult to be convinced by the
standards such critics apply in their assessments of what was 'right'
for Goethe. Is it what Ortega y Gasset calls the 'realized *Existenz*'
of Goethe, the man? This might only have been attained by the
sacrifice of Goethe, the poet. Or is it the idea of contented

equilibrium and psychological balance which Barker Fairley's *Study of Goethe* appears to put forward? But surely this therapeutic approach is most unbecoming for the literary critic who would soon be out of his job if poets decided to accept for the conduct of their lives the rules of mental health. To say that Goethe was pathologically introspective in his youth is to say that we should be prepared to dispense with *Werther* and the original design of *Faust*; and to imply that Frau von Stein was bad for Goethe is equal to holding that it would have been just as well if Goethe had not written *Iphigenie* or *Tasso* or *Erhabner Geist, du gabst mir, gabst mir alles* or *Warum gabst du uns die tiefen Blicke*. This kind of criticism implicitly pretends to possess the secret of an ideal pattern of creative life which, had it only been adopted by Goethe, would have made him into a still greater poet and a better and happier man.

The paradox of limitations caused by universality, with which Goethe confronts us, originates in a violent clash between the nature of Goethe's genius and his historical situation. In the spiritually barren climate of eighteenth- and nineteenth-century society, amidst that vanity fair of conflicting values and self-contradictory aspirations, a genius, apparently so chaotic and yet so profoundly organized as that of Goethe's, will easily seem to itself (and to others) to be something almost monstrous, demonic, extra-human —in fact, the spirit of *nature* itself. And this is what, set up against the spiritual character of his age, Goethe's genius was. If Goethe is not a *European* classic, this is due to the fact that his society was lacking in a fundamentally accepted and generally valid spiritual mould in which alone a classic can be cast.

In spite of all the unavoidable cleavages, disharmonies, animosities and antagonisms which are the perennial lot of human beings and human societies, there is a possibility—and this possibility is called culture when it is realized—of a community of men living together, and maybe fighting one another, in a state of tacit agreement on what the nature and meaning of human existence really is. This unity will then show itself to be at work beyond, or beneath, or despite all differences of actually proclaimed beliefs and articulate opinions. Such must have been the society for which the performances of the tragedies of Aeschylus and Sophocles were national celebrations; such were wide stretches of what we rather vaguely call the Middle Ages; such were, to judge by their artistic creations, the days of the Renaissance and of Elizabeth. The age of Goethe, however, was not of this kind. Its true representatives were the twin creatures of spiritual chaos: rationalism and romanticism, the one abhorring, the other worshipping the irrational aspect of man. In the absence of a genuine supranatural order human beings were thrown back on their purely naturalistic resources, with analytical sceptical reason on the one hand, and disorganized emotions on the other. Pascal's reasons of the heart degenerated into sheer emotionalism, which was mistaken for spirituality, and Plato's reason of understanding into the crudest empiricism, which prided itself upon its 'realistic' outlook. In vain had Kant fought his lonely battle. Those who came after him, the great philosophers of the age of Goethe, who, of course, felt and knew the disaster that had befallen the spirit, raised their arbitrary, 'exciting', 'interesting' metaphysical towers above the heads of a society that had become Babel in its mutual incomprehension.

Into such a situation there was born a genius who, more than any other of his time (with the possible exception of Blake), seemed to have been sent to fill with precious life whatever order of the spirit, whatever tradition he may have found upon his arrival—as Sophocles had done with the religious tradition of Greece, and Dante with the scholastic order of the Middle Ages. But, alas, 'the day was so absurd and confused', as Goethe himself has put it in his last letter to Wilhelm von Humboldt,[4] and his genius, being a perpetual source of light to the world, had itself to grope in darkness. What, I think, is correct in Ortega y Gasset's and—in some measure—Karl Jasper's thesis of Goethe's *Existenz* having remained unfulfilled, is the fact that his own genius was an unending puzzle to him. For the very nature of this genius deprived Goethe of that particular kind of historical sense, that intuitive grasp of the historical character of his age and his own position in it, which Schiller had and, above all, Hölderlin who wrote:

> . . . Indessen dünket mir öfters
> Besser zu schlafen, wie so ohne Genossen zu seyn,
> So zu harren und was zu thun indess und zu sagen,
> Weiss ich nicht und wozu Dichter in dürftiger Zeit?[5]

> [. . . Meanwhile, it seems to me often,
> Better to slumber than live without companions, like this,
> So to linger, and know not what to begin or to utter,
> Or, in such meagre times, why to be poet at all?]

Goethe too knew that question, and there were periods in his life when he actually did answer it in the negative and all but behaved accordingly. But for him the question was not an historical one; not 'why to be poet at all in spiritless times', but solely whether he himself *was* a poet. True, he once wrote (and just when he was about to resume his work on *Faust*): 'We are compelled to step out of our century if we wish to work according to our convictions' (to Schiller, November 25th, 1797), but such statements are extremely rare. Unaware of the deeper historical perspective of his situation, he merely perceived through his own agonies and through his spontaneous hostility towards almost all and everything that represented the spiritual character of his century—its rationalism, its romanticism, its unnatural hysterias, its cold empiricism, its idealistic philosophies, its tempestuous music—that there was a gulf fixed between what he himself was in his inmost being and the world in which he lived as a citizen. Yet unlike Hölderlin, he would not allow his genius to burden and destroy him with the historical mission of poetic prophet-martyr. He continually tried to 'do the duty of the day' by seeking a compromise between opposition and collaboration. Within his genius (which is never the whole man) he was undivided, in the sense in which a genuine pattern of nature and spirit fused, or any vital religious and cultural order, is undivided; but in the absence of any such valid order of human life outside himself he came to identify the inner order, inherent in his genius, with the spirit of nature itself.

'Unnatural,' in the mouth of Goethe, was one of the strongest invectives. 'Diese verdammte Unnatur!' he exclaimed, faced with the productions of Kleist, and Kleist was judged. Thus pantheism, God in nature, became his natural religion, and Spinoza his chosen prophet. 'This philosopher,' he wrote in a letter to Jacobi (June 9th, 1785), 'does not prove the being of God; God is being. And if others, because of this, blame him as an atheist, then I feel like praising him as *theissimum*, indeed *christianissimum*.' In the same letter, however, he confesses, in a rather touchingly ingenuous fashion, that he had never read systematically what the philosopher wrote (if he had, there is reason to think that he would occasionally have felt rather sadly disappointed): 'My way of living and thinking does not permit it. But whenever I cast a glance into his books, I believe I understand him, that is, he never seems to be self-contradictory, and I can derive from him something that affects my own feelings and doings in a very salutary manner.' How amazingly self-assured was Goethe's conviction that he represented, as it were, nature in her own right! And what a wonderful intimacy with all the disguises of the godhead is displayed in the following lines (from a very much later letter to Jacobi, January 6th, 1813): 'With all the manifold facets of my being, one way of thinking is not sufficient for me; as a poet and artist I am a polytheist, but a pantheist as a student of nature, and either belief I hold with equal determination. And if I need a divinity for my personal being, my moral existence —well, this need too is promptly catered for.'

Goethe, having to express the whole order of spirit and nature through his own genius, was limited in the performance of such an impossible duty by the absence of anything corresponding to that order within the society to which he belonged. Goethe's genius is miraculously 'natural' and 'uncivilized', in the sense that he has no support from a society civilized in the mould of the spirit that was his. And this is why, as a member of this society which had so little use for his genius, he could be so amazingly 'civilized', often to the point of cold formality and embarrassed stiffness, and even to the point of saying that he would rather commit an act of injustice than tolerate disorder. And this is also why his genius seems so boundless and its limitations, at the same time, so striking; for within his own contemporary situation such genius as his hovers perpetually on the precarious dividing-line between greatness and excess. (His counterpart, in the sphere of political genius, was Napoleon.) In the absence of a tradition to feed and educate his genius, the umbilical cord between it and nature was, as Goethe himself once put it, never severed.

Schiller, while admiring this fascinating spectacle of an undivided poetic nature, yet ceaselessly strained to play the part of midwife. In the letters about *Faust*, and still more in the correspondence about *Wilhelm Meister*, he makes the ever-renewed and ever-frustrated attempt to civilize, educate and discipline what seemed to him a too luxurious production of genius. Yet he was bound to fail, in spite of the fact that he had a profounder understanding of Goethe than anyone else. In one of the very first letters he wrote to him (August 23rd, 1794) he said that if Goethe had been born a Greek or in any other civilization where he would have been surrounded by 'an exquisite nature and an ideal art,' his struggle 'would have been shortened or even been superfluous'. At least in the creation of

certain types of work—*Faust* and *Wilhelm Meister* for instance—
Goethe, he thought, ought to resign himself to the rigours of a more
philosophical discipline. It was no good. Ideas were not embodied
in the society of his time, and in the abstract terms of philosophical
speculation Goethe had no use for them. He had to *see* and feel
them; but when he did see and feel them they became so real to him
that he was even surprised that to others they appeared to be mere
'ideas'.

The impression that Goethe's genius is 'wholly nature' is partly
due to an optical illusion caused by the refraction in the medium
of a 'spiritless time' where the spiritual had ceased to be incarnate,
having evaporated into vague abstractions. The anaemic and artificial civilization of his day drove Goethe again and again into a
realm where the 'real thing' could be found. This is why Italy was
such a revelation to Goethe. There, set up against a clearer sky and
the memory of a clearer realization of the human destiny, he found
a vision of life in which nature and humanity were merged in a
'natural civilization'.

It would be inadequate to the point of idiocy to approach Goethe
in a moralizing fashion; but there is no reason why one should not
see that, with such a predominance of nature within him and such
a lack of civilized tradition around him, he had to fail when faced
with the tragic or religious aspect of the moral problem as it is
inherent in the very plots of both *Iphigenie* and *Faust*. No human
being can come to grips with such a problem unaided by tradition
and traditional teaching. As it happened, within the 'tradition' of
Goethe's day it was precisely this problem that had been deformed
and dwarfed beyond recognition. The practical, 'lived' side of it
was indeed, after all is said (and said with great affection) about
Fräulein von Klettenberg and other beautiful souls, too pietistically
mediocre ever really to mean anything to Goethe; and its philosophical side too speculative, abstract and metaphysical not to be
discarded by Goethe's passion for 'reality'. In the spiritual climate
of the eighteenth and the beginning of the nineteenth centuries
the terror of a man's exposure to the need for ultimate moral or
religious decisions could not be creatively grasped, either on the
level of Greek tragedy or on that of undiluted Christianity, or indeed even on the level of that unique encounter of both which took
place in the Elizabethan drama. And Goethe was of his age in failing
to grasp it in either of these spheres.

We have seen what happened in his dealings with a classically
tragic subject; how he missed the meaning of the cross of Christianity is best illustrated by that passage from *Wilhelm Meisters Wanderjahre* where he 'draws a veil over this suffering' just because he
'reveres it so deeply', and because he 'regards it as a damnable
insolence to expose the agonies of the saint to the sun which had
hidden its face when an infamous world obtruded upon it this sight'.[7]
(It happened to be Weimar where an American commandant very
wisely decreed that Hitler's electorate in what was once Goethe's
city were to be shown the horrors of Buchenwald concentration
camp.) And summing up the meaning of *Hamlet*, Goethe defines it
as the tragedy of a man who was too weak to carry the burden
of his mission. Stating the problem in terms of strength and weakness, he once more fails to be impressed by the moral aspect of
Hamlet and the all-pervasive, all-corroding power of evil, the
'morbid' preoccupation of Elizabethan tragedy. For to be able to
perceive and creatively to articulate this problem, that is, to
form a vision of it rather than to discuss it, presupposes a theology
underlying, however dispersedly, the picture of reality that an
age possesses; and this is something different from a philosophy of
nature and from even the highest human wisdom. Goethe's genius
soared gloriously above the flat expanses of contemporary religious
sentimentality and mediocre morality, in triumphant opposition
to all puritan gloom, moral suspicion and tearful piety, asserting
that life, whatever it be, is good and beautiful: 'wie es auch sei, das
Leben, es ist gut', and

> Ihr glücklichen Augen,
> Was je ihr gesehn,
> Es sei wie es wolle,
> Es war doch so schön![8]

It is this finality in his assertion of life that makes it possible to claim
for Goethe the position of the greatest lyrical genius of Europe.
But though it is *his* final assertion, it is not ultimate. It indeed
transcends all sorrows of Werther, Tasso and Ottilie, and endless
conflicts most deeply felt and suffered. But would it transcend, one
wonders, tragedy fully realized? And only there is the place of an
ultimate 'Es ist gut'.

3

Under such auspices what was to become of a dramatic plot in which a man enters into a contract with the devil, signing away, on certain conditions, the fate of his soul? What is to become of *Faust*? One may well ask. It took Goethe, all in all, sixty years to decide, or rather to decide that he would not quite decide. Certain things, however, the play decided for him. For instance, that it would, being Goethe's, become a lyrical masterpiece. There is no greater and no more varied lyrical poetry to be found within the German language. And more: *Faust* became a pageant of the human spirit on its voyage throughout the ages. An extraordinary wealth of mythological creatures, Teutonic, Greek, Christian, populate the scene, all testifying to their creator's inexhaustible imaginative power. And still more: the hero of the play was to become the representative of a whole epoch of history, its lust for knowledge, for power over nature, its intellectual and emotional instability, its terrible failure in love, humility and patience. And still more: the first part of the play, dominated by what is usually called the Gretchen tragedy, was to bring out most movingly the undoing, by the Faustian manœuvres, of what was left in the world of simplicity of heart, devotion of love and innocence of feeling. This part of what is, after all, called the tragedy of Faust, developed by its own momentum into a poetic and dramatic achievement so immaculate that it will, I think, for ever hold its place by the side of what is great in the literature of the world—and this precisely because in its design it is not, in the traditional sense, tragic but lyrical. It is what might have become of the play *Hamlet* if Ophelia and not the Prince of Denmark were to be its protagonist. In other words, Goethe may have succeeded in creating a new genre: sentimental tragedy, or the tragedy of human *feelings*: Werther, Gretchen, Ottilie. What he could not write was the tragedy of the human *spirit*. It is here that the tragedy of Faust fails and becomes illegitimately ambiguous, because there is for Goethe in the last analysis no specifically *human* spirit. It is fundamentally at one with the spirit of nature. Hence it is He, the Spirit of Nature, or the Spirit of Earth, not God or the devil, who holds in his hands the final decision over Faust's bliss or damnation. Had He, when He appeared to Faust in the first scene of the play, not rejected him, neither God in heaven nor the devil in hell would have had a chance. And one of the only two scenes in which Faust really regrets that he has committed himself to his satanic company is the great monologue *Wald und Höhle*:

> Erhabner Geist, du gabst mir, gabst mir alles . . .[9]
>
> [Oh thou great Spirit, thou hast given me all . . .]

when it appears that this Spirit did not crush him after all.

There are in this vast display of demons great and small only two that affect Faust demonically; certainly not God who is a jovial old gentleman, enlightened and rather commonplace in some of his utterances ('Ein guter Mensch, in seinem dunklen Drange, Ist sich des rechten Weges wohl bewusst', which really means not more than that a good man will not altogether go astray; a conviction not so difficult to hold that it would need a divinity to persuade one), and certainly not Mephistopheles, a Voltairean spirit, with whom Faust is from the very beginning on terms of great familiarity. Goethe himself, in a conversation with Eckermann (March 2nd, 1831), has denied him all demonic properties: 'He is altogether too negative,' he said, and has explicitly stated in the play itself that he is of lesser rank than the Spirit of Earth.[10] But the two which teach Faust what a real demon is, are the Earth Spirit and the Mothers, the innermost spirits of nature and life. They represent the demonic element in Goethe's genius. It is in union with this element that Faust seeks his happiness from beginning to end, or *almost* to the very end, and not in the realization of a specifically human spirit. And Faust has been in contact with those demons before Mephistopheles enters the scene. This contact means black magic, and Faust is a magician when the curtain rises. It is this that reduces the *dramatic* stature of Mephistopheles to all but nil, and not the rather naïve consideration that Goethe has forestalled all dramatic tension in this respect by making, in the Prologue, the Lord himself, a sure winner, as it were, party to the wager. All that Mephistopheles can do for Faust is to give him a hand in a job of which he already knows the essential tricks of the trade. And throughout the play the devil performs hardly any magical feats with which one would not willingly credit the magician himself who had already succeeded in establishing contact with the very spirit of life.

All this would be rather irrelevant if it were not at the centre of the essential ambiguity of *Faust*—the most striking outcome of Goethe's avoidance of tragedy. What does Faust *really* expect of

Mephistopheles? Still more magic? No; but contentment, rest, peace; to be able to say to the moment: 'Verweile doch, du bist so schön'.[11] [Stay, thou art so fair.] In other words, life is good. True, this is preceded by Faust's contemptuous identification of such a state with self-complacency. But it is the words themselves, not what leads up to them, which become the condition of the wager. And their poetic truth gives the lie to the preamble. They are made of the same stuff as 'Es sei, wie es wolle, Es war doch so schön!' And this the devil is to provide? The very same devil whom Faust, a few scenes later, when he has found temporary peace in the company of the Spirit of Nature, knows to be the spirit responsible for

> So tauml' ich von Begierde zu Genuss
> Und im Genuss verschmacht' ich nach Begierde[12]

> [Thus I tumble from desire to fulfilment
> And in fulfilment I crave for more desire],

for ever destroying that very peace which communion with the Spirit of Nature gives him. With the devil defined as the spirit of negation and unrest, this becomes indeed a very strange condition meaning in fact that the devil is to have Faust if Faust ever escapes the devil.

What, on the other hand, is the condition of the wager between the Lord and Mephistopheles?

> Zieh diesen Geist von seinem Urquell ab[13]

> [Drag this spirit away from the very source of his life].

The Lord, that is, challenges Mephistopheles to alienate Faust from the springs of life, to uproot him. If he succeeds, Faust will be his. This sounds more like 'Deprive him of all peace, if indeed you can' than 'Make him contented with the moment'. And in the end, when Faust, anticipating this peace and contentment, blinded by anxiety, deluded into the belief that the great work of colonization has begun while, in actual fact, the busy noise is merely the sound of shovels digging his own grave, utters the fatal words, in the face of a vision so totally unconvincing in its meagre guilt-burdened town-and-country-planning bliss that one cannot but agree with Mephistopheles that it is the emptiest moment of his life, then the devil is cheated of his apparently well-deserved prey by the feeble trick of a future tense ['Im Vorgefühl von solchem hohen Glück'],[14] and by the intervention of divine grace called down upon him by the only human love Faust ever received and experienced.

How is this? Faust has indeed promised that he would content himself, even anticipated the enjoyment of peace ['Geniess' ich jetzt . . .']¹⁵ in his vision of the contented future. He has satisfied the devil who has never been found wanting in the shrewd judgment of any situation, and is, having faithfully renounced his programme of eternal striving, carried into heaven in reward for his determination to strive eternally:

> Wer immer strebend sich bemüht,
> Den können wir erlösen.¹⁶
>
> [It is the struggling, striving man
> Whom we are free to save.]

What is at the root of such confusion which has indeed defeated four generations of interpreters of *Faust*, and, if we are to trust Eckermann's report, Goethe's own faculties as a commentator? It would be tempting to relegate it to the place where many an impenetrable mystery is stored, were it not for the persistent suspicion that we are faced here not so much with a genuine poetic paradox as with a plain contradiction. It is the inevitable contradiction of the undedicated mind and heart. In Faust's world there are no real loyalties to be realized and no real commitments to be broken. Both his eternal striving and his desire for peace are merely the extreme stations of his mind and heart in their never-ending voyage of self-exploration. His 'tragedy' is that he is incapable of tragedy. For tragedy presupposes the belief in an external order of things which is indeed incomplete without the conformity of the human soul, but would be still more defective without the soul's freedom to violate it. Yet Faust's dilemma is different. His 'two souls' are merely the one soul divided in itself because it knows of no independent external reality to which it is related as a free agent. Faust is in every essential respect Goethe's *alter ego*, the embodiment of that part of his self which remained unprotected by his apparently fondest trust and belief: that he belonged to Nature as her most precious possession. Faust, outside this zone of safety, is therefore torn between the belief in a world to which, strive as he may, he has no access whatever, and the belief in himself as the creator of his own world. Thus the spiritual extremes of his existence are not guilt and atonement, but despair and titanism. It is a situation unresolvable in tragedy.

Nature is fundamentally innocent, and Goethe's genius is in communion with nature. Hence there can be, for Goethe, no catharsis, only metamorphosis. It is never with the spirit of a transcendent God or with the spirit of Man that Goethe's potentially tragic heroes are reunited after their dramatic crises. When the crisis is over, they are at one again with the spirit of nature. They are not purified in a tragic sense, not raised above their guilt through atonement, but enter, as it were, a biologically, not morally, new phase of life, healed by oblivion and restored to strength through the sleep of the just. This is what happens to Orestes, and what happens to Faust at the beginning of Part II. Both put down their cup of Lethe and burst into magnificent praises of nature. But such, clearly, could not have been the conclusion of Faust. He had to be saved or damned, for heaven and hell had become involved by virtue of the legendary pattern. But it is *only* by virtue of the legendary pattern that they have become involved at all. For the world of Faust is only just Christian enough to have room for purgatory. It is a purgatory suspended between two half unreal spheres. Hence 'Mephistopheles must only half win his wager', and Faust be 'only half guilty', as Goethe himself put it in a letter which looks forward to the play's 'most serene conclusion' when 'the old Lord may exercise his privilege of mercy'.[17]

What is Faust's sin? The restlessness of spirit. What is Faust's salvation? The restlessness of spirit. The confusion lies in a perpetual criss-crossing of restless strivings of different qualities: the striving for peace, and the striving for sensation; or, to put it differently, and in terms of the quality of the contentment sought, the striving for that peace that passeth all understanding, and the striving for a state of calm, an 'enough' which is merely a state of emotional exhaustion. What the heavenly powers mean by that striving which carries its own salvation, must surely be different from the striving, the goal of which Faust hopes to achieve with the help of black magic and the devil. Yet these two kinds of striving perpetually get into each other's way throughout the poem, and the entanglement is at its worst in the crucial last scene of Faust's life when his desire for doing good and for the realization of his humanity within its decreed limits is inextricably bound up with the delusion and madness of titanism. Of these two strivings the one desires the attainment of the superman, the alchemist heightening of all human faculties, whereas the other aims at renunciation and resignation to the simple state of man. The first is the native element of Goethe's genius, the second the longing of Goethe's moral existence.

> Könnt' ich Magie von meinem Pfad entfernen,
> Die Zaubersprüche ganz und gar verlernen,
> Stünd ich, Natur, vor dir ein Mann allein,
> Da wär's der Mühe wert, ein Mensch zu sein.[18]

[Could I forget my sorcery, and ban my magic, stand, stripped of it utterly, oh Nature, face to face with thee, it might be worth while then to be a man.]

This outcry of Faust, towards the end of the play when he is visited by *Sorge*—and this is the second place where Faust is prepared to renounce the devil—reveals perhaps Goethe's deepest secret. To cut the umbilical cord with Nature and her magic power, not to remain what he once called 'a magic oyster over which there pass mysterious waves', to be face to face with Nature and escape the fate of Proteus—this only would be human happiness. Over and over again he sought deliverance from his genius in work, in the practical jobs of everyday life, through Wilhelm Meister's, through Faust's solution, and so desperately that as a man of fifty he confessed to Schiller (January 6th, 1798) that he owed it to him if he had learned to 'look at the manysidedness of my own inner being with more justice. . . . *You* have made me a poet again which I had all but ceased to be.' Such was the nature of his genius and the character of his age that the spirit could only live at the expense of life, and life only at the expense of the spirit. Thus the meaning of creative genius as well as the meaning of doing the sober work of the day, inwardness as well as action, had to remain puzzles to each other, anonymous, undefined strangers. They never met in a common dedication and could not be at peace with each other because they knew no will other than their own. And at such distance from 'la sua volontate è nostra pace' neither divine comedy nor human tragedy can be written.

It was impossible for Goethe to accept this situation, and impossible, by the very nature of things, to solve it. Hence his perpetual oscillation between the precarious magic of the inner communion with the deep where the Earth Spirit dwells, and the moral determination to reconcile himself to the cruder demands made on human existence by society, with the emphasis of approval shifting to and fro between the two: Egmont and Oranien, Tasso and Antonio, Prometheus and *Grenzen der Menschheit*, elective affinities and legal bonds. Was harmony ever to be achieved? The answer may be found in the ambiguity of *Faust*.

III

BURCKHARDT AND NIETZSCHE

BURCKHARDT AND NIETZSCHE

I

WHEN in 1495 Raphael was apprenticed to Pietro Perugino at Perugia, this city was one of the many Renaissance centres of political strife, moral outrage and ruthless violence. Matarazzo, the chronicler of the Perugia of that time, relates in some detail the story of the two rival families, the Oddi and the Baglioni, interlocked in a deadly struggle for the possession of the city. The Baglioni had been victorious and remained for some time the overlords of the Republic. The Oddi and their soldiers lived as exiles in the valley between Perugia and Assisi, being attacked by, and counter-attacking, the Baglioni in a perpetual war which devastated the rich Umbrian land, turned the peasants into beggars or robbers, and the vineyards into jungles where wolves fed on the dead of the battles. One day, however, the soldiers of the Oddi succeeded in taking Perugia by storm. Coming up from the valley, they overwhelmed the defenders at the city gates and reached the piazza. But there, in front of the cathedral, they were defeated by Astorre Baglione. The contemporary reporter describes the daring feat of courage and martial skill that Astorre performed; at the last moment and against superior numbers, he threw himself into the battle, sitting upright on his horse, with a falcon on his helmet and with his golden armour glittering in the sun. He looked and acted, Matarazzo says, like the God of War himself.

Jacob Burckhardt, in his *The Culture of the Renaissance in Italy*, draws freely on such sources, and, in this particular case, reflects whether it is not the hero of this episode whom we can see in Raphael's early paintings of St. George and St. Michael; adding that in the figure of the celestial rider in the Heliodorus fresco Astorre Baglione has found his final glorification.

Again, using Matarazzo as his source, Burckhardt tells the story of Atalanta, the beautiful mother of Grifone Baglione who was for some time ruling prince of Perugia. He had fought his way to power against rival members of his own family. His mother Atalanta was on the side of his enemies. On her son's victory she cursed him and fled from the city. But Grifone's rule was shortlived. He was soon overpowered by his rivals and mortally wounded. When Atalanta

53

heard he was dying, she returned with her daughter-in-law. At the
approach of the two ladies, the tumultuous crowd on the piazza
parted, both sides fearing the wrath of the bereaved mother. She,
however, went straight to her son, and, far from contemplating
further violence, implored him to forgive those who had dealt the
deadly blow. After he had thus renounced the spirit of revenge, he
died with the blessings of his mother. Then the two women left the
city again, and the crowd, partisans of both camps, knelt down and
wept as they crossed the piazza in their blood-stained garments. It
was for this Atalanta that Raphael later painted his *Deposizione*.
Thus, Burckhardt writes, 'her own suffering was laid at the feet of
the most sublime and sacred agony of a mother'. After all this the
cathedral of Perugia, which had stood in the midst of these many
scenes of felony and murder, was washed with wine and consecrated
anew.[1]

Anecdotes of this kind occur frequently in Jacob Burckhardt's
book on the Renaissance, which was first published in Basle in 1860
when its author had reached the age of forty-two. Are they, the
historian of to-day may ask, worthy of a self-respecting scholar?
Have they not the romantic flavour of a fanciful dramatization
rather than the authentic ring of precise recording? What is the
value of a source like Matarazzo's chronicles? Was he not a partisan
himself, bent upon building up a heroic reputation for the Baglioni,
and, at the same time, a story-teller determined to entertain and
edify his public rather than to instruct it?

We may, in the context of such queries, note that, when he began
his University education in Basle as a student of theology, Jacob
Burckhardt soon developed a very sceptical attitude towards his
subject. He was the son of a Protestant minister of the Church, and
it was his father's—and originally his own—wish that he should
become a clergyman himself. Soon, however, he decided to give up
theology because the rationalist Bible criticism of his teacher de
Wette had undermined his faith in orthodox beliefs. 'De Wette's
system,' he wrote in a letter to a friend, 'grows before my eyes to
colossal dimensions; one *must* follow him, nothing else is possible;
but, alas, every day there disappears under his hands a fragment of
the traditional teaching of the Church. To-day I have finally discovered that he regards the birth of Christ as a myth—and I with
him. It was with a shudder that I thought of a number of reasons
why it all but had to be like this. . . .'[2] Had this critical passion left

him during his subsequent training as a historian? And, after all, this history of the Renaissance was published by a pupil of Ranke whom, by the way, he always respected, though without much affection, and in whose seminar he had learned how to handle sources and be critical of them; are we not, therefore, entitled to expect something more sophisticated than heroic tales from this Professor of History, holding a chair in the University of Basle?

Before raising such questions we may first ask ourselves: what is the picture produced in our minds by these unverified, and probably unverifiable, anecdotes? It is composed of intense evil and sublime beauty, of hatred and charity, of degradation and purification, of the unscrupulousness that inflicts pain, and the reverence felt for suffering, of sin, contrition and atonement. Indeed, the source from which it springs is not chosen for the sake of factual exactitude. Its authority is of a different nature. It has for Burckhardt the authenticity of the mind, imagination and spirit of the Renaissance, and if it yields a negligible *quantity* of reliable facts, it nevertheless reveals something more important to him: the *quality* of the life of the period, or as he would have called it, the *Geist* of the epoch. To reproduce this is the concern of what he calls History of Culture as distinct from Political History. If he is to recapture the quality of life lived by a certain age, the historian must bring to his study not only industry, intelligence and honesty, but also something of the sensitivity and intuition of the artist. History of Culture has a critical method of its own, still more difficult to acquire than the ordinary techniques of critical investigation. In fact, it is not a technique at all, but rather creative sympathy. If we do not possess this we are perpetually misled by the egocentricity of our intellectual concepts; for we are prone to overrate the power as well as the range of application of our abstract thinking. Notions, for instance, like 'freedom' and 'slavery'; 'tolerance' and 'intolerance'; 'tyranny', 'aristocracy', 'democracy'; 'belief' and 'superstition', which we believe we are using objectively, applying them to certain observed phenomena, are, in fact, value-judgments charged with all the sentiments and resentments of our contemporary perception of human affairs. The very sound in our ears of the word 'slavery' may render our imagination impotent in its dealings with the particular quality of Greek civilization, and the emotional charge contained in the term 'freedom of thought' or, indeed, 'objectivity' itself, may practically blot out all our understanding of the quality of the knowledge and wisdom of a medieval sage. Yet there is a possible scale of human achievement on which a wretched feudal drudge may appear to approach the degree marking absolute freedom, and the constitutionally free citizen of a free republic the state of absolute slavery.

To come back to Burckhardt's Renaissance scenes: who can, as long as he remains within his restricted moral senses, assess the spiritual power present in a society and ready to be spent on the transformation of a ruthless prince into the Raphael picture of a warrior of Heaven, and of a cunning and power-seeking woman into a *mater dolorosa*? And when it comes to our contemporary debates, we might become considerably more economical and subtle in drawing historical parallels and comparisons, if we were inspired by only one spark of what Burckhardt meant by historical understanding. We might not have to risk in every attempt at, for instance, appreciating the spiritual life and character of the Middle Ages, the release of cataracts of moralizing recriminations about religious wars, crusades, inquisitions and other pestilences.

Indeed, Burckhardt, like his teacher Ranke, is convinced of the fundamental importance of original sources and warns his pupils against text-books, digests and interpretations, not because he upholds the superstition of perfect objectivity emerging like the vision of a god from the assiduity of the source collector, but because he believes that the activity of the imagination can be stimulated as well as purified by an ever-renewed contact with the documents which reproduce the impact made by an event in human history upon particular minds. Such a mind—and here the method of the historian of a culture differs from that of the political or economic historian—may be a naïve chronicler like Matarazzo or, indeed, an inspired painter like Raphael. Did they report or paint what *really* happened? Of course not, if 'real' is to denote the pure abstract of an event, which is, in fact, no event whatsoever. For something that happens becomes an event only when it is mentally and emotionally perceived and registered. Matarazzo, therefore, in all his naïvety, and Raphael, with all the transforming power of his art, are both sources of the historian of a culture who is, as Burckhardt once put it in his unphilosophical manner, as much concerned with 'represented history' as with what 'literally happened', forgetting that nothing happens literally—unless we are determined to make our own perception the criterion of the perception of truth itself, and to say that what *really* happens is precisely what we would have noticed had we been on the spot. Thus it is with some justification that Burckhardt maintains in a neat over-statement that for the history of culture the facts to be assessed are *identical* with the sources. Claiming for his method *primum gradum certitudinis*,[3] he upholds in defiance of the fact-worshippers that even records of things that have not happened at all may be important by virtue of the typical mode of their distortions and misinterpretations. Of Aeneas Silvius he says in his *Renaissance*: 'One may distrust the testimony of that man completely, and yet one would have to admit that there are not many other men in whose mind is reflected, with such perception and liveliness, the picture of the age and its intellectual culture'.[4]

The idea, however, of arriving at any positive certainty by accumulating more and more sources until that point of completeness is reached at which we may, in Bury's words, 'grasp the complete development of humanity', is, of course, dismissed by Burckhardt as a chimaera. The very attempt, he holds, would interfere with any comprehensiveness of vision. Pedantry to him is one of the most cunning enemies of truth, luring the search into the dusty lumber rooms of the past where only mice may hope to find something to eat. Mind and imagination must needs choke in them, and Buckle, for instance, he says, owes his paralysis of the brain to his exclusive obsession with the Scottish sermons of the seventeenth and eighteenth centuries.[5] The very spiritual poverty of what Burckhardt calls his 'pretty century' drives so many of its academic studies into some narrow recess of the past where the ideal of precision and completeness may hide from the adept the absence of true comprehension. It is in those holes of the mind that the indiscriminate and diffused suspicion is bred which tends to dismiss as vague generalizations *all* historical assessments based on a broader vision. For the modern mind, in some of its most vocal representatives, has yielded to the inferior magic of facts, numbers, statistics, and to that sort of empiricism which, in its passion for concreteness, paradoxically reduces experience to a purely abstract notion of measurable data, having cast aside the 'immeasurable wealth' of authentic experiences of the spirit and imagination. The specialization in trifles which results from such abstractions, seeks its justification not only in the arithmetical deception that a thousand futilities add up to a large piece of significance, but also in the strange belief that the great issues have all been fully explored and the outstanding sources exhausted. For Burckhardt, however, it merely brings to life that waning sense of significance which he finds and deplores in his age, the crumbling of all central convictions and the spontaneous disinclination of mediocrity to expose itself to the impact of what is great. It may be, he says, 'that there is still hidden in Thucydides a fact of capital importance which somebody will note in a hundred years time'.[6] For the present, Burckhardt maintains, 'a single source, happily chosen, can, as it were, do duty for a whole multitude of possible other sources, since he who is really determined to learn, that is, to become rich in spirit, can, by a simple function of his mind, discern and feel the general in the particular'.[7]

This is an echo from the world of Goethe who knew the difference in quality between a writer who, starting with preconceived ideas, assembles his particulars to fit the needs of his generalities, and a poet who 'discerns and feels' the universal in the particular phenomenon.[8] Like Stifter, with whom he has so much in common, Burckhardt felt himself to be one of 'Goethe's family'. As a young man he hoped he would become a poet—and he actually did publish a number of poems—and throughout his life history remained for him a poetic activity. 'As a historian,' he once wrote, 'I am lost where I cannot begin with *Anschauung*.'[9] It is a Goethean word and hardly translatable. Its connotations are visual, and it means the mental process by which we spontaneously grasp, through observation aided by intuition, a thing in its wholeness. Goethe uses it as the opposite of analysis, the mental approach which he feared would establish itself as the dominant habit of an age fascinated by Newtonian Physics, only to destroy all culture of the intellect. Sometimes Burckhardt even felt it to be a nuisance that the historian, in presenting his historical narrative, was bound by the chronological order compelling him to tell one thing after the other when the true order 'could only be represented as a picture'.[10] With such a mind it is not surprising that he agrees with Aristotle and Schopenhauer in claiming for poetry and art a higher rank in the hierarchy of understanding and knowledge than history could ever hold. In those lecture notes which he prepared in the years 1868–71, posthumously published by Jacob Oeri in 1905 under the title of *Weltgeschichtliche Betrachtungen* (Reflections on World History), he states in a fashion leaving no doubt about the degree of his certainty:

'The rivalry between history and poetry has been finally settled by Schopenhauer. Poetry achieves more for our knowledge of the truth about mankind; even Aristotle said: "Poetry is more philosophical and profound than history", and this is true because the faculty which gives birth to poetry is intrinsically of a higher order than that of the greatest historian; further, the end to which it is created is much more sublime than that of history. . . . Hence history finds in poetry not only one of its most important, but also one of its purest and finest sources.'[11]

Saying this, Burckhardt refers to a number of specified passages from Schopenhauer's *World as Will and Idea*: they contain almost all that is needed for an understanding of Burckhardt's philosophy. Has he, then, a philosophy? He has no 'philosophy of *history*'; indeed, it is repugnant to him if by this forbidding term there is to be understood what dominated the philosophical and historical scene in Burckhardt's time: the attempt to transform history into philosophy and, indeed, into theology. In other words, Burckhardt hates the philosophy of Hegel. This fundamentally irreverent intimacy with Providence, this 'bold and insolent anticipation of a world plan',[12] as he calls it, is not for him. All the introductory remarks to his *Reflections on World History* are directed against Hegel. 'Our task in this course,' he writes, 'consists in linking a series of historical observations and findings to an all but arbitrarily chosen line of thought and then again to another one.'[13] Further: 'Above all, we shall not give any philosophy of history'.[14] And a few lines later, so as to leave no doubt what has prompted this renunciation of all philosophy of history, the name of Hegel is introduced: 'Hegel . . . tells us that the only idea which is "given" in philosophy is the simple idea of reason, the idea that the world is rationally ordered: hence the history of the world is a rational process, and the conclusion yielded by world history *must* be that it was the rational, inevitable march of the World Spirit. . . . Hegel speaks also of the "purpose of eternal wisdom", and calls his study a theodicy by virtue of its recognition of the positive in which the negative (in popular parlance, evil) vanishes, subjected and overcome. He develops the fundamental idea that history is the record of the process by which mind becomes aware of its own significance; according to him, there is progress towards freedom. In the East, only one man was free, in classical antiquity only a few, while modern times have set all men free. Thus we find him putting forward the doctrine of perfectibility, that is, our old familiar friend called progress.'[15]

But in spite of his disclaiming it, Burckhardt has, of course, a philosophy; that is, he thinks philosophically about history. He has, however, no system which could be expounded apart from, and beyond, his historical and philosophical thinking. His metaphysical beliefs and fundamental thoughts, therefore, have to be perceived through his reflections about things. Yet there is one philosopher in whom he finds the dispersed elements of his own thought crystallized into a definite system. This is Schopenhauer, whom in conversations with Nietzsche he called 'our philosopher'.[16] The introduction to his *Reflections on World History* is in parts a précis of what Schopenhauer has to say about the subject and, above all, about Hegel's hypostasis of history. 'The Hegelians,' we read in Schopenhauer, 'who regard the philosophy of history as the aim of all philosophy, ought to be taught some Plato, who indefatigably repeats that the object of philosophy lies in the unchangeable and in what lasts, and not in the things which are now like this, and now again like that. All those who postulate such constructions about the world in motion, or, as they call it, history, have not grasped the fundamental truth of philosophy: that, philosophically speaking, what *really* is, is the same at all times. . . . The fools, however, believe that it will develop and one day arrive. . . . Thus they regard the whirling world as they perceive it as the ultimate reality, and see its final meaning in a meagre bliss on earth which, even if cultivated evermore by man and favoured by fate, will remain a hollow, deceptive, fickle and sorry thing of which nothing essentially better can ever come through either constitutions, or legal codes, or steam engines, or telegraphs. Those philosophers and glorifiers of history are therefore realistic simpletons, optimists and eudaemonists, which is to say, mediocre fellows and obstinate philistines and, in addition, bad Christians. . . . A real philosophy of history ought to bear in mind what for ever *is* and never *develops*. It can, indeed, not consist in raising the temporal aims of man to the rank of absolutes, and, furthermore, in constructing in an artificial and fanciful manner man's progress; but it ought to be based upon the insight that, in all those endless variations and turmoils, we are having before us merely the one creature, *essentially* identical and unchangeable, busying itself with the very same things to-day, and yesterday, and forever. . . . This identity, preserved through all changes, is founded on the fundamental qualities of human hearts and brains, many bad, few good. . . . For someone bringing philosophical intentions to history, the study of Herodotus is sufficient. There he will find everything that has gone into the making of all subsequent world history: the activities, afflictions and fortunes of the human race. . . .'[17]

Schopenhauer's philosophy pervades the whole work of Jacob Burckhardt, and letter after letter shows how deeply he was in agreement with it. For instance, in the Introduction to his *Reflections* he says: 'Our point of departure is the one and only thing which lasts in history and is its only possible centre: man, this suffering, striving and active being, as he is and was and will be for ever. . . . The philosophers of history see the past in opposition and as a preliminary to us as the more developed; *we* shall study what is *recurrent*, *constant* and *typical* as echoing in us and to be understood by us.'[18]

In this context Burckhardt, as though casually, makes a remark which strikes at the very centre of what can, after all, be called his philosophy of history. Man, he had previously asserted, not a Hegelian *Weltgeist*, is the centre of history. Is this to be taken as the declaration of a humanistic creed, pure and simple? In a sense, it is—in as far as it draws a definite line between the study of the *historical* aspect of human life and all theology. But while he definitely attacks the Hegelian brand of *secularized* theology, he acknowledges, without accepting it for himself, the particular justification of a genuinely religious interpretation of history, the great model of which he sees in Augustine's *De Civitate Dei*.[19] It is, however, none of his business. He is concerned with man, he says, and not with God. Is he, therefore, simply a humanist? We might be allowed to assume this more lightheartedly were it not for the remark which I have hinted at, and which concludes the paragraph that allots to man the central position in Burckhardt's studies. It says: 'Hence our study will, in a sense, be pathological in kind'. In other words: the perpetual agent of human affairs is a pathological creature, the Fall the beginning of history, original sin its driving force and redemption its end. Although this may sound very much like a surreptitious opening of the theological floodgates, it is, in fact, implied by Burckhardt when he regards the study of history as an essay in pathology.

He may have lost his faith in Christianity, very much as 'our philosopher' Schopenhauer had lost it; he may have abandoned the belief that the offer of redemption reached man in the shape of an historical event and was rejected by a creature bent on the *continuation* of his history. But, again like Schopenhauer, he accepts an *order of things* identical with that accepted by the Christian believer. It is the only order of things in which the religion of Christ can make sense; and if it is the *true* order of things, it is, at the same time, a profoundly *senseless* pattern *without* the religion of Christ. To look upon man, as Schopenhauer and Burckhardt did, as the fallen creature, on sin and evil as constituent and ineradicable factors in human history, on human affairs as pathological, without believing in the reality, existence, possibility and indeed the definite offer of spiritual health, must needs create a profound spiritual predicament. A tougher form of humanism than that of Burckhardt, a humanism coupled with rationalism, knows nothing of such difficulties. But it is astonishing how few people can really and truly attain to such toughness. Those who believe they can do without metaphysics are usually only those who cannot do with metaphysics, indulging instead in sentimentality and other secretive betrayals of *ratio*, and in the kind of metaphysics which escapes being diagnosed as such merely by virtue of its diffuseness and conventional respectability; as, for instance, the metaphysics of equating scientific discoveries with the discovery of Truth, or the metaphysics of perfectibility and progress. For the rest the predicament persists; and it did, throughout their lives, persist for men like Schopenhauer and Burckhardt. They bore it nobly, and with a strength of spirit and character which is rare among human beings. They represent the true aristocracy of the nineteenth century. Within the German language writers like Stifter, Grillparzer, Mörike, Gottfried Keller, are of their kin. They are few indeed; and to all of them one could, in some measure, apply the words of Nietzsche in which he describes Schopenhauer in the image of Dürer's *Knight with Death and Devil*, that man in armour 'who bravely travels along his path of horror, unperturbed by his terrible companions, and yet without hope'.[20]

Set up against such stoicism, those Germans who, in the nineteenth century, cried out their despair, appear somewhat obtrusive and vulgar. But who is able to judge whether in them—and I am thinking of men like Kleist, Büchner, Nietzsche himself—the sense of spiritual loss had not penetrated deeper? However this may be, it certainly was not met by the same inner resources of natural strength and tradition which saved Schopenhauer and Burckhardt.

2

Nietzsche, who, for a short time, was Burckhardt's very much younger professorial colleague in the University of Basle, once described him in a letter as 'that elderly, highly original man, given, not to distorting truth, but to passing it over in silence'.[21] He goes on to say that he deeply enjoys listening to Burckhardt's lectures 'with their profound thoughts and their strangely abrupt breaks and twists as soon as they touch the danger point'. Passing over the truth in silence, sudden twists as soon as the matter approaches a critical point: Nietzsche appears to imply that Burckhardt is in fact more of a rebel than he is inclined to show, and more profoundly desperate about the intellectual and spiritual situation of the age than his professorial equilibrium would betray. Indeed, Nietzsche was convinced to the very end of his conscious life that Burckhardt knew the desperate truth which he believed himself to have discovered and exposed, and that the resigned serenity of Burckhardt's life in Basle was a mask put on for the sake of self-defence. Again and again, from the depths of his loneliness, Nietzsche begged Burckhardt's understanding and sympathy. He was probably mistaken. The core of Burckhardt's being was not affected by his pessimism. There was no need for him to attempt, in the manner of Nietzsche, any metamorphosis of spiritual gloom into Dionysian ecstasy. He knew, as certainly as Nietzsche, that the civilization of Europe which he loved was doomed. To one of his German friends who placed high hopes in the pre-1848 revolutionary and nationalist movement, he wrote—to quote only one example out of a very great number of similar statements: 'None of you has any idea yet what a people is and how easily it deteriorates into a barbarous mob. You do not know yet what a tyrannical rule is to be set up over the spirit. . . . We may all perish; but I for one shall choose the cause for which I am going to perish: the culture of old Europe.'[22]

Burckhardt could not bear with Nietzsche's iconoclast philosophizing. He had lost his religious faith, but, unlike Nietzsche, the loss was registered by the intelligence alone. The 'shudder' with which, as a young student, he discovered that he did not believe in the recorded circumstances of the birth of Christ did not disturb the core of his being. 'Religions,' he said in his *Reflections on World History*, 'are the expression of the eternal and indestructible metaphysical need of human nature.'[23] This he accepted as a self-evident and empirical truth—in the same way in which it was accepted by Schopenhauer who in his *World as Will and Idea* called man the *animal metaphysicum*, in a chapter entitled 'About the Metaphysical Need of Man'. And believing, as he did, in a fundamental correspondence in the world between needs and possibilities of satisfaction, Burckhardt could not share Nietzsche's suspicion that man—the diseased animal, for Nietzsche—was an eternally cheated misfit within a universe catering, on the whole, for the natural needs of its creatures. Should man alone have been cursed with an everlasting appetite, to feed which all the Heavens may be ransacked without result? Nietzsche did believe this; and his Superman was the child of his fancy, miraculously feeding on barren fields and finally conquering the metaphysical hunger itself. Burckhardt, on the other hand, was of a more robust spiritual nature and more firmly rooted in the Christian tradition of Europe. He continued to eat the bread and drink the wine, and called them by the names of culture and tradition. Religious crisis he regarded as only one more historical variation and change embedded in the spiritual *continuum* without which history would have meant nothing to him. To Burckhardt, therefore, Nietzsche's nihilism must have appeared monstrous, and yet it must have set in motion those elements of despair which were inherent in his own philosophy. The all but inhuman coldness with which he responded—or rather did not respond—to Nietzsche's entreaties for a word of encouragement, can hardly be accounted for in any other way. We are reminded of Goethe's forbidding aloofness in his dealings with men of whom he sensed that too close a contact with them might endanger the subtle balance which he had achieved, because they embodied the *alter ego* of his own being, the *ego* of despair.

Nietzsche, however, remained convinced of Burckhardt's 'mask'. One of his notebook jottings from the years 1875–76 says: 'Those who are restrained, like Jacob Burckhardt, out of desperation',[24] and there is little doubt who is in his mind when in *Beyond Good and Evil* he remarks: 'There are "scholarly men" who make use of scholarship because it gives them a classically serene façade, and because scholarship suggests the conclusion that the man is superficial:—they *wish* that people should arrive at a wrong conclusion about them'. In the same context Nietzsche also speaks of 'buffoonery' as another possible disguise of 'desperate, all too certain knowledge'.[25] Clearly, he meant himself, referring to his own display of paradoxical formulations, witty extravagances, provocative exaggerations. The two supposed masks of despair, Burckhardt's scholarship and his own 'buffoonery', are mentioned once more: in the last letter Nietzsche wrote to Burckhardt after the catastrophe, foreseen by Burckhardt, had happened, and clinical insanity had descended upon him. It is one of the most extraordinary and most revealing documents ever composed by a madman, which begins with the words: 'Dear Herr Professor, when it comes to it I too would very much prefer a professorial chair in Basle to being God; but I did not dare to go as far in my private egoism as to refrain for its sake from the creation of the world', and in which the writer refers to himself as 'being condemned to entertain the next eternity with bad witticisms'.[26]

There were two men in Nietzsche's life whom intellectually he had abandoned, but whom he continued to love, respect and admire: Schopenhauer and Burckhardt. With regard to all others—and he was alone at the end—he identified their unwillingness to follow him intellectually with weakness of character, and discarded them. But to Burckhardt, about whose rejection of his own philosophizing he was left in no uncertainty, he submitted, as it were, his resignation in what are the only lucid words in an otherwise deranged note, written two days before the letter just quoted: 'Now you are our great—our greatest teacher'.[27]

In the case of Burckhardt, Nietzsche's love survived even humiliation. What then did, in so commanding a manner, hold Nietzsche's affection for Schopenhauer and Burckhardt? Undoubtedly what Goethe had praised in Schopenhauer: intellectual honesty. And something else as well: the spiritual vitality which enabled them to live on, and to remain sane in spite of their profound pessimism. This is precisely the same strength which the young Nietzsche, in his *Birth of Tragedy*, discerned in the Greeks, and which he passionately and lyrically exalted—so passionately and lyrically, indeed, that the work was, of course, rejected by the sound scholars of his day. Despair, reconciled to life through beauty: this is Nietzsche's interpretation of the Greek view of the world. It is identical with the view of Greek antiquity which pervades the pages of Burckhardt's *History of Greek Culture*, another of his lecture courses

posthumously published between 1898 and 1902. Obviously, he
had read his younger colleague's book on the *Birth of Tragedy*.
Burckhardt, too, is attacking the conventional enthusiasts of
classicism, who look upon ancient Greece as a prolonged jamboree
of sunburned optimists and philosophizing athletes, and gives to
tragic pessimism the central position in the picture he draws of their
culture.

It is this tragic pessimism which, in the beginning of their
acquaintance, Burckhardt and Nietzsche had in common. But
Nietzsche soon went further, and the very way he went reveals—
much to Burckhardt's horror—the precariousness of the position
they had held in common. Nietzsche was more deeply wounded by
the loss of positive religious convictions than Burckhardt, which is
as much as to say that his nature was more in need of an articulate
religious faith. The aesthetic comfort offered by the contemplation
of the human tragedy was, in the long run, not sufficient to counter-
act Nietzsche's despair. For Burckhardt history, or rather the history
of culture, was the medium of such selfless contemplation. Had his
talents allowed him to become an artist, it would have been so much
the better for him; as it was, the history of culture had to take the
place of poetry. Here at least he could contemplate the *manifestations*
of art. For it is the work of art (and with it, to a certain degree,
culture itself) through which, according to Schopenhauer, man
escapes from the drudgery of the Will and leaves behind the fetters
of selfhood. Thus it testifies to man's share in a creative intelligence
beyond the purely historical realm, the realm of original sin.
Therefore, Burckhardt believes that it is in the sphere of culture that
human contemplation can perceive that spiritual *continuum* which he
believes gives meaning to all history. For the performance of this
task, he maintains, 'the human mind is well equipped', for it
represents 'the power of interpreting all things in an ideal sense. . . .
Our spirit must transmute into a possession the remembrance of its
passage through the ages of the world. What was once joy and
sorrow must now become understanding. . . . Therewith the saying
Historia vitae magistra assumes a higher yet a humbler meaning. We
wish knowledge to make us, not shrewder (for next time) but wiser
(for ever).' And finally: 'Contemplation, however, is not only the
right and the duty of the historian; it is also a supreme need. It is
our freedom in the very awareness of universal bondage and in the
stream of necessities.'[28]

This is the nucleus of Burckhardt's view of history. It is, at the same time, the application of Schopenhauer's metaphysics to historical studies. It also contains Burckhardt's idea of the historian's objectivity, which for him does not consist in the seemingly simple and practically impossible device of suspending moral judgment or, indeed, any other judgment in the face of a phenomenon, merely because it happens to be historical. The evil which Burckhardt perceives in history—and he perceives more evil in it than good—he freely calls by its name; as freely as he calls beauty beautiful and ugliness ugly. 'From the fact, however,' he says in *Reflections on World History*, 'that good may come from evil, and from disaster relative happiness, it does not follow that evil and disaster are not what they are.'[29] *Values*, for him, are as real, and more so, than facts and happenings. In this he remains with Schopenhauer a Platonic idealist, despising what he calls 'the frivolous pretence of objectivity' which, instead of achieving what it aims at, merely loses itself in a welter of relativities. By the objectivity of true contemplation he means the conquest of the self-will, the philosophical activity *kat' exochen*. Its goal is certainly not the abolition of judgment, be it aesthetic or moral, but its purification.

There was a time when Nietzsche was prepared to remain at rest here with Burckhardt. And indeed, we hardly know of any better resting-place. It is certainly good enough to deserve our most exacting efforts in defending it against the onrush of those noisily activist forces which, in the disguise and with the persuasion of social moralism, are undermining it from all sides. Burckhardt, in letters to his friends, called all 'these great achievements' in politics, industry and social organization which are demanded from us at the cost of all peace for contemplation 'thoroughly mediocre, and a nuisance because of the ever-increasing bother of "earnest work"'. He speaks of the 'frightful spiritual nullity' of 'radicalism',[30] of those 'odious windbags of progressive optimism', and fears that 'the conditions of Europe may overnight deteriorate into a kind of gangrene with all truly conservative forces suddenly dying away'.[31] In his critique of the age Nietzsche, consistently enough, was with him. At what point, then, did they part company?

It was, I would suggest, over a religious and moral issue.

The kinship between Schopenhauer's (and therefore Burckhardt's) philosophy of contemplation and Eastern forms of religion has often been emphasized. Yet we have, I think, little understanding of the

F

nature of some aspects of Eastern quietism. What we really appreciate of it we judge by the tradition of European mysticism. The reward of this kind of mystical contemplation is the contact established with the divinity. Thus it is not practised for its own sake, but for the sake of this highest reward which, as the highest reward, stands in no need of further justification. Schopenhauer's idea of contemplation also knows of some reward; but its reward is, or at least appears to be, the purest aesthetic experience. If life on this earth is sin and self-willed deception, if the misery of it by far outweighs the rare moments of happiness, if it is altogether the continuous and futile drudgery of a fallen creature—and this is, I believe, a faithful summing-up of Schopenhauer's and Burckhardt's views—then, surely, the desire to emancipate oneself from it, and seek reward in the sublimity of a self-detached vision, not of God but, for Burckhardt, of *history*, must needs provoke dissatisfaction and moral suspicion in a man to whom life on this earth is agony, precisely because he cannot attain to a vision of God.

This is where the roots of Nietzsche's catastrophic plight lie, and the deepest cause of his final breaking-away from his 'great educator' Schopenhauer and his 'great teacher' Burckhardt. With God 'being dead' for him he could find no lasting spiritual satisfaction in the pure contemplation of a creation deserted by its creator. If history, the dwelling-place of sin and evil, had thus lost its meaning, it had to be abolished; if the fallen creature had ceased to be redeemable, good and evil had to be transcended by the Superman; and the gloom of the Eternal Recurrence of a senseless world in motion (and not Burckhardt's spiritual *continuum*) was for him the only alternative to the Second Coming. Nietzsche, to the very end of insanity, spins out the thread of unbelief. In his very spiritual consistency there dwells the madness of desperation. Yet there was in him a mind nobler than the mind of those who, like Hegel's idealist and Marxian train, chose the other consistent alternative, seeking, and presumably finding, in the *historical* dimension of man's existence the promise of salvation, and in his mundane performances sufficient attraction for the *Weltgeist* to settle down among human beings, bringing with it the bliss of perfect harmony or, at least, a classless society.

Rare, however, are they who, on the highest level of spiritual awareness and in this hour of history, are blessed with the power to maintain the equipoise of suspense. Burckhardt was one of them. 'At every moment,' he wrote in a letter, 'I would be prepared to exchange my life for a never-having-been.'[32] He knew 'what beggars we mortals are at the gates of happiness',[33] but he was determined to 'die at peace with the world'. Yet his, on the surface, purely aesthetic faith was not the only source that sustained his soul. There was, though it remained inarticulate, much left in him of a faith which has a profounder reach. In his *Reflections on World History*, contemplating the power and the success of evil (and power he regarded as for ever predominantly evil, and Napoleon he called a personified absurdity), he dismisses the comfort which the Hegelian assumption of a historical master-plan for the world may give. 'Every successful wickedness,' he says, 'is, to say the least of it, a scandal,' and he adds: 'The only lesson to be derived from the successful misdeeds of the strong is to hold life here and now in no higher esteem than it deserves.'[34] And once, concluding one of his lectures about Greek art with some reflections on the sadness expressed in the faces of the marble images of Greek gods, he made the Vatican Hermes say: 'You are astonished that I am so sad, I, one of the Olympians living in perpetual bliss and immortal joy? Indeed, we possessed everything: glory, heavenly beauty, eternal youth, everlasting pleasure, and yet we were not happy. . . . We lived only for ourselves and inflicted suffering on all others. . . . We were not good, and hence we had to perish.'[35] This is not the language of a rhapsodist of beauty. It rather sounds like an echo of the voice of Jacob Burckhardt *senior*, Vicar of the Minster of Basle.

IV

NIETZSCHE AND GOETHE

NIETZSCHE AND GOETHE

I

In 1817 Goethe published in *Kunst und Altertum* a little essay entitled 'Epochs of the Spirit, based on Hermann's newest records'.[1] Inspired by the book *De Mythologia Graecorum Antiquissimorum* of the Leipzig scholar Gottfried Hermann, this sketch, anticipating in its modest way the method of Spengler's historical morphology, speaks of four major phases in the history of man. These 'four epochs of the human spirit', 'profoundly contemplated', as Goethe claims, 'and fittingly named', he calls the Ages of Poetry, Theology, Philosophy and Prose. They are preceded, according to his account, by a state which does not even qualify for a name. It is the chaos before the beginning and before the Word; although even then a few favoured spirits might rise above the speechless dark, crudely meditating the uncreated universe and uttering raucous sounds to express their confused astonishment. Theirs is an apparently barren state of mind which nevertheless holds the seeds of observation and philosophy, of giving nature names, and thus of poetry. From these inarticulate mutterings emerges the first Age proper, the Age of Poetry, in which man projects his tender familiarity with himself, his desires and fears, satisfactions and discontents, on to the things which surround him. It is a time of popular myth and poetical fancy; the soul, overconfidently and lightheartedly, frees itself of the cumbersome abstruseness of the primeval stage. The spirits of myth and poetry wield their undivided power over the community which is, as Goethe says, distinguished by a sensuousness at once free, serious, noble and enhanced by the imagination.

Soon, however, man finds himself, perhaps by force of external circumstances, thrown into new perplexities. The world ceases to be his castle, in which the mind and the imagination dwell comfortably between walls covered with allegorical tapestries, but appears once more inadequately understood and mastered. The poetically comprehending creature is again beset by apprehension, the idyllic order threatened by a multitude of demons demanding to be placated in their wildness, reverenced in their incalculable dominion, and conquered no longer by pretty fancies but only through a more energetic activity of the spirit. Gone is the graceful intimacy of the

73

Age of Poetry, and Mystery is reinstated. It is to this epoch that
ultimately God is revealed, with the fear and terror of the primeval
phase purified into love and awe. We may call it, says Goethe, the
Age of the Holy, or the Age of Theology, or the Age of Reason in
its highest sense.

Again, it cannot last. For Reason will insist on reasoning and
ultimately, as a conqueror often does with the object of his con-
quests, destroy what it is reasoning about. Analysing what eludes
analysis, systematizing what defies the system, it will in the end
deceive itself by pretending that the vainly besieged mystery does
not exist. At this point the Age of the Holy gives way to the Age of
Philosophy, or, to use a more familiar term, to enlightenment and
finally rationalism. We cannot, says Goethe, but acknowledge the
noble and intelligent endeavour of this epoch; yet while it may suit
some talented individuals, it cannot satisfy whole peoples. The
Prosaic Age is bound to follow. The all too radical attempt of the
Age of Philosophy at a 'humanization' and rationalization of the
mysterious ends in a perverted miracle. The mystery, cheated of
its rightful place, goes underground, reverting to its primeval, unholy and barbarous stage. The human spirit, agitated by historical
catastrophes, leaps backward over all hurdles which the guidance of
reason had erected, clinging here and there to remnants of tradition,
scattered residues of many incompatible beliefs, then plunges head-
long into pools of insipid mythologies, bringing to the top the
muddy poetry of the depths and proclaiming it as the creed of the
age.

No longer are there teachers who teach with calm and reason,
but merely men sowing grain and weeds in random profusion. No
centre holds the human world together and men must lose their
bearings; for countless individuals step forth as leaders, preaching
their perfect foolishness as the acme of wisdom. In such an age
every belief turns into blasphemy, and the proclamation of mysteries
into sacrilege. Elements, once evolving naturally one from the
other, are now interlocked in perpetual strife. It is the return of the
tohu-bohu; yet a chaos not fertile as the first, but so deadening that
not even God could create from it a world worthy of Himself.

It is surprising that a peaceful Leipzig scholar, whose attitude
Nietzsche once described as the typically *sächsisch* combination of
humanism and religious rationalism,[2] should have been the begetter
of such a rare flight of Goethe's historical imagination, culminating

in a precise vision of the apocalypse through which we are living. But although the condensed precision of this seemingly casual prophecy is unique in Goethe's writings, shadows of things to come fall on many a page of his mature work. In the guarded and fortified stillness of *Wilhelm Meisters Wanderjahre* (the work that occupied him at the same time) echoes can be discerned of subterranean rumblings, menacing with future eruptions a society whose exposures and dangers are acknowledged by the very didactic passion of this extraordinary work—a work which struck Nietzsche, in one of his more irreverent moods, as a mixture of 'the most beautiful things in the world' and 'the most ridiculous triflings'.[3] Indeed, a certain parallelism is obvious between the three epochs of the spirit and the three stations in Wilhelm Meister's pilgrimage which fill the first book of the novel, so that the monastic sphere of St. Joseph the Second is informed with all the ingredients of the Age of the Holy, with elements of the Age of Poetry lingering on, while the estate of Hersilie's uncle clearly represents the Age of Philosophy, with no picture tolerated in the eighteenth-century portrait gallery that 'might point even remotely towards religion, tradition, mythology, legend or fable'.[4] And there is finally Makarie's ancient castle, looking so fresh and new—'as though builders and masons had only just departed'[5]—where Goethe's, not Newton's physics are pursued, a science whose calculations reveal, rather than disturb, the harmony between man's intuitive and rational natures, showing him, not as the ruthlessly dominating, but as 'the spiritually integrating part'[6] of the universe. This castle of Makarie stands like a fortress, built in Goethe's imagination, to ward off, as their most positive alternative, the horrors of the Prosaic Age.

Furthermore, in that masterpiece of ambiguity, *Faust*, the clash between the holy simplicity of the Gretchen world and the reason of the philosopher, aided by the prose of the devil, determines not only the tragedy of Part I, but finds expression also in Part II. Indeed, if we sought in Goethe's works for the most poignant poetic dramatization of the defeat of the holy at the hands of prosaic engineering, we would have to call on the faithful old couple in their little house on the hill, sacrificed to the planning of the future bliss of millions:

BAUCIS   Menschenopfer mussten bluten,
               Nachts erscholl des Jammers Qual;

Meerab flossen Feuergluten,
Morgens war es ein Kanal.
Gottlos ist er, ihn gelüstet
Unsre Hütte, unser Hain;
Wie er sich als Nachbar brüstet,
Soll man untertänig sein.

PHILEMON Hat er uns doch angeboten
Schönes Gut im neuen Land!

BAUCIS Traue nicht dem Wasserboden,
Halt auf deiner Höhe stand!

PHILEMON Lasst uns zur Kapelle treten,
Letzten Sonnenblick zu schaun!
Lasst uns läuten, knien, beten,
Und dem alten Gott vertraun![7]

[Human sacrifices had to bleed, the night resounded with cries of anguish; floods of fire poured into the sea, in the morning it was a canal. Godless is he, lusting after our cottage, our grove; Boastful neighbour that he is, he demands obedience.—Yet he has offered us a pretty estate in the new country!—Do not trust the watery soil, hold out on your height!—Let us go to our chapel, catch the sun's last radiance, ring the bells, and kneel and pray, and put our trust in the hands of God.]

What, in the Prosaic Age, is to become of poetry itself, its activity and its enjoyment; how will this very poem *Faust* be received, Goethe asks, five days before his death, in his last letter to Wilhelm von Humboldt. 'The absurdity and confusion of the day is such,' he writes, 'as to convince me that the honest and prolonged labour with which I have built this strange edifice will be but ill rewarded; it will be cast up by the sea as fragments of a wreck, and for some time to come will be buried under the barren dunes of the age. Confused gospels, begetting confused deeds, are abroad in the world, and my business is to enhance and purify what is mine and what has remained with me, as you, my worthy friend, also contrive to do up there in your castle.'[8]

In other words, the Prosaic Age is upon us, with its disenchantment of myth and poetry, and its 'mystification' of reason itself. It will—to use Goethe's words—'drag into the vulgar light of day the ancient heritage of a noble past, and destroy not only the capacity for profound feeling and the beliefs of peoples and priests, but even that belief of reason which divines meaningful coherence behind strangeness and seeming disorder'.[9]

It is, then, the destruction, or rather the mutilation and deformation, of something which Goethe, perhaps for want of a better word, calls 'belief', which is one of the symptoms, or one of the causes, of the repulsiveness of the Prosaic Age. As soon as the notion of belief enters into our reflections about Goethe, we have to move with the utmost wariness; for Goethe, of course, was no believer in any doctrinal sense. On the other hand, we need not be too prudish and may take courage from the fact that Goethe, at about the same time, uses the word again in a very much more contaminated neighbourhood; namely, in connection with the Old Testament. Meditating on the desert adventures of the Israelites, he says, in his 'Notes and Discourses concerning the *West-östlicher Divan*': 'The one and only real and profound theme of the world and of human history—a theme to which all others are subordinate—remains the conflict between belief and unbelief. All epochs dominated by belief in whatever shape have a radiance and bliss of their own, and bear fruit for their people as well as for posterity. All epochs over which unbelief in whatever form maintains its miserable victory, even if they boast and shine for a while with false splendour, are ignored by posterity because nobody likes to drudge his life out over sterile things.'[10]

Paradoxically enough, what follows leaves no doubt that Goethe, indulging at this point in a rather ruthless sort of Bible criticism, does not mean the belief of the strict believer in the Old Testament. What, then, does he mean? For clearly, this belief can be no trifling matter; it makes and unmakes epochs by its very coming and going; it gives the Age of the Holy its holiness and in parting abandons the next to its prosaic fate; and its struggle with unbelief is proclaimed as the only theme of genuine historical relevance.

The question of what he meant by 'belief' would have drawn from Goethe different answers at different times, all equally veiled, ironical—and irritated. For the question touches upon a sphere which Goethe held to be reserved for the initiates—'Sagt es niemand, nur den Weisen, Weil die Menge gleich verhöhnet'. Thus it is impossible to state his beliefs in any doctrinal manner, particularly if one wishes to avoid a discussion of that sublime menace besetting all studies of Goethe: pantheism. For there is no creed to be elicited from Goethe's writings. Put together systematically as articulate

opinions, his convictions would appear very inconsistent and at
times self-contradictory. Yet it is neither his opinions nor their
inconsistencies that matter in this context. What matters is the
level on which his convictions are formed, or the pressure of spiritual
energy by which they are sustained; and the quality and direction
of his beliefs are most clearly revealed through Goethe's critique of
his age. For there is little doubt that the mature Goethe would have
put his contemporary world, in spite of occasional outbursts of
Panama Canal optimism, into a rather shadowy place on his map of
the world's historical epochs, at some removes, in any case, from
the Age of Poetry and the Age of the Holy, and considerably nearer
those grey stretches where history writes its most atrocious prose
passages. And he would certainly not have discovered in it many
glimpses of that radiance which emanates from 'epochs of belief'.

It would be easy enough to deny the historical accuracy of
Goethe's scheme of epochs; but perhaps still easier to show that our
seemingly most effective refutation would simply be due to our use
of a different code of selection and emphasis in ordering the mass
of historical raw material. Goethe's—and Nietzsche's—judgments
on their contemporary world are undoubtedly what it is the fashion
to denounce as 'wild generalizations'. But then, this is the same vice
in which the prophets of the Old Testament indulged. Perhaps the
Israel of their time was, in fact, a very much better community than
their indignation suggests. But if we reached this conclusion, and
even if it were based on the greatest profusion of historical evidence,
our findings would ultimately reflect, not a higher degree of 'objective knowledge', but our allegiance to values which the prophets
would have denounced as false. And as this mental and moral
situation is the precise cause of their indignation, it is we who are
under judgment—a position which is generally not regarded as
favourable to the forming of unbiased views. Also, I think, our
case against the justice of the judges must be aggravated by the fact
that their prophecy has come true. The Temple was destroyed.

What the mature Goethe means by belief has this in common
with the prophets—that for him too it is the active realization of
certain *values* in the lives of men. And our question turns on the
nature of these values, a question which, as Nietzsche knew, 'is more
fundamental than the question of the certainty [of knowledge]: the
latter becomes serious only if the question of values is answered'.[11]
Goethe would have accepted this, although it stands as a key-phrase

within a body of thought which at first sight is worlds apart from the world of Goethe. And Goethe actually did accept it, if not in the radical spirit in which Nietzsche proposed it, nor, of course, with the same intensity of desperate doubt about the worth of knowledge. His opposition to Newton, for instance, is ultimately based not on a conviction of his own *scientific* superiority, but on his commitment to values which he believed were threatened by man's adopting an exclusively mathematical-analytical method in his dealings with nature. Elsewhere in this book I have attempted to show how Goethe confuses the issue in his scientific writings; but outside the laboratory, as it were, he makes this abundantly clear, as, for instance, in the words which Wilhelm Meister, here no longer a disciple of life, but the expositor of Goethe's own wisdom, addresses to the astronomer: 'I can well understand that it must please you, sages of the sky, to bring the immense universe gradually as close to your eyes as I saw that planet just now. But allow me to say . . . that these instruments with which we aid our senses, have a morally detrimental effect on man. . . . For what he thus perceives with his senses is out of keeping with his inner faculty of discernment; it would need a culture, as high as only exceptional people can possess, in order to harmonize, to a certain extent, the inner truth with the inappropriate vision from without. . . .'[12]

2

'There must have been a time when the religious, aesthetic and moral perceptions were at one.'[13] This is not, though it could be, a sentence from the context of Goethe's 'epochs of the spirit', but one of Nietzsche's posthumous notes from the time of his *Transvaluation of Values*. It is so much a Goethean thought that it seems to have been expanded into the following reflection about Goethe in *Götzen-Dämmerung*, one of the last works of Nietzsche:

Goethe—in a grandiose attempt to get beyond the eighteenth century through the naturalness of the Renaissance, a kind of self-conquest on the part of that century—had within himself its strongest instincts: its sentimentality, its nature-idolatry, its anti-historical bias, its idealism, lack of realism and revolutionary spirit (which is only one form of the lack of realism). He called in the help of history, of natural science, of antiquity, even of Spinoza, and, above all, of practical activity; he surrounded himself with closed horizons; he did not desert life, but placed himself at its centre and took as much as possible upon himself, above himself, into himself. What he aimed at was *totality*; *he fought against the sundering of reason, sensuality, feeling, will* . . . ; he disciplined himself into wholeness, he *created* himself . . . Goethe was, in the midst of an unrealistic age, a *convinced realist.* . . . He envisaged man as strong, highly civilized, skilled in all skills of the body, holding himself in check, having respect for himself as a creature who may be allowed to taste the whole width and wealth of naturalness, who is strong enough for this kind of freedom; who is tolerant, not from weakness but from strength, because he knows how to use to his advantage what would destroy an average character. . . .[14]

Although things of this kind have been said so often in later appraisals of Goethe that they have come to smack of the commonplace, in the context of Nietzsche's *Transvaluation of Values* they have a profundity of their own, and receive in the concluding words of this passage, so far withheld, a surprising twist which we shall, a little later, allow to shock us. For the time being we would like to reflect on the identification in this passage of Goethe's realism with his antagonism to the severance of reason, sensuality, feeling and will; or, in Nietzsche's previous formula, on Goethe's roots in an imaginary period in which religious, aesthetic and moral perceptions were at one—a unity so disastrously destroyed in the Prosaic Age.

The term 'realism' had a definite meaning, as the opposite to nominalism, at a time when metaphysical disputes enjoyed the advantages of as rigid a discipline as is nowadays accorded to scientific research. But, of course, this was before the word became used as a coin of uncertain value in that nineteenth-century bazaar of ideas where other counters too, such as transcendentalism, idealism, empiricism, materialism, positivism, bought a few frills of the mind. Thus Goethe's 'realism', fallen among the philistines, assumed so often the meagre meaning of 'down to earth', or 'practical', or 'you will learn, my boy'. Or else, as the name of a literary genre, 'realism' was to provide a convenient common denominator for all writers who harness the exuberance of their imaginations to the austere task of calling a spade a spade.

Clearly, this is not what Nietzsche means in speaking of the realist Goethe. What, I think, he does mean I would like to illustrate with the help of three Goethe aphorisms which were first printed together in the same number of *Kunst und Altertum* (V, 3, of the year 1826). The first reads as follows: 'It is now about twenty years since the whole race of Germans began to "transcend". Should they ever wake up to this fact, they will look very odd to themselves.'[15] The second, famous enough, is: 'In a true symbol the particular represents the universal, not as a dream or shadow, but as the living and instantaneous revelation of the unfathomable'.[16] The third is at first rather obscure: 'All that is ideal will ultimately, once it is claimed by the real, consume it, and itself. As the paper money does with the silver and itself.'[17] There is, not merely by virtue of their sequence in print, an intimate connection between these three aphorisms. The first, of course, ridicules the German *Transzendentalphilosophie* of Goethe's time; the second provides the happiest condensation of Goethe's own idea of the relationship between the transcendent and the immanent, the 'ideal' and the 'real'; the third is the epigrammatic abbreviation of the prophecy of the Prosaic Age, this time seen as the destructive, nihilistic outcome of the tearing apart of the real and the ideal sphere.

It is a very long story which these three aphorisms succeed in cutting short, and it would be an invidious business indeed to restore it to its original length. But perhaps a few meditations are permissible.

Goethe's hostility towards all forms of transcendental philosophy has certainly no affinities whatever with a very much later philosophical offensive against the transcendent, waged under the name of positivism—a campaign with which Nietzsche is often associated by his more simple-minded interpreters. On the contrary, Goethe's ill feelings against the transcendentalists sprang from the same source which sustained his energetic attacks on the kind of positivism which he believed was inherent in Newtonian physics. He regarded both transcendentalists and positivists (of whom he had the idea, if not the name) as the systematizers of a perception of reality which to him appeared absurd, indeed as that very 'absurdity and confusion of the day' which he denounced at so late an hour of his life to Wilhelm von Humboldt. What both these tendencies of the mind —superficially so inimical to each other—have in common is a passion for abstraction. And it is in abstraction that Goethe saw the fatal loophole through which reason could escape into an illusory freedom from its commitments to what is of the senses, of feeling, of the will. He dreaded this emancipation of reason, whether exercised in adventures of transcendental speculation, or in the mathematical calculus which creates, despite its apparent empiricism, the phenomena to be fitted into its abstract order.

Either method of emancipating reason from the totality of the human person appeared to Goethe as the denial of his vision of man, the negation of the values to which he was committed, the heresy *kat'exochen*. He sincerely believed that this way lay catastrophe.

In the pursuits of transcendentalism he discerned the danger that reason, doped with transcendental ambition, would construct a world, too big in its anaemic hugeness, for man to live and love in, distracting him at every point from—as Wilhelm Meister puts it— 'attending with spontaneous care to the duty of the day, examining the purity of your hearts and the stability of your minds. . . . Only then will you find the right attitude towards the sublime; for it is to the sublime that we dedicate ourselves in all manner of activities and in a spirit of awe. . . .'[18] In a spirit of awe; not of that spiritual conceit of which he suspected the architects of the transcendental Towers of Babel to be possessed.

If in transcendentalism human reason was perverted in the direction of the abstruse, in scientific positivism, so it seemed to Goethe, it was led astray in yet another way: in turning the universe into a plaything for mathematics and the wilful assertiveness of experimentation, reason once more placed the world out of the reach of true human comprehension. For the truth of human comprehension resides for Goethe in that balanced vision in which the religious, the aesthetic and the moral perceptions are at one. Only through their concord the world stands revealed as the proper home of man, appearing neither too great for his insignificance, nor too small for his greatness; neither too fantastic for his reason, nor too prosaic for his imagination; neither too unwieldy for his will, nor too unlovable for his affection. In a very profound sense of that word, *propriety* is for Goethe the criterion of truth. This is why Nietzsche admired him as the last of the great aristocratic minds of Europe.[19] For there is indeed something plebeian at work in all other standards of truth which have become, articulately or not, the fashion in modern intellectual activities: elements of either self-abasement or rational conceit, of excessive curiosity, of psychological tactlessness, and a sniggering suspicion of the absence of meaning in anything that evades definition or experimental proof, and above all, a disregard for those intangible qualities that make the world a noble habitation.

Goethe's scientific labours were directed and sustained by his intuitive certainty that knowledge can only be true as long as it is not in excess of man's feelings. The problem involved is, of course, an old one, at least as old as modern science itself, and was first lived and struggled through by that extraordinary man, in whom the mind of a mathematician clashed with the mind of a mystic— Pascal. His endless concern was with reason and that reason of which reason knows nothing: the reason of the heart; with the *esprit de géométrie* and the *esprit de finesse*. Since then the question and conflict, in innumerable variations, have never ceased to vex some of the finest minds of Europe. In Goethe's case, however, it can hardly be called a problem. For he had no serious doubts about the worthlessness of the *esprit de géométrie*. And where its achievements were beyond dispute, beyond even the negative certainty of Goethe, the utmost homage he was prepared to pay to them was the suggestion that a soul rich with intuition could reach at least as far as the newest telescopes. In the peculiar household of Makarie, the astronomer's business is simply to spot the stars which the lady of the house, harbouring all the galaxies in her breast, has seen in her dreams; an astronomical job not very much superior to that of the digger who digs for the water that the diviner has divined.

But beyond such indulgence of a wayward sense of humour, Goethe is deeply convinced that man can only do justice to himself and to the world and its maker by creating from within an image of both himself and the world which does not clash with his idea of the deity. And Goethe's idea of the deity was given to him in that 'revealed mystery', that 'living and instantaneous revelation of the unfathomable', through the symbolic nature of the particular. From this symbolic nature of the particular, to be grasped only in the concerted receptivity of sense, mind, feeling and will, man was increasingly alienated through the excessive rationalism of both his physics and metaphysics.

The Germans were indeed to look odd to themselves once they woke up to their real status after all the transcending had been done; as odd, one might add, as the scientist, confronted with the all but

G

demonic unmanageability of the results of his analytical radicalism. For what is lost between the extremes of transcendence and analysis is the Goethean ideal of personality: a state of balance between what man *is* and what he *can do*. 'Man ought not to know more of a thing than he can creatively live up to.' Goethe might have said this. It was said by Nietzsche, reflecting on the sterility of philological studies, and comparing the quality of mind of his most learned colleagues to Goethe's meagre philological equipment; yet, he adds, 'he knew enough to wrestle fruitfully with antiquity!'[20] And elsewhere: 'Goethe's taste and ability ran parallel.'[21] This is a posthumous note from the time of the dithyrambus *Richard Wagner in Bayreuth*. Even then he knew what was to become violent polemic in later years: that this could not be said of Richard Wagner. And with the word 'the presumptuous' the remark on Goethe leads on to an observation about Richard Wagner's histrionic character.

Indeed, Nietzsche knew who Goethe was. There is the instruction of Goethe in his turning away from Wagner, the Goethean knowledge that it is the discrepancy between human substance and human virtuosity, between what a man is and what he can do, which is a dominant feature of the Prosaic Age. The Age of Talent may be an alternative name for it. The symptoms are displayed by art and life alike. Life is frightened out of its highly enlightened wits by the return of ancient nightmares: the tales of the sorcerer's apprentice, of dwarfs with magic powers. The promise of Heaven for the poor in spirit is understood to mean that, on earth at least, they should be educated into clever people able to manipulate and let loose the technical installations of hell. And in art, there are sounds most skilfully organized, furies expressed in the most virtuoso fashion, and proud of signifying nothing. Whole systems of aesthetics are evolved to justify this state of affairs. A world emptied of meaning seeks to escape from the infinite boredom of its meaninglessness by the magic of words without flesh, and forms without content. And, indeed, the attempt to distil poetry from the things or ideas that form our 'real' world would be in vain. Poetry, we are told, is enchantment, and all things and thoughts have been robbed of their charm in the bright daylight robbery of utility and abstraction. Yet for Goethe things and thoughts shared that luminous concreteness which is the quality of a world with all its dimensions intact. Remember what he called 'thinking' in a passage of his *Second Sojourn in Rome*, where he describes his impression of Raphael's

'Transfigurazione': 'The kindred spirits among us were confirmed in their convictions,' he writes; 'Raphael, they said to one another, is distinguished by the rightness of his thinking.' And thus he interprets the two levels of being, represented in that painting: 'How can one sever what is above from what is below? The two are one; below there is suffering and neediness, and above active mercy, the one reflecting upon the other in mutual interchange. Is it then, to express the meaning of this painting in a different way, at all possible to separate from the real its ideal relevance?'[22]

In the 'Buch Hafis' of the *West-östlicher Divan* the section which has the motto:

> Sei das Wort die Braut genannt,
> Bräutigam der Geist;
> Diese Hochzeit hat gekannt,
> Wer Hafisen preist[23]

[Let the word be named the bride, and the spirit the bridegroom; he who sings in praise of Hafis has known this wedlock.]

the poet, addressing himself to Hafis, proclaims his faith in a world marked with the imprint of the divine features and sings its praise in defiance of all negation, hindrance, robbery that words and things endure at the hands of the detractors and abstractors:

> Und so gleich ich dir vollkommen,
> Der ich unsrer heil'gen Bücher
> Herrlich Bild an mich genommen,
> Wie auf jenes Tuch der Tücher
> Sich des Herren Bildnis drückte,
> Mich in stiller Brust erquickte,
> Trotz Verneinung, Hindrung, Raubens,
> Mit dem heitern Bild des Glaubens.[24]

[Thus I am your equal, I who have received and taken the glorious vision of our sacred books, and, with the image of the Lord printed on that cloth of cloths, have delighted in the joyful faith, despite negation, hindrance, robbery.]

This, then, is Goethe's belief, or his answer to the problem which is 'more fundamental than the question of the certainty of knowledge': the problem of values. The answer lies in Goethe's realism

as understood by Nietzsche. It is the *realism of the symbol*; not of the
obscure symbol thrown up by the collective unconscious of the
symbolists, invading the husks of dead memories with dreamt and
undreamt-of significances; nor of the symbol which refers to abstractions, in the manner of an allegory: the kind of symbol which
the young philologist Nietzsche in a preparatory note for *The Birth of
Tragedy* regarded as the sign of a dying art because it introduced,
furtively and in flimsy disguise, abstract notions into it—but the
symbol in its original meaning, defined by Nietzsche in the same
note, in a strikingly Goethe-like manner, as 'the language of the
universal'.[25] This realism of the symbol is the common property
of all great art. It does not strain after an ideal sphere which may
redeem the prosaic unworthiness of this world (as Schiller's art does),
nor does it seek deliverance from the terror of truth in the healing
unreality of the 'schöner Schein' (as Nietzsche sometimes believed),
nor does it self-consciously call on dreams and nightmares pleasantly
or unpleasantly to ruffle the boring smoothness of life's surface. It
describes; and in describing it opens our eyes to what really is. And
what really is, is not a dream or shadow, nor the meaningless agony
of the Will, nor the abstractions of Reason, but the living revelation
of the unfathomable. Yet why should the unfathomable be beautiful? Because it can only be comprehended by the unfathomable,
and the only truly unfathomable faculty of man is love. Thus the
realism of the symbol becomes the artistic vindication of the reality
of a lovable world. 'That something like Spinoza's *amor dei* could
be experienced again!'[26] This is a note which Nietzsche, during his
most radical Anti-Christ period, made about Goethe.

3

At this point we had better return to that passage in Nietzsche's
Götzen-Dämmerung from which, in quoting it before, we left out the
concluding words. After he had called Goethe a 'convinced realist
in the midst of an unrealistic age', Nietzsche continues: 'Such a mind,
having attained to real freedom, lives at the very centre of all things
with a joyful and confident acceptance of fate, lives in the faith that
only the particular in its separateness is objectionable, and that in the
wholeness of life everything is affirmed in its holiness—*he no longer
denies*. . . . There is no higher faith than this: I have baptized it in the
name of Dionysus.'[27]

This is very beautiful and true, and shocking only because of Dionysus so suddenly entering an apparently Apolline scene. Goethe, no doubt, would have been baffled by the choice of this godfather, and might have asked for some less inebriating deity to lend him a spiritual hand—Apollo, perhaps, or even Eros. Yet it is precisely this invocation of Dionysus, forced upon Nietzsche (and not only upon him) by his determination to accept and affirm life, which is our theme; and we should lose track of it if we allowed ourselves to be persuaded that it was, as it were, Apollo's child's play for Goethe to persevere in affirmation, or simply due to his superbly fortunate temperament and genius. And our theme would equally be abandoned if we succeeded in no more than showing that the iconoclast Nietzsche surrounded the picture of Goethe with nothing but admiring marginal notes—significant though even this would be. Goethe would not be the author of Faust and Mephistopheles had he not known—and at times with terrible intimacy—the spirit of denial, of

> ... Was ist daran zu lesen?
> Es ist so gut, als wär' es nicht gewesen,
> Und treibt sich doch im Kreis, als wenn es wäre.
> Ich liebte mir dafür das Ewig-Leere.[28]

[What can one make of it? It is as good as though it had never been. ... And yet it rushes round in circles, as if it had some real existence. I would prefer instead eternal emptiness],

with its anticipating echoes of Nietzsche's Eternal Recurrence of a positivistically self-contained world without any opening into meaning and sense. Indeed, he was only too familiar with the temptation of calling on magical powers to endow a drably disenchanted life with the poignancy of consuming beauty:

> Und sollt' ich nicht, sehnsüchtigster Gewalt,
> In's Leben ziehn die einzigste Gestalt.[29]

[And shall I not, with all the might of my craving, succeed in bringing to life the uniquely beautiful shape?]

This desire, even if realized only for that one fatal moment of ultimate satisfaction, is Faust's very challenge to the devil. But the challenge is withdrawn at the end, and the *very desire for*

*magical transformation identified with the act of blaspheming and cursing
life*:

> Könnt' ich Magie von meinem Pfad entfernen,
> Die Zaubersprüche ganz und gar verlernen,
> Stünd ich, Natur, vor dir ein Mann allein,
> Da wär's der Mühe wert, ein Mensch zu sein.
> Das war ich sonst, eh' ich's im Düstern suchte,
> Mit Frevelwort mich und die Welt verfluchte.[30]

[Could I but forget my sorcery, ban my magic, and stand, stripped
of it utterly, face to face with thee, oh Nature! Then it might be
worth while being a man. I was one once, before I searched in
the sinister sphere, thus blasphemously cursing the world and
myself.]

This rejection of magic is, of course, not merely a poetical and
secularized version of the traditional theological disapproval of that
activity. Nor has it anything in common with the conventional idea
of piety. It simply reflects Goethe's final acceptance of life as it is—
only that Goethe's vision of what is, affirms the *reality* of much that
in the consciousness of the Prosaic Age is not. Goethe is exemplary
in his courage to trust in the absolute reliability of that experiment
which, in its utter 'subjectivity', is not merely one of many possible,
but the experience of life itself. And at least half of his experiment
yields results dismissed by the Prosaic Age with frowning vagueness
as 'emotional' or 'mystical':

> Sie haben dich, heiliger Hafis,
> Die mystische Zunge genannt,
> Und haben, die Wortgelehrten,
> Den Wert des Worts nicht erkannt.
>
> Mystisch heissest du ihnen,
> Weil sie Närrisches bei dir denken,
> Und ihren unlautern Wein
> In deinem Namen verschenken.
>
> Du aber bist mystisch rein,
> Weil sie dich nicht verstehn,
> Der du, ohne fromm zu sein, selig bist!
> Das wollen sie dir nicht zugestehn.[31]

[They have called you, Saint Hafis, the mystical tongue; but they, the scribes, have not recognized the meaning of the word. To them you are mystical because you inspire foolish thoughts in them, and because they pour out their impure wine in your name. Indeed, you are mystical, but only because they do not understand you, you who are blessed without being pious. And this they will not allow you.]

This is the poem 'Offenbar Geheimnis' from the *West-östlicher Divan*. Nietzsche might well claim its authorship. It is Goethe's most light-hearted assertion of the oneness of the two spheres, of the revelation of the unfathomable in the reality of the symbol, and of the holiness and blessedness which is the quality of being *really* alive.

The 'ideal' aspect of life, abandoned by transcendentalists and positivists alike to some limbo of ideality, was so inescapably real to Goethe that he was convinced it would one day avenge itself on the age that has banished it from its 'reality'. This brings us to the last of the three aphorisms from *Maximen und Reflexionen* which we have selected to epitomize stages on the precarious journey of the European mind. It is the aphorism which follows immediately upon the definition of the symbol from which this discussion has so far taken its bearings and which it leaves now with one of the last jottings among the posthumously published notes of Nietzsche: 'The interpreters of poets do not understand that the poet has both: the reality and the symbol. Thus he has the first and the second sense of a totality.'[32] This last aphorism reads, once more: 'All that is ideal will ultimately, once it is claimed by the real, consume it, and itself. As paper money does with the silver and itself.' And this is exactly what has happened within the fifty years of the Prosaic Age, between Goethe's death and Nietzsche's *Zarathustra*. Goethe's realism, on its profoundest level, was driven to despair. And Nietzsche, in order to transform this despair into affirmation, had to call in so un-Goethean a spirit as that of Dionysus. The comparison between the god of Goethe's *amor dei* and Nietzsche's love of Dionysus yields the measure by which we can assess the distance the Prosaic Age has travelled from Goethe's time to Nietzsche's, or the depth to which it has sunk. For with all the radical, and indeed obvious, differences between Goethe and Nietzsche—differences of character, genius, temperament, modes of thought and expression—they nevertheless meet in their concern for, and their vision of, the proper state of man. Nietzsche is the outraged believer of Goethe's beliefs, the scandalized and scandalizing upholder of Goethe's values, fighting out within his own soul the battle between belief and unbelief, accepting for himself the fates of the tortured martyrs of either side, and the role of the adjudicator of victories and defeats.

It is not only Nietzsche's consistent admiration which bears witness to his kinship with Goethe. There is no *internal* evidence either to refute the intellectual sincerity of Nietzsche's repeated assertions that there could not be any by-passing of Goethe when it came to tracing his own intellectual ancestry; and although the names he quotes on the occasions of such stock-taking vary, Goethe is invariably included. In the second volume of *Menschliches, Allzumenschliches*, he writes: 'I too have been in the underworld, like Odysseus, and shall be again and again; and not only rams have I sacrificed, but I have not spared my own blood. There are four pairs that have never denied themselves to me when I made my sacrifices: Epicurus and Montaigne, Goethe and Spinoza, Plato and Rousseau, Pascal and Schopenhauer. It is with these that I must come to terms again, each time after a long stretch of lonely wanderings; by them I want to be proved right or wrong, to them I want to listen when they prove one another right or wrong. Whatever I say, conclude, think out for myself and others, it is on those eight that my eyes are fixed. . . .'[33] In another place, among the many notes from the time of *Zarathustra*, Goethe is again one of his ancestors, this time together with Heraclitus and Spinoza.[34] And in one of his own posthumously published critical comments on the writings of his early period, Goethe is thanked for having freed him from the pessimistic tyranny of Schopenhauer and Wagner: '*Now* antiquity dawned upon me and Goethe's insight into the nature of great art, and *now* I gained that *simplicity* of vision to see what human existence *really* is; I had the antidote to make sure that it did not turn into poisoning pessimism.'[35]

In *Menschliches, Allzumenschliches*, in one of the loveliest passages ever written on the *moral* task and function of literature (and, indeed, there is not much loveliness to be found in the repertoire of writers on this austere subject), the imprint of Goethe's genius is recognizable in every phrase: 'The works of such poets'—poets, that is, whose vision of man is exemplary—'would be distinguished by the fact that they appear immune from the glow and blast of the *passions*. The fatal touch of the wrong note, the pleasure taken in smashing the whole instrument on which the music of humanity has

been played, the scornful laughter and the gnashing of teeth, and all
that is tragic and comic in the old conventional sense, would be felt
in the vicinity of this new art as an awkward archaic crudeness and
a distortion of the image of man. Strength, goodness, gentleness,
purity, and that innate and spontaneous sense of measure and balance
shown in persons and their actions, . . . a clear sky reflected on faces
and events, knowledge and art at one; the mind, without arrogance
and jealousy dwelling together with the soul, drawing from the
opposites of life the grace of seriousness, not the impatience of
conflict:—all this would make the background of gold against which
to set up the real portrait of man, the picture of his increasing
nobleness.'[36]

This, quite consistently, is written by the same Nietzsche who has
listed the best books in German prose, reserving no place for either
the tumultuous Kleist or the brilliant Heine or any of the Romantics,
but choosing, apart from Goethe and Goethe's Conversations with
Eckermann, as the only works which deserve to be read again and
again: Lichtenberg's Aphorisms, the first book of Jung-Stilling's
Autobiography, Adalbert Stifter's *Nachsommer* and Gottfried
Keller's *Leute von Seldwyla* ('and this is likely to remain all there is,
for some time to come').[37] But is it, one wonders, written by the
same Nietzsche who has appealed to what is most immature in the
popular imagination of his country, and largely antagonized that of
the West, by 'philosophizing with a hammer', proclaiming himself
dynamite, preaching the advent of the Superman? How is one to
reconcile this violent mind with that Nietzsche whom we have
observed painting, against a background of gold, the Goethean
picture of man 'immune from the glow and blast of the passions'?

Throughout Nietzsche's life, and not merely from a certain point
onward, his acclamations of Goethe, the dominant voice indeed,
are yet interspersed with misgivings. They are invariably concerned
with the Goethe-Winckelmann idea of Greek antiquity and with
Goethe's 'purely epic genius' which, according to Nietzsche,
rendered him incapable of facing the problem of tragedy. He
might have added, as a source of anxiety, the nature of Goethe's
opposition to modern science.

As early as 1870, while he was writing his *Birth of Tragedy*,
Nietzsche enters in his notebook the following remark: 'With
Goethe, in accordance with his epic nature, poetry is the remedy,
protecting him from full knowledge; with tragic natures art is the

remedy, liberating them from knowledge'.[38] All that Nietzsche ever said in criticism of Goethe is contained in this observation of the young philologist. Seven to eight years later, at the time of *Menschliches, Allzumenschliches*, it is applied to Goethe's reaction to Kleist: 'What Goethe felt at coming into contact with him was his sense of tragedy. Goethe turned his back on it; for tragedy represents the incurable aspect of nature. He himself was conciliatory and curable.'[39] At the same time, after some rather unfortunate gibes about 'the tragic problem' of *Faust*, Nietzsche exclaims: 'Is this really the greatest German "tragic idea", as the rumour goes among Germans?'[40]

These criticisms, clearly, are not determined by purely aesthetic considerations. Nietzsche was utterly incapable of dividing up his thought into any such neat academical departments. He once said: 'I have at all times written with my whole body and my whole life. I do not know what purely intellectual problems are.'[41] And again: 'You know these things by way of thinking, yet your thought is not your experience but the reverberation of the experience of others; as your room trembles when a car passes. I am sitting in that car, and often am the car itself.'[42] Thus Nietzsche's criticism of Goethe can be seen as part and parcel of his total strategy: the strategy of despair. Towards the end of his conscious life Nietzsche was convinced that the culture of Europe was doomed; that an eclipse of all traditional values was at hand, and that modern European man, this pampered child of the optimistically rational eighteenth century, would needs go astray in a wilderness without path or guidance. He quoted Pascal, who said that without the Christian belief we shall become to ourselves what nature and history will become to us— a monster and a chaos. We, he adds, shall make this prophecy come true.[43] The sections of his *Will to Power* which are concerned with the coming of European nihilism read like a vast elaboration of that dictum of Pascal's as well as of Goethe's prophecy of the Prosaic Age. Nietzsche believed that its approach was *inevitable*. But the paradox, which is the very life of true prophecy, also sustained— until madness possessed him—the prophet Nietzsche; that prophetic paradox within which historical inevitability is defeated through an act of spiritual conquest: 'God has decided to destroy the Temple. In the name of God, rescue the Temple from the wrath of God.' This is the paradox of every true prophet.

What was inevitable, according to Nietzsche's prophecy, was the coming of nihilism. The conqueror, more powerful than fate itself, was the Dionysian spirit, the spirit that ruled Greek tragedy. The Dionysus of Greek tragedy transformed the despair at the fate of man into the bliss of ultimate acceptance, thus transcending the very thing it accepted. There is an amazing consistency running right through Nietzsche's wild contradictions. The young philologist and philosopher had, in the *Birth of Tragedy*, celebrated the god of ecstasy, redeeming the spectacle of man's ultimate failure in the rapturously accepted wholeness of life in which there is nothing but ultimate succeeding. The writer of the *Will to Power*, seventeen years later, demanded from European man that he should perform the very same drama on the stage of the world and, caught in the doom of his historical fate, transcend it through the act of tragic affirmation.

For him who believed he had recognized this, *Faust* could no longer stand as the 'tragedy of knowledge', 'die Tragödie der Erkenntnis'. 'Really? I laugh at Faust.'[44] Salvation was no longer to be had from the 'Ewig-Weibliche'. This was still merely comfort, a religious illusion hiding the mercilessness from above against which not man, in his weak and fallen state, will assert himself, but only the creature graced with the grace of Dionysus: the Superman. As far as man is concerned, no *chorus mysticus* concludes Nietzsche's 'tragedy of knowledge', but Mephistopheles:

> Kein Weg! Ins Unbetretene,
> Nicht zu Betretende; ein Weg ans Unerbetene,
> Nicht zu Erbittende. Bist du bereit?—
> Nicht Schlösser sind, nicht Riegel wegzuschieben,
> Von Einsamkeiten wirst umhergetrieben.
> Hast du Begriff von Öd' und Einsamkeit?
>
> Nichts wirst du sehen in ewig leerer Ferne.
> Den Schritt nicht hören, den du tust,
> Nichts Festes finden, wo du ruhst.[45]

[No way! Towards untrodden ground, where none may tread; a way towards the unprayed-for, beyond all prayer. Are you prepared? There are no locks, no bolts to thrust aside; you will be driven hither and thither by hosts of loneliness. Do you know what void and loneliness mean?... You will see nothing in that distance of eternal emptiness, you will not hear your own step, you will find nothing solid for your rest.]

In those voids, the first sound that will be heard again, indeed be met by the resonance of a transfigured world, will be the voice of the Superman. He will find the firmest of all footholds precisely where man loses the ground under his feet.

To insist on the Mephistophelean prospect, and yet not to despair, and yet to glorify, indeed to transfigure existence—this is the goal of Nietzsche's desperate strategy. He was determined to go to the very end of the positivist disillusionment, shed skin after skin of comforting beliefs, destroy every fortress manned by protective gods, in fact, to banish the last vestiges of 'magic' which still save man from the final exposure to his tragedy—and *then* bring to life once more Goethe's vision of the glorious integrity of all things. Until this was done, even the nearest German approximation to Dionysian acceptance, even Goethe, would fail us. For he had an inclination to play truant when life was teaching its most desperate lessons—and indeed it was about to teach them to Europe. At the approach of the terror of ultimate knowledge, Goethe withdrew into the healing darkness of the unconscious, trusting to intuition that it would restore the brightness of day in the created work of art. But Nietzsche dreamt—and dreamt in vain—of an artist of the future who would reach in his art that turning-point where the highest degree of consciousness and self-consciousness transforms itself into a new spontaneity, primitivity and innocence;[46] just as he strove to realize the utmost of nihilistic despair to arrive at a new faith, and mobilized all forces of negation to defeat all denial. In one of the last paragraphs of *The Will to Power* he says: 'To have paced out the whole circumference of modern consciousness, to have explored every one of its recesses—this is my ambition, my torture, and my bliss. Really to overcome pessimism—; and as a result, *ein Goethischer Blick voll Liebe und gutem Willen.*'[47]

The desperate *experimentum crucis* failed desperately. Nietzsche's tragic failure is spiritual impatience. He was a Faustian, after all, in his deep-rooted belief that in the beginning was the deed. But it is certainly not in the end, and this increases the probability that it was not in the beginning either. He saw the end and took the initiative. Even the words suggest that this is incongruous. He had before him a world without faith or hope or love; and how much was he of the nineteenth century in attempting to create from his own impatience that trinity of spiritual survival which is 'all in the waiting'. From the goodness of his heart he believed

> ... such is the infection of the time,
> That, for the health and physic of our right,
> We cannot deal but with the very hand
> Of stern injustice and confused wrong.

But such war-like preparations have a habit of producing the precise state in which the 'paper money consumes the silver and itself'. Nietzsche, with an intellectual courage, penetration and impatience which have no equal in the nineteenth century, made himself, with the most splendid invocations, the claimant of the ideal on behalf of the real; but in his time and place, already so hopelessly exposed, he merely succeeded in vindicating Goethe's prophecy that this will be the point at which the severed spheres consume each other.

V

RILKE AND NIETZSCHE

WITH A DISCOURSE ON THOUGHT, BELIEF AND POETRY

RILKE AND NIETZSCHE

WITH A DISCOURSE ON THOUGHT, BELIEF AND POETRY

I

'WE came to speak of *Tasso*, and of the *idea* which Goethe sought
to represent in it,' reports Eckermann under the date of May 6th,
1827. '*Idea?*' said Goethe—'not that I know of!—I had the *life* of
Tasso before me, and my own life, and by jumbling up two such
peculiar figures . . . the picture of *Tasso* took shape within me. . . .
The Germans are really peculiar people!—They make life more
difficult for themselves than is necessary by seeking everywhere, and
putting into everything, their profound thoughts and ideas.—Why
not for once have the courage *to give yourselves up to impressions*, to
allow yourselves to be amused, moved, edified, indeed taught and
roused to something great; but don't believe all the time that
everything must be vain if it is not some abstract thought or idea. . . .
A poetic creation is the better for being incommensurable and
rationally incomprehensible.' A little later in the same year (July 5th,
1827), talking about inconsistencies in his treatment of the Helena
scene in *Faust II*, Goethe says: 'I only wonder what the German
critics will think of it. Will they have the freedom and courage to
ignore the inconsistencies? The French will be hampered by their
reason and fail to recognize that imagination has to abide by laws
of its own which reason neither can nor should comprehend. The
imagination would hardly be worth bothering about, if it did not
create things which will for ever remain problematical to reason.
This is the difference between poetry and prose. In prose, reason is
and may and should be at home.'

For once Mr. T. S. Eliot seems to agree with Goethe of whom
generally he thinks rather unkindly. In his essay on 'Shakespeare
and the Stoicism of Seneca'[1] he says about Shakespeare and his
philosophical interpreters very much the same that Goethe said
about his *Tasso* and the German critics. Mr. Eliot quotes someone
who wrote that 'we possess a great deal of evidence as to what
Shakespeare thought of military glory and martial events'. 'Do
we?' asks Mr. Eliot, rather in the manner of Goethe's 'Not that I
know of!', sure of the applause of anyone with even the slightest

insight into the goings-on in a poet's workshop. For, indeed, what we possess of evidence goes to show conclusively that Shakespeare's imagination comprehended with the greatest precision every shade of difference between what, for instance, Anthony thought and felt about the significance of military events, both before and after he fell in love with Cleopatra, or what military glory meant to such varied characters as, say, Henry V, Ajax or Thersites. In fact, the politeness of good High Table manners, with everyone ready to see everyone else's point of view except his own, is, on the highest level of imaginative achievement, the cardinal virtue of the dramatic writer; and the wider the scope of his imagination, the less evidence will he leave behind to show what he himself thought about this or that controversial issue. Having dwelt in so many divided minds and believed so many conflicting beliefs, he is likely to be slow in fulfilling the first commandment of all enlightened education: to form his own opinions. He may, alas, even begin *and* end by not knowing what he himself believes, or not believing what he himself knows.

So far, then, Mr. Eliot's 'Do we?' justly commands that general consent which rhetorical questions take for granted. Yet some of it may be withdrawn when Mr. Eliot continues 'Or rather, did Shakespeare think anything at all? He was occupied with turning human actions into poetry'[2]—in precisely the same way, that is, in which Goethe, without concerning himself with ideas, made poetry out of Tasso's life and his own. Again, very much in keeping with Goethe's notorious dictum that all his works form part of a great confession, but with a striking shift of emphasis from earlier meditations on the subject in the essay 'Tradition and the Individual Talent',[3] Mr. Eliot now maintains that 'every poet starts from his own emotions' and that 'Shakespeare, too, was occupied with the struggle—which alone constitutes life for a poet—to transmute his personal and private agonies into something rich and strange, something universal and impersonal'.[4] And in discussing whether the poet necessarily believes in such theories, theologies or philosophies as he may borrow for his poetic purposes—whether Dante actually believed in the theological system of Thomas Aquinas which he so magnificently used in the *Divina Commedia*, or whether Shakespeare, in poetically paraphrasing their thought, agreed with such thinkers as Machiavelli or Montaigne or Seneca—Mr. Eliot comes to a conclusion that seems to elaborate a Goethean image: 'The poet makes poetry, the metaphysician makes metaphysics, the bee makes honey, the spider secretes a filament; you can hardly say that any of these agents believes: he merely does'.[5] It is Goethe's Tasso who dismisses the advice that he should take a holiday from writing poetry, by exclaiming: Bid the silkworm stop spinning!

Clearly it all amounts to this: by drawing a parallel between Nietzsche, whose principal claim is to be a *thinker*, and Rilke, whose reputation rests on his *poetry*, the critic seems to commit the original sin of literary criticism. Yet I should be on safe ground if I now proceeded to show how Rilke used one or other of Nietzsche's ideas and, believing them or not, transformed them into poetry, as Goethe presumably drew on Spinoza, or Shakespeare on Seneca, Montaigne, and Machiavelli. This would be a literary exercise, respectable and time-honoured, and on this occasion promising high entertainment as it is a *chercher la femme* that lurks behind the 'and' connecting Rilke and Nietzsche: Frau Lou Andreas-Salomé, who played a not inconsiderable part in Nietzsche's life and certainly a very considerable one in Rilke's. The exercise would be still more rewarding if I could produce authentic records of conversations about Nietzsche which, of course, must have taken place between Lou and Rilke; or unearth a copy of *Also sprach Zarathustra* anno-tated in Rilke's hand. I might then go on to show what has happened to Nietzsche's thought in the process of its transmutation into Rilke's poetry, for, as Mr. Eliot says, the poet 'is not necessarily interested in the thought itself' but merely in expressing 'the emotional equivalent of thought'. But, as it is precisely this theory of the relation between thought, belief and poetry which I propose to challenge, I am obliged to follow a different course, with the strictly scholarly road being barred in any case by the remarkable scarcity of first-hand material. I am not even convinced that a full publication of the correspondence between Rilke and Lou would yield very much for the scholarly purpose; for on the whole Rilke was in the habit of suppressing any more elaborate acknowledgment of his intellectual debts because he too believed that their assimilation and transformation in the unique medium of his art was the only thing that mattered.

2

The writings of the young Rilke show Nietzsche neither assimi-lated nor transformed, but rather imitated and sometimes vulgarized.

In *Der Apostel* (1896),[6] *Ewald Tragy*,[7] and *Christus-Visionen* (1896–1897),[8] the effects of Nietzsche's hammering and dynamiting are unmistakable; yet there is not the slightest trace of the depth and complexity of Nietzsche's thought and feeling. When, early in 1897, in Munich, he met Lou Andreas-Salomé he must have still been in this 'Wie er sich räuspert und wie er spuckt' stage of his Nietzsche-fascination. We do not know whether he had read her book on Nietzsche which was published in 1894,[9] and is, with all its inadequacies, profundity itself compared to the Nietzschean gesticulating of *Der Apostel* or *Ewald Tragy*. But even if Rilke did read it, the document he produced in the following spring and summer (1898), largely in Italy and entirely for Lou's eyes—his so-called *Tuscan Diary*[10]—is still quite innocently Young-Nietzschean in its rapturous vision of the Artist-Superman. Yet in retrospect the reader of the *Tuscan Diary* can clearly discern in it almost all the threads that were to go into the rich texture of *Duino Elegies* and *Sonnets to Orpheus*, so very much more intimately related to Nietzsche (as I shall hope to show) than all the Superman sound and fury lavishly displayed in Rilke's early writings. However, the year of the *Tuscan Diary* marks the point at which, to my knowledge, all relevant direct references to Nietzsche, or obvious borrowings from him, end. Up to 1904 the name of Nietzsche casually appears now and then in articles or letters, and sometimes, though very rarely, a faint echo of the earlier crude instrumentation of Nietzsche *motifs* can be heard, but certainly in no manner to command attention. Yet although the Zarathustra *opinions* and *gestures* vanish from Rilke's writings, the kinship between his own and Nietzsche's *ideas* and *inner attitudes* is steadily deepening, and is nowhere profounder than in *Duino Elegies* and *Sonnets to Orpheus*, so dramatically released at Castle Muzot as near the end of the poet's life as 1922.

We must not be deceived by appearances; there are, at first sight, as many striking differences between Rilke and Nietzsche as definite similarities. They were both uprooted and homeless. 'Wer jetzt kein Haus hat, baut sich keines mehr,' writes the one, and the other: 'Weh dem, der keine Heimat hat!' They were lonely among men, driven by inner compulsion to shun all binding human relationships for the sake of an uninhibited indulgence of their one consuming passion: namely, to use Mr. Eliot's words about the poet in general, 'to transmute their personal and private agonies

into something rich and strange, something universal and impersonal'. In their abhorrence of the democratic vulgarity of their
times, they were both anxious to establish their own aristocratic
descent. These are not mere biographical accidents. They have the
same significance as their common dedication to a belief in everything that has never been uttered before, and to the adventure of
willing what nobody has ever dared to will:

> Ich glaube an alles noch nie Gesagte.
> Ich will meine frömmsten Gefühle befrein.
> Was noch keiner zu wollen wagte,
> wird mir einmal unwillkürlich sein.[11]

[I believe in everything that has never been said before. My most
dedicated feelings I desire to set free, and one day there shall come to
me spontaneously that which nobody has ever dared to will.]

These verses of Rilke spring from the very centre of Zarathustra's
message. And, to the point of a near-identity of images conveying
the conquest of loneliness, the harmonizing of inner conflict in the
feast of reconciliation, of the One becoming Two through the
arrival of the divine guest, Rilke's lines

> Wer seines Lebens viele Widersinne
> versöhnt und dankbar in ein Sinnbild fasst,
> der drängt
> die Lärmenden aus dem Palast,
> wird *anders* festlich, und du bist der Gast,
> den er an sanften Abenden empfängt.
>
> Du bist der Zweite seiner Einsamkeit,
> die ruhige Mitte seinen Monologen;
> und jeder Kreis, um dich gezogen,
> spannt ihm den Zirkel aus der Zeit.[12]

[He who succeeds in reconciling the many contradictions of his
life, holding them all together in a symbol, pushes the noisy crowd
from the palace and will be festive in a different sense, receiving you
as his guest on mild evenings.
Then you will be the Other of his loneliness, the still centre of his
monologues; and every circle drawn around you takes his com-
passes right outside time.]

sound like the *adagio* treatment of a theme which gets rather out
of hand in the *fortissimo* passage of Nietzsche's finale:

> . . . . .
> um Mittag war's, da wurde Eins zu zwei. . . .
> Nun feiern wir, vereinten Siegs gewiss,
>   das Fest der Feste:
> Freund *Zarathustra* kam, der Gast der Gäste !
> *Nun* lacht die Welt, der grause Vorhang riss,
> die Hochzeit kam für Licht und Finsternis. . . .[13]

[It was at midday when One became Two. . . . Together now
and sure of our triumph, we celebrate the feast of feasts: friend
Zarathustra has arrived, the guest of guests ! The world is overjoyed,
the weird curtain is torn apart, the wedding day has come for light
and darkness.]

It is on evenings, calm and gentle, when the great Other of
Rilke's loneliness comes to his only disciple who, in all his gentleness,
has already managed to drive the noisy crowd from the temple.
Zarathustra, on the other hand, arrives in the glaring midday
hour. Midday and evening—this example will have to stand
for the most striking difference, obvious throughout their
works, between Rilke and Nietzsche. Nietzsche's tone is imperial.
He has received the great commandment, has once faced his God,
and henceforward he will speak out. Rilke's orders are of a more
cumulative nature. His head is bent in the attitude of one who
listens intently to 'das Wehende', the continual lesson, formed out of
stillness. But is this necessarily a difference in substance? Not if the
whispered news amounts in the end to the same as the revelation
which Nietzsche receives with the dramatic incisiveness of the
thunderbolt. Some, however, believe that it is altogether other
news, and are, I think, misled by their belief; for they do not
distinguish between the theme and its variations, between the soul
and its seasons. And while Nietzsche and Rilke may merely be two
moods of the same heart, they are often held to be possessed by
fundamentally different certainties. It may be difficult to see the one
garden for its very varied flowers. But only if we are inclined to
take the transports produced by night-scented stock for a distinct

spiritual initiation, shall we be convinced of the profound difference between Rilke's religion and Zarathustra's, proclaimed in the proudest of daylights with 'the crown of roses on the prophet's brow'. Yet we should perhaps remember that St. Paul served with prophetic zeal the same God whom others loved in humbler dedications. We shall come to see Rilke as the St. Francis of the Will to Power.

This assertion will seem extravagant only to those who are victims to the popular misapprehension which suggests that the Will to Power is a kind of moral teaching sanctioning violence and ruthlessness, and not the profound metaphysical inspiration which in fact it is, comprehending, or at least attempting to comprehend, the real meaning behind the representative beliefs and unbeliefs, activities and philosophies of Europe in war and peace throughout its more recent history. Rilke may be to Nietzsche what Orpheus is to Dionysus; and Rilke's Orpheus and Nietzsche's Dionysus are brother deities, by virtue of that peculiar adjustment to more modern attitudes of the soul, which was forced upon Greek mythology by the spiritually needy and hungry of modernity. But before we establish this equation, we shall have to attend to what else they have in common.

They are both initiates in the alchemy of loneliness and suffering. Rilke as well as Nietzsche discovers the fountainhead of joy in the very heart of the land of sorrow. Happiness for them is not, as it was for Schopenhauer, in the absence of pain; it is the fruit of so radical an acceptance of suffering that abundant delight springs from its very affirmation. For the denial of pain means the denial of existence. Existence is pain, and joy lies not in non-existence, as Schopenhauer would have it, but in its tragic transfiguration. This is the theme of Nietzsche's *Birth of Tragedy* as well as of *Zarathustra* and of *The Will to Power*, where it is treated with ever growing assurance by a man, it is well to remember, who wrote to a friend: 'The terrible and all but incessant torture of my life makes me thirst for the end. . . . As far as agony and renunciation are concerned, my life during these last years is a match for that of any ascetic at any time. . . . Yet no pain has been able or shall be able to tempt me into giving false testimony about life as I recognize it.'[14] And this recognition is praise. From the darkest night of the soul rises

Zarathustra's 'Trunkenes Lied', his Dionysian song of the deep suffering of the world, which is yet surpassed in depth by that rapture of delight which wills, not that the world with its pain should pass away, but that it should last for ever:

> doch alle Lust will Ewigkeit —,
> — will tiefe, tiefe Ewigkeit! —

an eternity not of joy (as Nietzsche is so often misunderstood to mean) but of the world *with* all its sorrow, transfigured in the act of willing it.

If we bear in mind what has been said about the difference in tone and gesture between Rilke and Nietzsche, there remains hardly a single element in Nietzsche's acceptance and transformation of suffering that could not also be found in Rilke. Indeed, the parallels appear to be exact. As early as his *Tuscan Diary* he writes: 'To think that I myself was once among those who suspect life and distrust its power. Now I would love it at all events. . . . Whatever of it is mine . . . I would love with tenderness, and would bring to ripeness within myself all possibilities that its posession offers to me.'[15] And much later, in the Tenth Elegy, we encounter what is an elegiac version of the theme of *The Birth of Tragedy*: Rilke's Klage, the embodiment of Lamentation, guiding the dead youth through the country of her ancestors with its mines of sorrow, until they reach the terminus where Klage and youth must part, that gorge

> wo es schimmert im Mondschein:
> die Quelle der Freude. In Ehrfurcht
> nennt sie sie, sagt: 'Bei den Menschen
> ist sie ein tragender Strom'.*

> [where it gleams in the moonlight:
> the source of Joy. With awe
> she names it, says 'Among men
> it is a carrying stream'.]

And not even an intonation alien to Nietzsche's, but *merely* the presence of the Angels seems (and merely *seems*) to render the

---

* With a number of separate editions of *Duino Elegies* and *Sonnets to Orpheus* available, I shall refer to these poems by their numbers only. The translations are, with some modifications of my own, by J. B. Leishman and Stephen Spender (*Duino Elegies*, London, 1948) and J. B. Leishman (*Sonnets to Orpheus*, London, 1946).

beginning of Rilke's Tenth Elegy unsuitable as an epitaph for Nietzsche:

> Dass ich dereinst, an dem Ausgang der grimmigen Einsicht,
> Jubel und Ruhm aufsinge zustimmenden Engeln.
> Dass von den klargeschlagenen Hämmern des Herzens,
> keiner versage an weichen, zweifelnden oder
> reissenden Saiten.

> Some day, emerging at last from the vision of terror,
> may I burst into jubilant praise to assenting Angels.
> May no one of the clear-struck keys of the heart
> fail to respond through alighting on slack or doubtful
> or rending strings !]

Nietzsche, who for so long believed that he was a musician, as well as a philosopher, once composed a 'Hymn to Life', the text of which is—strangest of biographical coincidences—by Lou Salomé. In *Ecce Homo* he says that he chose it because its last lines possess greatness; their meaning is that suffering is no argument against life: 'Hast du kein Glück mehr übrig mir zu geben, wohlan ! noch hast du deine Pein . . .'.[16] It is a bad poem. The future lover of the poetess would have done better. If Nietzsche discovered some greatness in those verses, persuaded no doubt by the theme of praise, the great persuasion of the *Sonnets to Orpheus* would have overwhelmed him.

For instance, the sonnet 'Singe die Gärten, mein Herz, die du nicht kennst'. It almost sounds like Lou's 'Hymn to Life', set to music by Rilke (though perhaps in this sonnet the music is actually not very much better than Nietzsche's):

> Meide den Irrtum, dass es Entbehrungen gebe
> für den geschehnen Entschluss, diesen: zu sein !
> Seidener Faden, kamst du hinein ins Gewebe.

> Welchem der Bilder du auch im Innern geeint bist
> (sei es selbst ein Moment aus dem Leben der Pein),
> fühl, dass der ganze, der rühmliche Teppich gemeint ist.

> [Do not believe you will be deprived
> of something by your resolution: to *be*.
> Silken thread, you have entered the weaving.

With whatever pattern you are inwardly blended
(and be it a scene from the story of Agony),
feel that the whole, the praiseworthy carpet is meant.]

And the sonnet which begins with the beautiful lines:

Nur im Raum der Rühmung darf die Klage
gehn, die Nymphe des geweinten Quells

[Only in the realm of Praise may Lamentation move,
naiad of the wept fountain]

is indeed Rilke's 'Trunkenes Lied', the lyrical echo of Zarathustra's
Dionysian song. For in this song too sorrow transcends itself in the
knowing certainty of jubilation, raising to the skies a constellation of
immaculate joy:

Jubel *weiss*, und Sehnsucht ist geständig, —
nur die Klage lernt noch; mädchenhändig
zählt sie nächtelang das alte Schlimme.

Aber plötzlich, schräg und ungeübt,
hält sie doch ein Sternbild unsrer Stimme
in den Himmel, den ihr Hauch nicht trübt.

(I, VIII)

[Triumph knows, and Longing makes confession,—
Lamentation learns: in nightly session
counts, with maiden-hands, old tribulation.

Then, however inexpertly limned,
lifts our voices in a constellation
to the sky her breathing has not dimmed.]

Delighted as Nietzsche would have been by these sonnets, would
he necessarily have recognized Orpheus as their divine inspiration?
He himself was preoccupied with gods of fuller status: with Dionysus and Apollo. His early *Birth of Tragedy* interpreted the Attic drama
as the outcome of an age-old struggle which these two gods waged
within the Greek soul. In tragedy, at last, the two hostile gods came
together and concluded peace: Dionysus, the god of chaotic ecstasy,
rapturously abandoning all claims to form and shape, all individuality, to the amorphous oneness of life; and Apollo, the god with

the lyre at whose call all things were arrested within their own contours and their own articulate order. Would Europe, after the end of the 'tragic' period of Greece, ever again know such reconciliation, and achieve so profound a harmony between the deepest and most conflicting impulses of the human soul? Shall we ever create an order which is not, as all our orders are, at the expense of the fullness of life, but its richest unfolding; a pattern which is not imposed upon chaos, but overreaching and surpassing it, its beauty still tremulous with the ancient terror? Or is the ancient god of ecstasy doomed to an ignominious existence in the murky corners of sin and depravity, and the god of order to be imprisoned in the petrified structure of classicism and morality? Or *shall* Dionysus and Apollo be united again, as they were in Attic tragedy?

Such were the youthfully enthusiastic questions which Nietzsche asked in his *Birth of Tragedy*. At the time his equally enthusiastic answer was: the old gods have risen again; they live in the work of Richard Wagner. It was to prove an agonizingly provisional answer. Perhaps Rilke's Orpheus would have made good the promise that Wagner's Parsifal broke.

The attempt of scholars to unravel the complex of historical reminiscences, images, insights, feelings that make up the story of Dionysus, Apollo and Orpheus in modern German literature and thought, and then to relate it to what may be the Greek reality of these divine creatures, is as heroic as it is doomed to failure. For a scholar's guarded steps cannot possibly keep pace with the rush and dance of the passions of the mind swirling around those names and arrested only for brief moments in innumerable figurations. Nietzsche, from *The Birth of Tragedy* onwards, is seeking spiritual employment in the service of a god who is a synthesis of Dionysus and Apollo. In this composite Nietzschean deity, Apollo, it is true, more and more loses his name to the older god, but by no means the power of his artistic creativeness, for ever articulating the Dionysian chaos in distinct shapes, sounds and images, which are Dionysian only because they are still aglow with the heat of the primeval fire. At the end of his *Will to Power*, that is, at the end of the life of his mind, he once more returned to the antagonism within the Greek soul between the Dionysian and Apolline, and once more celebrated the triumph of a god who wrests the utmost of glorifying beauty from the monstrous terror of chaotic passions. This triumphant god, far from suffering the chill of classicism, has, as it were,

Apollo's eyes and the heart of Dionysus. In Nietzsche's mature years the real opposition is not Dionysus versus Apollo, but the Apolline Dionysus versus Christ.[17]

And Rilke? In a letter from Rome, written probably in the spring of 1904, twenty-two years before the *Sonnets to Orpheus* (it is the last-known letter using undisguised Nietzschean terms), Rilke indulges in a kind of eschatological vision of Apollo's ultimate triumph over the chaotic dominion of Dionysus. The phrases of this letter have not only the ring, but almost the precise wording of Nietzsche's evocations of Apollo-Dionysus. It is chaos itself, says Rilke, which, at the end of days, will stand transformed into 'a million ripe, fine and golden forms', an 'Apolline product, fermented into maturity and still radiant with its inner glow'. And nothing could be more Nietzschean than 'the wakeful, lucid enthusiasm of Rilke's Apolline world.[18]*

This is the eschatology of an artist; of an artist, at that, whose business is not merely to heighten by his own creations the beauty of a world, beautiful and significant in itself, but to *create* himself the only beautiful and significant world that there is or can be. It is astonishing and instructive to see how long an idea, present right at the beginning of a poet's career, takes to mature into great poetry. We may also observe how this same idea, originally part of a quasi-historical or Darwinian theory about the development of man, becomes in the end the timeless assertion, not of a future state, but of existence itself. In 1898 Rilke notes in the *Tuscan Diary*: 'Not for all time will the artist live side by side with ordinary men. As soon as the artist—the more flexible and deeper type among them— becomes rich and virile, as soon as he *lives* what now he merely *dreams*, man will degenerate and gradually die out. The artist is eternity protruding into time.'[19] In the *Sonnets to Orpheus* this eternity not merely protrudes, it has arrived. It *is* the world itself; a world which exists in and through song alone. Song is existence— 'Gesang ist Dasein'. A god could easily achieve it: 'Für den Gott ein Leichtes'. But if there are no gods? Then we must become gods ourselves. We? We who hardly *are*? 'Wann aber *sind* wir?' Indeed, man must transform and transfigure himself; and in transfiguring himself he will be the redeemer and transfigurer of all existence: '*der Verklärer des Daseins*'.[20]

---

* The authentic wording of this letter was established with considerable effort and great scholarly care by Eudo C. Mason. (Cf. his *Der Zopf des Münchhausen*, Einsiedeln, 1949, 77.)

This dialogue, made up of verbatim quotations from Rilke and Nietzsche, is about the Orpheus of the sonnets. The other name of this 'Verklärer des Daseins'—the formula is Nietzsche's—is Dionysus Apollo:

Du aber, Göttlicher, du, bis zuletzt noch Ertöner,
da ihn der Schwarm der verschmähten Mänaden befiel,
hast ihr Geschrei übertönt mit Ordnung, du Schöner,
aus den Zerstörenden stieg dein erbauendes Spiel.

. . . .

O du verlorener Gott! Du unendliche Spur!
Nur weil dich reissend zuletzt die Feindschaft verteilte,
sind wir die Hörenden jetzt und ein Mund der Natur.

(I, XXVI)

[You that could sound till the end, though, immortal accorder
seized by the scorn-maddened Maenads' intemperate throng,
wholly outsounded their cries when in musical order
soared from the swarm of deformers your formative song:

. . . .

O you god that has vanished! You infinite track!
Only because dismembering hatred dispersed you
are we hearers to-day and a mouth which else Nature would lack.]

This composite deity is still more obviously present in the following sonnet in which allusions to Rilke's imagined family history, repeated in the Third Elegy, are merged in a kind of Dionyso-Apolline anthropology of universal significance:

Zu unterst der Alte, verworrn,
all der Erbauten
Wurzel, verborgener Born,
den sie nie schauten.

Sturmhelm und Jägerhorn,
Spruch von Ergrauten,
Männer im Bruderzorn,
Frauen wie Lauten. . . .

Drängender Zweig an Zweig,
nirgends ein freier. . . .
Einer! o steig . . . o steig. . . .

Aber sie brechen noch.
Dieser erst oben doch
biegt sich zur Leier.

　　　　　　　　　　　(I, XVII)

[Undermost he, the earth-bound
root of uprearing
multitudes, source underground,
never appearing.

Helmet and hunting-horn,
words of the ageing,
rage between brothers-born,
women assuaging.

Branch on branch, time on time,
vainly they spire. . . .
One free! Oh, climb . . . oh, climb. . . .

One, though the others drop,
curves, as it scales the top,
into a lyre.]

　　There are also sonnets in which the image of Orpheus could,
without imposing the slightest strain on either the poem or our
imagination, fade out altogether, making room for Zarathustra
himself; for instance, the sonnet which begins

Rühmen, das ist's! Ein zum Rühmen bestellter,
ging er hervor wie das Erz aus des Steins
Schweigen. Sein Herz, o vergängliche Kelter
eines den Menschen unendlichen Weins.

　　　　　　　　　　　(I, VII)

[Praising, that's it! As a praiser and blesser
he came like the ore from the taciturn mine.
Came with his heart, oh, transient presser,
for men, of a never-exhaustible wine.]

and, still more so, the sonnet

Wolle die Wandlung. O sei für die Flamme begeistert
　　　　　　　　　　　(2, XII)

[Choose to be changed. With the flame be enraptured.]

in which almost every word—'Wandlung', 'Flamme', 'jener entwerfende Geist, welcher das Irdische meistert', 'Was sich ins Bleiben verschliesst, schon ists das Erstarrte', 'Hammer' and 'Härtestes'—belongs as its most unmistakable property to Zarathustra's prophetic household, although there can be no doubt that they have come into Rilke's possession through perfectly legitimate channels. The seal on the deed is authentic. It shows a lonely priest in a ruined cathedral. The roof is off. Through the vast opening comes down what looks a little like the traditional image of the Holy Ghost. But as it is blurred and indistinct, this may be too hasty an interpretation, merely suggested by the cathedral. It may also be rain. As it descends through the open roof of a ruin, we might perhaps just call it 'the openness', 'das Offene'. This seems to be confirmed by the words which are printed around the circumference of the seal. They say: 'Denn offen ist es bei dir und hell', 'Where you are at home, everything is open and light', and 'Mit allen Augen sieht die Kreatur das Offene', 'With all its eyes the creature-world beholds the open'.

The last sentence is the beginning of Rilke's Eighth Elegy; but the first was spoken by Zarathustra on coming home to his lonely cave.* Once more he has left the noisy town—one is irresistibly tempted to say, the 'Leid-Stadt' of Rilke's Tenth Elegy:

> wo in der falschen, aus Übertönung gemachten
> Stille, stark, aus der Gussform des Leeren der Ausguss,
> prahlt, der vergoldete Lärm, das platzende Denkmal.
> O wie spurlos zerträte ein Engel ihnen den Trostmarkt,
> den die Kirche begrenzt, ihre fertig gekaufte:
> reinlich und zu und enttäuscht wie ein Postamt am Sonntag

> [where, in the seeming stillness of uproar outroared,
> stoutly, a thing cast out from the mould of vacuity,
> swaggers that gilded fuss, the bursting memorial.
> How an Angel would tread beyond trace their market of comfort,
> with the church alongside, bought ready for use: as tidy
> and disappointed and shut as the Post on a Sunday]

for Rilke's is as exact a description as Nietzsche gives of the town

---

* Cf. also Zarathustra's words: 'Only when a clear sky looks down through broken ceilings . . . will my heart turn again towards the places of God'. (M.A., XIII, 116.)

that Zarathustra has left behind in order to converse with his own
solitude:

> 'Here you are at home with yourself,' he says. . . . 'Here all
> things come to your speech, caressing and flattering, for they
> wish to ride on your back. And you yourself are riding on many
> a symbol towards many a truth. . . .
> 'Here the words and word-shrines of everything that is, open
> up before you; everything that is, desires to become word;
> everything that will become, desires to learn from you how to
> speak.'[21]

Rilke too was to travel on many a symbol, yielded by the word-
shrines of things, towards many of Zarathustra's truths. Rilke's
youthful *Tuscan-Diary* version of Zarathustra's secret sessions with
'die Dinge' is as follows: '. . . I feel that more and more I am
becoming the disciple of things (not merely their listener), a disciple
who adds, through comprehending questions, intensity to their
answers and confessions, and who, enticing them to spend their
advice and wisdom, learns how to reward their generous love with
the disciple's humility'.[22]

The aspect of things changes in the new 'openness' of Nietzsche's,
of Rilke's solitude. Within the perspective of this expanded, and
yet, as we shall see, more radically confined space, it appears that
neither things nor names have ever been really known. With a new
consciousness and perception gained, they must be christened anew,
baptized, as it were, into a new Church. For another dimension of
speech has been thrown open, and all things desire to hear their
names once more, uttered in a voice resonant enough to fill the new
spaces. Said as they used to be said, words fall flat in these changed
acoustical conditions.

What happened to the *form* and *shape* of things at the beginning
of the Renaissance, seems now to happen to their *names*. With the
third dimension *consciously* perceived as an essential aspect of vision,
all objects demanded to be seen and painted afresh, and indeed quite
new ones called out for recognition. Zarathustra's words of the
things that 'come to your speech, caressing and flattering, for
they wish to ride on your back', would, with a change from
speech to canvas, have made good sense to the first of the great
Renaissance painters. If the medieval madonnas and angels

seemed to complain that they cut poor figures in their two-dimensional flatness, at the same time an abundance of other images pressed upon the painters' imagination, claiming their right to significance in the new field of vision. Pillars, towers, gates, trees, jugs and windows demanded to be *seen* with an intensity as never before—'wie selber die Dinge niemals innig meinten zu sein'.

Rilke's new dimension is inwardness. As they came to Zarathustra with their novel claims, so the things approach Rilke, asking to be taught how to become words and how to make themselves truly felt in the widened space; and in return they show him that this is precisely his real task in the world: to assimilate them into the new inward dimension:

> — Sind wir vielleicht *hier*, um zu sagen: Haus,
> Brücke, Brunnen, Tor, Krug, Obstbaum, Fenster, —
> höchstens: Säule, Turm . . . aber zu *sagen*, verstehs,
> oh zu sagen *so*, wie selber die Dinge niemals
> innig meinten zu sein. . . .
>
> (Ninth Elegy)
>
> [—Are we, perhaps, here in order to say: House,
> Bridge, Fountain, Gate, Jug, Peartree, Window,—
> at most: Pillar, Tower? . . . but to *say*, remember,
> oh, to say this so as never the things themselves
> meant so intensely to be. . . .]

It has often been said of both Nietzsche and Rilke that they were masters of new nuances, the one of thought, and the other of feeling. True, they both felt that their souls and minds were at the mercy of sensations and revelations so subtle as had never been received before; that they were instruments on which the wind of unsuspected spaces played its first tentative tunes. In this unexplored space which is, as it were, made up of the 'empty distances' *between* and *around* our normal concepts of thought and feeling, lies our 'wirklicher Bezug', our *real* 'relatedness' to what really *is*. Like a hymn of spiritual friendship, addressed to Nietzsche, sounds Rilke's sonnet:

> Heil dem Geist, der uns verbinden mag;
> denn wir leben wahrhaft in Figuren.
> Und mit kleinen Schritten gehn die Uhren
> neben unserm eigentlichen Tag.

I

Ohne unsern wahren Platz zu kennen,
handeln wir aus wirklichem Bezug.
Die Antennen fühlen die Antennen,
und die leere Ferne trug. . . .

(I, XII)

[Hail, the spirit able to unite us!
For we truly live our lives in symbols,
and with tiny steps move our clocks,
beside our real, actual day.

Without knowing our true place
we yet act from real relatedness.
Antennae feel antennae,
and the empty distance carries. . . .]

And Nietzsche's response:

Jenseits des Nordens, des Eises, des Heute,
jenseits des Todes,
abseits:
unser Leben, *unser* Glück!
Weder zu Lande
noch zu Wasser
kannst du den Weg
zu den Hyperboreern finden:
von *uns* wahrsagte so ein weiser Mund.[23]

[Beyond the North, the ice, the present day,
beyond death,
away from it:
our life, *our* bliss!
Neither by land nor by sea
can you find the way
to the Hyperboreans:
it was of *us* that the mouth of wisdom thus prophesied.]

And the solitary figure of Rilke in the Piccola Marina of Capri,
feeling and hardly surviving the

uraltes Wehn vom Meer,
welches weht
nur wie für Urgestein,
lauter Raum
reissend von weit herein. . . .[24]

[primeval waft from the sea,
which wafts
as if only for primeval stone,
rushing pure space
in from afar. . . .]

easily merges with that of Nietzsche, leaning over a bridge in the brown Venetian evening:

Meine Seele, ein Saitenspiel,
. . . unsichtbar berührt[25]

[My soul, a play of strings
. . . touched by an invisible hand]

words which might be followed by Rilke's

Und welcher Geiger hat uns in der Hand?
O süsses Lied.[26]

[And who is the fiddler that holds us in his hand?
O sweet song.]

Yet these are only lyrical prolegomena or accompaniments to the real theme: the radical revision of all frontiers within human experience. The full realization of this theme comes to both of them in ecstatic states of inspiration. Both Nietzsche and Rilke knew they were inspired, irresistibly commanded to write, the one *Zarathustra* and the other *Duino Elegies*. Theirs are the only personal accounts we possess in modern literature of states of inspiration. The reports are almost interchangeable, except that Nietzsche's, written at some distance from the experience itself, is more sober than are Rilke's breathless announcements of victory. 'Has anyone, at the end of the nineteenth century, any clear idea of what poets of more vigorous ages called *inspiration*?' asks Nietzsche in the *Zarathustra* chapter of his *Ecce Homo*, and continues: 'If one were in the least superstitious, one would not know how to reject the suggestion that one is merely an incarnation, merely a mouthpiece, merely a medium of superior powers'.[27] Of 'days of enormous obedience', speaks Rilke, of 'a storm of the spirit' which threatened to annihilate the body. 'O that I was allowed to survive to this day, throughout everything. Wonder. Grace.'[28] Both Nietzsche and Rilke felt that the very physical surroundings which were the chosen scenes of

these Pentecosts were hallowed places. The tenderness with which
Nietzsche describes his walks on the hillsides of Genoa and through
the Mediterranean pinewoods along the Bay of Santa Margherita
where Zarathustra accompanied him, is equalled by Rilke's stepping
out into the cold moonlight, when he had survived the onrush of
the Elegies, and stroking the walls of the 'little castle Muzot' 'like an
old animal'.

This is not the way mere nuances are discovered. The word
nuance presupposes an order of firmly established ideas and objects
between which an indefinite number of subtly-coloured shades may
playfully mediate; whereas Nietzsche's and Rilke's sensibilities tend
towards a radical denial of that very principle of separation—
philosophically speaking, the *principium individuationis*, within a
world perceived under the dual aspects of immanence and transcendence—on which our intellectual perception has been based
throughout the centuries. Nietzsche denounces its results with
regard to our thought as that 'barbarism of concepts' which we are
still far from fully realizing, and Rilke its effects on our feeling as
that pauperism of the heart which makes us outcasts among angels,
men and beasts alike, distressed vagabonds of the crudely interpreted
world—

> dass wir nicht sehr verlässlich zu Haus sind
> in der gedeuteten Welt.

For all men make the mistake of *distinguishing* too sharply—

> ... Aber Lebendige machen
> alle den Fehler, dass sie zu stark unterscheiden.
>
> (First Elegy)

But this is an elegiac understatement of the real denunciation im-
plicit in Rilke's mature work, which is that our traditional way of
distinguishing is false throughout the whole range of our fundamental distinctions between transcendence and immanence, God and
man, man and things, external reality and inwardness, joy and
suffering, communion of love and separation, life and death; a list
to which Nietzsche's main contribution is: good and evil. 'To
presuppose the *oneness* of life and death,' Rilke writes, one year after
Duino Elegies and *Sonnets to Orpheus*, and again, 'to know the *identity*
of terror and bliss ... is the essential meaning and idea of my two
books'.[29]

3

We seem to have travelled a fair distance without being perturbed by our initial scruples which ought to have cast a shadow over the whole enterprise of relating the *poet* Rilke to the *thinker* Nietzsche. It appears that we had neither the courage nor the wisdom to act on Goethe's advice and 'give ourselves up to impressions', to allow ourselves freely 'to be amused, moved, and edified' by Rilke's poetry; nor did we share, or work on Mr. Eliot's belief that 'the poet who "thinks" is merely the poet who can express the emotional equivalent of thought. But he is not necessarily interested in the thought itself'.[30] For the conviction informing this essay is that Rilke *as a poet* is interested 'in the thought itself', and Nietzsche *as a thinker*, also expresses 'the emotional equivalent of thought'; and yet Nietzsche remains a thinker throughout, and is not, as some believe, 'merely a poet', nor does Rilke ever cease to be a poet, even if some complain that he is 'too speculative' in his mature phase. On the contrary, I believe that Nietzsche's and Rilke's distrust of, and opposition to, valid distinctions have some of their roots in their *legitimate* antagonism to one profoundly *invalid* distinction to which their age clung with almost religious passion: the distinction between thought and feeling. It is the distinction on which both rationalism and romanticism throve, spending their forces in an ultimately futile struggle to assert the superiority of the one or the other. Yet it is no good trying to choose between two misfits. Both Goethe and Mr. Eliot, in the quoted instances, attempt to clear up a confusion by using tools of thought manufactured in the very workshop that is responsible for the muddle.

This becomes quite obvious if we look at the concepts to which both Goethe and Mr. Eliot oppose poetry. Goethe says that it has nothing to do with 'ideas'. 'Ideas' have always been the *bête noire* as well as the weak point of Goethe. Once, as we have seen, he was on the verge of being very angry with Schiller who accused his *Urpflanze* of belonging to that oppressive and oppressed class. But of course Schiller was right and Goethe was offended only because the word 'idea' suggested to him something 'abstract', something 'thought out' by what he was in the habit of calling 'Verstand': discursive and analytical reason. And throughout the conversation with Eckermann, quoted at the beginning, it is this analytical reason that is set against poetry, this 'Verstand' which

Goethe disliked so much as the prosaic enemy of poetry—and, indeed, of science too. It assumes mythological shape in the figure of Newton.*

Mr. Eliot, on the other hand, knows that the meaning of 'thought' does not permit so lighthearted and restrictive a definition. He deplored the difficulty of 'having to use the same words for different things'.[31] But when it actually comes to using 'thought' in *his* sense, this is what happens: 'Champions of Shakespeare as a great philosopher have a great deal to say about Shakespeare's power of thought, but they fail to show that he *thought to any purpose*; that he *had any coherent view of life*, or that he *recommended any procedure to follow*'.[32] In other words, 'thought' in this sense appears to be the preoccupation of a group of men among whom the professional bores are in the majority. The three criteria amount to a definition of a certain type of rationalism. It is a definition that excludes, first, the thinker for whom thinking is not a means to an end, but a passion; secondly, the thinker who knows that no system of thought can ever be completely coherent without the knowledge of the indispensable measure of incoherence worked into the whole structure of the system; and thirdly, the thinker whose thought does not issue in recipes for action, but in invitations to think. In short, it excludes the thinker.

To make poetry is to think. Of course, it is not *merely* thinking. But there is no such activity as 'merely thinking', unless we confine the term to purely logical or mathematical operations. Language is not quite so stupid as some of our analytical philosophers seem to assume. It knows what it does when it allows us to say that we 'think of someone', and when it calls actions deficient in kindness of imagination, 'thoughtless'. 'Thinking' and 'thought' in these phrases are no mere manner of speaking. The words mean what they say: thought and thinking. And if we have it on an authority still higher than Goethe's or Mr. Eliot's that in the beginning was *logos*, the word, the thought, the meaning, we should think twice

---

* A dictionary of Goethe's vacillating use of the word 'idea' would reveal the full measure of ambiguity that besets the problem of 'thought and poetry' in the age of rationalism and romanticism, and the difficulties of a man who is opposed to either. The first essay in this book, 'Goethe and the Idea of Scientific Truth', contains a number of quotations from Goethe that show a much more positive attitude towards 'ideas' than his conversation about *Tasso* would suggest. About *Faust* he said to Luden on August 19th, 1806, that its 'higher interest' lies in 'the idea which has inspired the poet and which is capable of knitting all the details of the poem into a whole, providing norm and significance for its individual elements'. (Cf. also L. A. Willoughby's essay 'Faust als Lebensorganisation' in *Goethe und die Wissenschaft*, Frankfurt a.M., 1951, 37.)

before we answer the question whether or not a poet thinks. It is a happy coincidence in German that 'Dichter und Denker', poet and thinker, form an alliterative pair.

Mr. Eliot suggests that Shakespeare, in making Hamlet think in the manner of Montaigne, did not think himself, but merely 'used' thought for dramatic ends. This sounds true enough, and would be even truer if it were possible to 'use' thought without thinking in the process of using it. For thought is not an object, but an activity, and it is impossible to 'use' an activity without becoming active. One can use a table without contributing to its manufacture; but one cannot use thinking or feeling without thinking or feeling. Of course, one can use the results of thought in a thoughtless fashion. In this case, however, one does not use thought, but merely words which will, more likely than not, fail to make sense.

In so far as Hamlet's thought makes sense, Shakespeare must have been thinking it, although not necessarily as the first to do so and certainly in a manner of thinking which is more imaginative and intuitive than rationally deliberate. To define 'thinking' in such a way that the activity which Shakespeare pursued in composing the speeches of Hamlet, or Ulysses, or Lear has to be dismissed as 'non-thought', is to let thinking fall into the rationalist trap from which it is likely to emerge as a cripple, full of animosity against that other deformed creature, mutilated in the same operation: the Romantic emotion. If thought, stripped of imaginative feeling, and emotion, stripped of imaginative thought, become the dominant modes both of thinking and feeling, the outcome is the 'Leid-Stadt', that insufferable city of sorrows, or the Waste Land, in which the spirits of Nietzsche, as well as Rilke, as well as Mr. Eliot feel ill at ease. Paradoxically enough, it is precisely this neat separation between thought and feeling which has forced, on the one hand, upon modern philosophy 'the Absurd' as one of its principal themes; and, on the other hand, upon modern poetry an excessive degree of *intellectual* complexity.

Poetry is not, as Goethe would suggest in that conversation with Eckermann, in opposition to 'ideas', nor does it, as Mr. Eliot says, merely give the 'emotional equivalent' of thought. Dante, Shakespeare, Goethe, Rilke and Mr. Eliot, in making poetry, have ideas; and they think. Only in the 'pure' lyric and the 'pure' epic may ideas and thought be so negligible as to be irrelevant to aesthetic or critical appreciation. If Dante's thought is Thomas Aquinas', it is yet Dante's; not only by virtue of imaginative sympathy and assimilation, and certainly not as a reward for the supply of an 'emotional equivalent'. It is Dante's property by birthright. He has reborn it within himself—poetically. For poetry is not a garment around thought, nor is it its shadowy aesthetic reflection. It is a certain kind of thought, hopelessly uncertain of itself at a time when thought is 'merely' thought and poetry 'merely' poetry and therefore, to quote Mr. Eliot's *East Coker*, 'does not matter':

> Because one has only learnt to get the better of words
> For the thing one no longer has to say, or the way in which
> One is no longer disposed to say it.

If this happens, the problem of thought and poetry takes on an altogether new complexion. For happy is the poet whose only job is to learn how to get the better of words for things which he *has* to say. He is the poet who thinks with the thought of his age, as Dante thought with the thought of St. Thomas. Whether or not the poet thinks in the thought-mould of his time, does not necessarily depend on the goodness or profundity of its thought, and certainly not on its systematic coherence. The question is rather, whether this thought springs from the same level of spiritual experience on which poetry is formed; and whether it is linked to that reservoir of fundamental intellectual certainties (and be it the certainty of doubt, scepticism or stoicism) from which the poetic impulse must be sustained if it is not to be in danger of breaking under a burden too heavy for its delicate constitution. This danger will arise when the poet, compelled by the peculiar spiritual barrenness of his age, has to struggle for the poetic expression of unheard-of and unthought-of experiences. It is then that he will have to do *all* the thinking himself, because the experiences for which, as a poet, he has to find the adequate *poetic* thought, have not yet become articulate even in terms of *intellectual* thought.

What has become articulate in terms of intellectual thought is experience so prosaic that its mere contemplation paralyses the poetic imagination. It is the situation that Hegel had in mind when in his *Aesthetics* he wrote: 'If the mode of prose has absorbed all the concepts of the mind and impressed them with its prosaic stamp, then poetry has to take on the business of so thorough a recasting and remodelling that, faced with the unyielding mass of the prosaic, it finds itself involved everywhere in manifold difficulties'; and which led him to the pessimistic dictum that there-fore 'art . . . is and will remain for us a thing of the past'.[33] In such conditions a kind of poetry will be produced, for which, anomalously enough, the *intellectual* thinking has to be done after the event. Whole gangs of interpreters will rush in, intellectually to prepare the ground for what has already grown—ploughboys of the sparse harvest.

Yet Mr. Eliot is not, I suspect, concerned as much with the question of thought in poetry as with the problem of belief. For the assumption underlying his essay is that the thinker is interested in the *truth* of thought, but the poet merely in its fitting expression. In other words, the thinker invites us to *believe* what he says, whereas the poet aims only at our being *moved* or *pleased* by the way he puts it. This is indeed a very relevant problem at a time when more and more people try to believe in poetry as in a religion. Around Rilke, for instance, a vast body of literature has grown up that appears to aim not at gaining comprehending readers for the poet, but at making proselytes.

The question, then, is: is the poet a trustworthy counsellor? Does he himself believe what he says? Is he committed to his truths, as the thinker appears to be committed to his? Without going into the endless intricacies of this problem, I would say that it has nothing to do with the nature of either poetry or thought as such, but with the character of any particular poet or thinker, or with the character of any particular poetry or thought. There *are* poetic creations which bear the unmistakable stamp of convictions deeply held by the poet; and the *aesthetic* success of this kind of poetry is inextricably bound up with the sincerity of the personal beliefs expressed in them. This applies, for instance, to the poetry of St. John of the Cross. But it applies, also, on varying levels and in different degrees, to less extreme examples: to George Herbert, John Donne, Milton, Andreas Gryphius, Claudius, Hölderlin—and Mr. T. S. Eliot. It does not matter in the slightest whether such a poet is, while writing, *preoccupied* with his beliefs. Of course, in the act of writing he is preoccupied with the business of writing as well as possible. But what does matter is the fact that such poets could not produce good poetry if they were prepared to betray their beliefs for the sake of occasional heresies offering a more felicitous phrase. On a profounder level it would even be true to say that such a poet, in writing his poetry, *discovers* the precise nature of the beliefs to which he is, or ought to be, really committed. Whether he remains committed to such beliefs, whether he is a believer all the time, realizing what he believes through his actions, is another matter, again wholly irrelevant to the specific problem of poetry. Few men are like Pascal, and even he had to remind himself continually, by a sheet of paper sewn into his jacket, of what he had on one sacred occasion recognized as wholly true.

Naturally, the beliefs of such a poet, as proclaimed in his poetry, may be of so subtle, esoteric and even eccentric a sort that it would be unwise to try to live by them. But he is not necessarily less 'trustworthy' as a prophet of truths than any other type of prophet. The difficulty does not lie in the fact that he is a poet, but is of a universal nature. It is the difficulty of translating spiritual convictions into living convictions. If this were an easy matter, the Christian Church would have no 'history'. Her practices would be as unchanging and unchangeable as the core of her spiritual beliefs. The reasons why one should, or should not, accept the beliefs inherent in Rilke's later poetry, are not different in kind from the reasons why one should, or should not, accept the beliefs of Marxism, or of the Oxford Group, or of anthroposophy. To say, 'but he is merely a poet' (and not, I suppose, a sectarian hawker, an ideologist or a political propagandist), is to suggest that, by his profession, he is less capable of perceiving truth than others; to say, 'but his poetry is too beautiful to be true', is to insinuate that the closer the poetry is to truth, the less successful it will be as art, because all truth is necessarily ungainly. This is a point to which we shall return at the end of this essay.

I am not concerned with advocating Rilke's beliefs. But I am concerned with a dangerous type of aesthetic fallacy: that Rilke's ideas do not matter because they are a poet's ideas. If I could see a choice where, in fact, I believe there is none, between the ideas and the poetry, I think I would rather be inclined to say with Mr. Eliot that it is the poetry which 'does not matter'. But there is no such choice. In *Duino Elegies* the poetry is the ideas, and the ideas are the poetry. If the ideas were all humbug, or if, as Herr Holthusen suggests in his book on Rilke, they were all 'wrong', in the sense of contradicting that 'intuitive logic' which tells us what is a true and what is a false picture of man,[34] then the poetry would have little chance of being what he believes it to be: *great* poetry.

The appreciation of poetry is not like looking at a beautiful apple; it is rather like looking and eating. If the core is rotten, the outside beauty will soon be felt to be a mockery. Herr Holthusen's way out of the dilemma between his Christian beliefs that make him condemn Rilke's ideas, and his pagan enchantment for which he acknowledges the greatness of Rilke's poetry, is, I think, the way of spiritual timidity. Its coarser symbols are the fig-leaves of the Vatican museum. Let us enjoy the pagan beauty, but not go too far. How far? Not as far as the *whole* poetry. For the poetry of the *Duino Elegies* is indivisible. There is no poetry left if we *feel* that the 'ideas' are false to the point of being a distortion of the true image of man. If, on the other hand, we merely *know* this, not by that 'intuitive logic' of which Herr Holthusen speaks, but by theological deliberations, we are by no means immune from sharing the beliefs of the *Duino Elegies*. Why not accept a situation which for most Christians in Europe is at least as old as the Renaissance? The characteristic spiritual quality of that long period of history of which we are the bewildered heirs was not only a dissociation of faith from knowledge; this was a comparatively harmless episode, lasting from the seventeenth century to the age of Victoria, a mere surface repercussion of that mightier earthquake which severed faith from sensibility. It is this rift which has made it impossible for most Christians not to *feel*, or at least not to feel *also* as true many 'truths' which are incompatible with the truth of their faith. If this is agony, it must be borne by those who are incapable of Keats's '*Negative Capability*, that is, when a man is capable of being in uncertainties, mysteries, doubts, without any irritable reaching after fact and reason'. Such an 'irritable reason' is the all too facile distinction between the 'truth' of a poem and its 'aesthetic appeal', between the 'idea' and the 'poetry', a separation which can only do damage to the resources, meagre as they are, with which we have to carry on in our modest efforts to get a little nearer the spiritual integrity within which, in Nietzsche's words, 'the religious, aesthetic and moral perceptions are at one'. For the time being, which does not seem to be God's good time:

Jede dumpfe Umkehr der Welt hat solche Enterbte,
denen das Frühere nicht und noch nicht das Nächste gehört.
(Seventh Elegy)

[Each torpid turn of the world has such disinherited children,
to whom no longer what's been, and not yet what's coming,
belongs.]

This again is spoken, not only from the heart of Nietzsche, but almost with his tongue, suggesting that we should resume the discussion of the particular poet and the particular philosopher.*

4

We observed them, each in his own way, working, thinking and feeling towards a radical revision of the frontiers between traditionally articulated concepts of thought and, as it were, units of feeling. There remains the question of how and why they came to undertake such a stupendous labour of thought and feeling—'Herzwerk', 'work of heart', as Rilke called it. The answer was given for both of them by Nietzsche: because God is dead. And God was so powerful, efficient and secretive a landlord that to look after His Estate all by ourselves involves us in great difficulties. What under His management used to be clearly defined spheres, are now objects of confused and conflicting claims. Much that we were powerfully persuaded to accept as true, dissolves into sheer illusion. For all the land appears to have been heavily mortgaged.

* In his essay on Dante, written in 1929, two years after 'Shakespeare and the Stoicism of Seneca', Mr. Eliot discusses once more the question of belief and poetry. 'There is a difference,' he says, 'between philosophical *belief* and poetic *assent*' (*Collected Essays*, p. 257). This is undoubtedly true in an age in which 'the religious, aesthetic and moral perceptions' are *not* at one. We may, however, disregard the word 'philosophical' in Mr. Eliot's phrase, for his context is more strictly a religious or theological one. An agnostic can give his poetic assent to Dante and a Christian withhold it from every single hymn sung on a Sunday in his church. Yet there will be a certain strain in such a situation. The more *serious* becomes a reader's love for Dante's poetry, the more will he be tempted to accept his beliefs, or else be exasperated by the poet's wrongheadedness in holding them or his own inability to share them; and exasperation detracts from enjoyment. Differences of opinion are more worrying between lovers than between superficial acquaintances; in fact, they tend to become or reveal something else: flaws in mutual understanding. And because this is so, Mr. Eliot's discussion of this particular problem comes to nothing. His statement on page 258: 'You are not called upon to believe what Dante believed, for your belief will not give you a groat's worth more of understanding and appreciation' is, after its more forceful reiteration in a postscript (p. 269) crossed out again by 'So I cannot, in practice, wholly separate my poetic appreciation from my personal beliefs' (p. 271). The question is extremely difficult, so difficult that both assertions, blatantly contradictory, are in some measure true. It seems to me that two points could be added to make them a few degrees truer and less incompatible. 1. Where beliefs embodied in poetry are as important as they are in what one may call confessional poetry, we cannot fully appreciate the poetry without being at least *tempted* to accept the beliefs as well. The measure of our appreciation will be the degree to which we experience the poem's strength in persuasion and our weakness in the face of the challenge. With such poetry before us, complete immunity from infection would prove either the bluntness of our perception or the worthlessness of the poetry. 2. There are ideas and beliefs so prosaic, outlandish or perverse in their innermost structure that no great or good poetry can come from them; for instance, Hitler's racialism. It is this *negative* consideration that to me finally proves the intimate *positive* relation between belief, thought and poetry. If there were no relation, there would be no reason either why the most perverse or idiotic beliefs should not be convertible into *great* poetry. They are not.

We have lived in splendour, but the splendour was merely loaned. Payment was due on the death of God, and the unknown transcendental creditor lost little time in claiming it. A tremendous effort has to be exacted to restore the glory.

Both Nietzsche and Rilke have made themselves administrators of the impoverished estate. The enormous complexity of their works must not deceive us; the structure behind it is consistently simple; it has the simplicity of that immense single-mindedness with which they, consciously or intuitively, dedicated their lives to the one task: to re-assess and re-define all experience in thought and feeling; to show that the traditional modes of thought and feeling, in so far as they were determined, or decisively modified, by Christian transcendental beliefs—and to which of them does this not apply?—had been rendered invalid by the end of religion; to replace them; to overcome the great spiritual depression, caused by the death of God, through new and ever greater powers of glory and praise; to adjust, indeed to revolutionize, thought and feeling in accordance with the reality of a world of absolute immanence; and to achieve this without any loss of spiritual grandeur. 'Indeed,' writes Nietzsche (to Overbeck, May 21st, 1884), 'who can feel with me what it means to feel with every shred of one's being that the weight of all things must be defined anew,' and Rilke (to Ilse Jahr, February 22nd, 1923): 'God, the no longer sayable, is being stripped of his attributes; they return to his creation';[35] and in 'The Letter of the Young Workman' (reversing the debtor-creditor relationship and presenting the bill to Heaven): 'It is high time for the impoverished earth to claim back all those loans which have been raised at the expense of her own bliss for the equipment of some super-future'.[36] Nietzsche spoke for himself as well as for Rilke when at the time of writing *Zarathustra* he made the following entry in his notebook: 'He who no longer finds what is great in God, will find it nowhere—he must either deny or create it'.[37] It is the most precise formula for the religiously disinherited religious mind.

Nietzsche and Rilke experienced and explored this situation with the utmost consistency, courageously facing the paradox to which it leads: the paradox of affirming from negation, and creating from denial. For the denial of God involves for both Nietzsche and Rilke the denial of man *as he is*. Even before Zarathustra proclaimed the rule of the Superman, Nietzsche, knowing that man has become 'impossible' after doing away with God, 'the holiest and mightiest that the world possessed', asked: 'Is not the greatness of this deed too great for us? To prove worthy of it, must not we ourselves become gods?'[38] And Rilke said of his *Malte Laurids Brigge* that it almost 'proved that this life, suspended in a bottomless pit, is impossible'.[39]

How is this impossible life to become possible again? How is the vanished glory issuing from a transcendental god to be recreated by a world gloomily imprisoned in its own immanence? At this point both Nietzsche and Rilke indulge in the same alchemy that we have seen employed in their transmutation of pain and suffering. The idea of even heightening the agony of existence in order to increase the resources from which ultimate bliss will be sustained, is familiar to both of them. Nietzsche once quoted Cardanus as having said that one ought to seek out as much suffering as possible in order to intensify the joy springing from its conquest;[40] and Rilke wrote of the 'holy cunning of the martyrs', taking 'the most concentrated dose of pain' to acquire the immunity of continual bliss.[41] Now again they seek in the greatest possible intensification of immanence salvation from the inglorious prison. They almost invent more and more deprivations of transcendence to heighten the pressure within the hermetic vessel. In that, Nietzsche's Eternal Recurrence and Rilke's '*Ein*mal und nichtmehr', '*Once* and no more', are contrasts merely in verbal expression, but identical in meaning. This identity lies in the emphasis both these symbols place on the *eternity* of the moment here and now, the *irrevocability* of the one and unique opportunity and test of living.

The idea of Eternal Recurrence seeks to bestow the paradox of an eternity of finite time on the transient moment, which Rilke, in his turn, eternalizes in the hermetical flame of inner experience, consuming all that is merely corruptible matter and concreteness in our world and leaving us with an essence as imperishable as it is invisible. Rilke states this theme of his mature work with explicit precision as early as his *Tuscan Diary*: 'We need *eternity*; for only eternity can provide space for our gestures. Yet we know that we live in narrow finiteness. Thus it is our task to create infinity within these boundaries, for we no longer believe in the unbounded.'[42] And the imaginations of both Nietzsche and Rilke have given birth to symbolic creatures moving with perfect grace and ease in a sphere to which man can attain only in the utmost realization of his spiritual powers. These creatures of immanence, transcending immanence in the achievement of a yet profounder immanence, are Nietzsche's Superman and Rilke's Angel. Both are terrible to man, threatening with annihilation the image that, fondly and lazily, he has built up of himself, an image resting on the illusion of transcendence and now shattered in the great undeceiving: 'To create the Superman after we have thought, indeed rendered thinkable, the whole of nature in terms of man himself' and then 'to *break all your images of man* with the image of the Superman—this is Zarathustra's will . . .'[43] says one of Nietzsche's notebooks from the time of Zarathustra; and Rilke's *Duino Elegies* begin with the invocation of the angelic terror:

> Wer, wenn ich schriee, hörte mich denn aus der Engel
> Ordnungen? und gesetzt selbst, es nähme
> einer mich plötzlich ans Herz: ich verginge von seinem
> stärkeren Dasein . . .
>
> (First Elegy)

> [Who, if I cried, would hear me among the angelic
> orders? And even if one of them suddenly
> pressed me against his heart, I should fade in the strength of his
> stronger existence . . .]

and

> Jeder Engel ist schrecklich. Und dennoch, weh mir,
> ansing ich euch, fast tödliche Vögel der Seele,
> wissend um euch. . . .
>
> (Second Elegy)

> [Every angel is terrible. Still, though, alas!
> I invoke you, almost deadly birds of the soul,
> knowing of you. . . .]

The supreme realization of immanence and its metamorphosis into everlasting inwardness is man's task in a world dominated by Rilke's Angel, in the same way in which Nietzsche conceives Eternal Recurrence as the terrifying discipline which must break man and make the Superman. Only he, in the glory of his own strength, joy and power of praise, can *will* again and again a life which, even if lived only once, must be all but unendurable to man, as soon as he is exposed to the full impact of its absolute godlessness and senselessness, and no longer sheltered from it by the ruins of

Christianity among which he exists. 'I perform the great experiment: who can bear the idea of Eternal Recurrence? He who cannot endure the sentence, "There is no redemption", ought to die out.'[44] The Superman is for Nietzsche what Orpheus is for Rilke: the transfigurer of unredeemable existence, with the 'mystery of its unending repetition issuing from superhuman delight'.[45]

> Und so drängen wir uns und wollen es leisten,
> wollens enthalten in unseren einfachen Herzen,
> im überfüllteren Blick und im sprachlosen Herzen.
> Wollen es werden. . . .
>
> (Ninth Elegy)

[And so we press on and try to achieve it,
try to contain it within our simple hands,
in the gaze ever more overcrowded and in the speechless heart.
Try to become it. . . .]

But what we try to achieve here and what overcrowds our gaze and heart—with 'überzähliges Dasein', 'Supernumerary existence'—is not the vision of Eternal Recurrence, but, on the contrary, of

> Einmal
> jedes, nur *ein*mal. *Ein*mal und nichtmehr. Und wir auch
> *ein*mal. Nie wieder. Aber dieses
> *ein*mal gewesen zu sein, wenn auch nur *ein*mal:
> irdisch gewesen zu sein, scheint nicht widerrufbar.
>
> (Ninth Elegy)

[Just once,
everything only for once. Once and no more. And we, too,
once. And never again. But this
having been once, though only once,
having been once on earth—can it ever be cancelled?]

Nietzsche's Eternal Recurrence and Rilke's eternally reiterated 'Once' are both the extreme symbols of the determination to wrest the utmost of spiritual significance from a life that, in traditional terms, has ceased to be spiritually significant. How to cast eternity from the new mould of absolute transience, and how to achieve the mode of transcendence within the consciousness of pure immanence, is one of the main concerns of Nietzsche as well as of Rilke. This problem links Rilke (and, of course, Nietzsche) with the philosophers of Existence; Heidegger, for instance, is said to have remarked that his philosophy is merely the unfolding in thought of what Rilke has expressed poetically;[46] but even without this confession the affinity would be obvious. What, above all, Rilke and the existentialists have in common, is the experience of the utter exposure and defencelessness of the frontiers of human existence against the neighbouring void, that area which was once established as the divine home of souls and is now the unassailable fortress of the *nihil*, defeating for ever every new and heroic attempt of man to assert himself in that region: hence Jasper's *Scheitern*, Heidegger's *Geworfensein* and, long before them, Kierkegaard's— and even Pascal's—*Angst*. The focal point of all existentialist philosophies is this 'marginal situation' of man in the border-districts of immanence and the realization of the existence of a sphere which seems to invite and yet relentlessly beat back every attempt at transcendence.

It is this impenetrable void against which Zarathustra hurls his armies of men, knowing that they will not be victorious, but utterly routed; yet a few will return in triumph, having gained the strength of supermen in the purifyingly defeat. For life is a 'Wagnis', a perpetual staking of existence, man a mere 'essay in existence' and lovable only because he is 'ein Übergang und ein Untergang',[47] at once transition and perdition. The same frontier is the defeat of Malte Laurids Brigge, until the mature Rilke succeeds in concluding an everlasting truce with the anonymous powers on the other side —by appropriating their territory 'inwardly'. Where man knew merely the terror of the monstrous emptiness beyond, there is now the peace of 'reiner Bezug', 'pure relatedness', which is so pure because no real 'otherness' enters into it. In this 'reiner Bezug' life and death are one. As soon as it is achieved,

> entsteht
> aus unsern Jahreszeiten erst der Umkreis
> des ganzen Wandelns. Über uns hinüber
> spielt dann der Engel. . . .
>
> (Fourth Elegy)

> [arises
> from our seasons the cycle
> of the entire motion. Over and above us,
> then, there is the Angel's play. . . .]

K

Or, one is tempted to add, the Superman's dance, the joy of the creatures who have gained eternity in the resigned and yet victorious return to themselves. Rilke, in the Super-Narcissus image of his Angels, at the same time expresses the essence of Nietzsche's race of Supermen who assert their power and beauty in the cycle of Eternal Recurrence:

> . . . die die entströmte eigene Schönheit
> wiederschöpfen zurück in das eigene Antlitz.
> (Second Elegy)
> [. . . drawing up their own
> outstreamed beauty into their faces again.]

It is not correct that after the *Duino Elegies* Rilke returned, as some critics suggest, to a 'simpler' and 'purely lyrical' mode of expression. The apparent simplicity and pure lyricism of the final phase are not different in kind from the simplicity and lyricism of *Sonnets to Orpheus*. There is, indeed, repose; but it is the repose of a poetry that appears to have settled peacefully on the very pastures which had for so long been the goal of the struggle. If the *Duino Elegies* were the invocation of the Angel, some of the poems that come afterwards sound like the Angel's own poetry; and it is hardly surprising that it could also be said: like the poetry of the Superman. This, indeed, does not make them easier to understand. It is the poetry of achievement, and not the poetry of return. There is little gain in it for those who find the 'ideas' of the preceding period disturbing. The ideas are not abandoned, but realized; for instance, in the poem written in 1924:

> Da dich das geflügelte Entzücken
> über manchen frühen Abgrund trug,
> baue jetzt der unerhörten Brücken
> kühn berechenbaren Bug.
>
> Wunder ist nicht nur im unerklärten
> Überstehen der Gefahr;
> erst in einer klaren reingewährten
> Leistung wird das Wunder wunderbar.
>
> Mitzuwirken ist nicht Überhebung
> an dem unbeschreiblichen Bezug,
> immer inniger wird die Verwebung,
> nur Getragensein ist nicht genug.

Deine ausgeübten Kräfte spanne,
bis sie reichen, zwischen zwein
Widersprüchen. . . . Denn im Manne
Will der Gott beraten sein.[48]

[As the winged ecstasy
has borne you over many an early abyss,
now, with mathematical audacity
build the arches of unheard-of bridges.

Wonder is not merely in the inexplicable
surviving of danger;
only in the clear and purely granted
achievement is the miracle miraculous.

To participate in the indescribable
relating, is not presumption,
ever more intense becomes the pattern,
only being borne along will not suffice.

Stretch your practised powers till they span
the distance between two contradictions,
for the god must find
counsel in the man.]

Or in Rilke's last-known poem in German, which, if it is simple,
has the inexhaustibly complex simplicity of a sphere so esoteric that
it renders it completely untranslatable, defeating even the attempt to
give a prose version of it in English. Yet all that has been said here
about Rilke and Nietzsche could easily be based on this one poem
alone and would need no further support. It is dated August 24th,
1926, four months before Rilke's death, and is dedicated to Erika
Mitterer 'for the feast of praise':

Taube, die draussen blieb,   ausser dem Taubenschlag,
wieder in Kreis und Haus,   einig der Nacht, dem Tag,
weiss sie die Heimlichkeit,   wenn sich der Einbezug
fremdester Schrecken schmiegt   in den gefühlten Flug.

Unter den Tauben, die   allergeschonteste,
niemals gefährdetste,   kennt nicht die Zärtlichkeit;
wiedererholtes Herz   ist das bewohnteste:
freier durch Widerruf   freut sich die Fähigkeit.

Über dem Nirgendssein   spannt sich das Überall!
Ach der geworfene,   ach der gewagte Ball,
füllt er die Hände nicht   anders mit Wiederkehr:
rein um sein Heimgewicht   ist er mehr.[49]

5

Both Nietzsche and Rilke, experiencing life as wholly immanent,
irrevocable in its transience and unredeemable in its imperfection,
stake it on the supreme 'Wagnis', the daring experiment: man
himself must become the redeemer of existence. This is the ultimate
consequence of the Will to Power, or of humanism thought out
and felt to its radical conclusion by the *anima naturaliter religiosa*.
Nietzsche replaces the mystery of the Incarnation by the Superman,
the Will to Power incarnate; and Rilke by the angelic vision of a
world disembodied in human inwardness. 'We must transform our
prayers into blessings,'[50] says Nietzsche; and Rilke:

> Erde, ist es nicht dies, was du willst: *unsichtbar*
> in uns erstehen? — Ist es dein Traum nicht,
> einmal unsichtbar zu sein? — Erde! unsichtbar!
> Was, wenn Verwandlung nicht, ist dein drängender Auftrag?
> (Ninth Elegy)

> [Earth, isn't this what you want: an *invisible*
> re-arising in us? Is it not your dream
> to be one day invisible? Earth! invisible!
> What is your urgent command, if not transformation?]

Only on the discovery of this redeeming mission follows Rilke's
final affirmation: 'Erde, du liebe, ich will'.

Interpreting the Elegies to his Polish translator, Rilke wrote:
'*There is neither a Here and Now nor Beyond, but only the great Oneness,*
in which the creatures surpassing us, the Angels, are at home. . . .
*We are the bees of the Invisible. Nous butinons éperdument le miel du
visible, pour l'accumuler dans la grande ruche d'or de l'Invisible.*' And
after denouncing the ceaselessly progressing depreciation of the
spiritual value of all 'things', he continues: 'The earth has no other
refuge except to become invisible: *in us* . . . only *in us* can this
intimate and enduring transformation of the Visible into the
Invisible . . . be accomplished. . . . The Angel of the *Elegies* has
nothing to do with the angel of the Christian heaven. . . . He is the

creature in whom the transformation of the Visible into the Invisible, which is our task, appears already accomplished. . . .'⁵¹ But for all this, the most illuminating part of Rilke's much-quoted letter is the statement that the ultimate affirmation of life, achieved in the *Elegies*, is sustained by precisely the same awareness that persuaded Malte Laurids Brigge of life's 'impossibility'. Malte's disgust and the Ninth Elegy's praise spring from an identical source. In other words, the Angel did for Rilke what the Superman did for Nietzsche: he supplied the philosophers' stone with which to make gold from base matter. Yet it appears that of the two Rilke was the more successful alchemist. The letters he wrote after the *Duino Elegies* lavished the precious stuff from the poet's workshop on as many needy as cared to apply for it. Nietzsche, on the other hand, while writing *Zarathustra* and expounding the doctrines of Eternal Recurrence, praise and affirmation, made the following entry in his notebook: 'I do not wish to live *again*. How have I borne life? By creating. What has made me endure? The vision of the Superman who *affirms* life. I have tried to affirm it *myself*—but ah !'⁵²

These two confessions of Rilke and Nietzsche clinch the whole excruciating problem that besets the spiritually disinherited mind of Europe, and raise anew the question of poetry and truth in an age dispossessed of all spiritual certainties. Without that all-pervasive sense of truth which bestows upon happier cultures their intuition of order and reality, poetry—in company with all the other arts—will be faced with ever increasing demands for ever greater 'creativeness'. For the 'real order' has to be 'created' where there is no intuitive conviction that it exists. The story of the rise of the poet from the humble position of a teller of tales and a singer of songs to the heights of creation, from a lover of fancies to a slave of the imagination, from the mouthpiece of divine wisdom to the begetter of new gods, is a story as glorious as it is agonizing. For with every new gain in poetic creativity the world as it is, the world as created without the poet's intervention, becomes poorer; and every new impoverishment of the world is a new incentive to poetic creativeness. In the end the world as it is, is nothing but a slum to the spirit, and an offence to the artist. Leaving its vapours behind in audacious flight, his genius settles in a world wholly created by the creator-poet: *Gesang ist Dasein*.

'Only after the death of religion will the imagination be able to luxuriate again in divine spheres,'⁵³ said Nietzsche, perhaps not

knowing that in saying it he was merely echoing one of the favourite
ideas of the Romantics whom he so much disliked. For it was
Friedrich Schlegel who wrote: 'Only he can be an artist who has a
religion of his own, an original view of infinity',[54] and it was Novalis
who added to this dictum the marginal note 'The artist is thoroughly
irreligious. Hence he can work in the medium of religion as though
it were bronze.'[55] But the original views of infinity cannot for ever
remain unaffected by the spiritual destitution of the finite. There
must come a time when owing to excessive mining bronze is
devalued and the soil becomes too dry for anything to grow
luxuriantly, except in artificial conditions.

Neither Rilke nor Nietzsche praises the praiseworthy. They
praise. They do not believe the believable. They believe. And it is
their praising and believing itself that becomes praiseworthy and
believable in the act of worship. Theirs is a *religio intransitiva*.
Future anthropologists may see in it the distinctive religious achievement of modern Europe, the theological equivalent of *l'art pour
l'art*. For the time being, it may help us to assess the rank of Rilke
as a poet, and to clear up some of the confusion into which we are
plunged by dissociating his 'great poetry' from his 'false ideas'.

In a sense Rilke's poetry is as 'false' as are his ideas. This sense,
however, is not simply derogatory. There is a kind of falseness
which, quite legitimately, affords the most refined aesthetic pleasure;
at the point, that is, at which consistently sustained artificiality
assumes the semblance of spontaneity, and the most elaborate
magical procedure the appearance of the naïvely miraculous. In this
sense both Rilke's poetry and his ideas show the intrinsic falseness
of a self-created reality and a self-induced love for it. In defending
a sense and vision of reality different from Rilke's, the critic implicitly upholds, often against his explicit intentions, standards of
poetry by which the poetic work of Rilke's mature years stands
judged as too eccentric to be really great. Rilke poetically exploits
a marginal position, precariously maintained on the brink of
catastrophe. The catastrophe, perpetually threatening and only just
warded off by the most dazzling acrobatics of soul and mind, is the
loss of significant external reality. In the great poetry of the European tradition the emotions do not interpret; they respond to the
interpreted world. In Rilke's mature poetry the emotions do the
interpreting and then respond to their own interpretation.

All great art (and, for that matter, every human order stabilized by tradition) rests on a fundamentally fixed correspondence between the impact of external experience on man and man's articulate answers. These answers may be given on varying levels of profundity and with varying degrees of precision, but they are all recognizable by, as it were, their basic colour as the more or less right answers. Indeed, the imagination, this kingfisher after new experiences and new articulations, may discover new waters in lands which had long remained inaccessible and unexplored. But there will be a place for them, hitherto left blank, on the maps of the familiar world.

Rilke, however, is the poet of a world, the philosopher of which is Nietzsche. Its formations evade all traditional systems of cartography. Doubt has dislodged all certainties. The unnameable is christened and the unsayable uttered. It is a world in which the order of correspondences is violently disturbed. We can no longer be sure that we love the lovable and abhor the detestable. Good does no good and evil no harm. Terror and bliss are one. Life and death are the same. Lovers seek separation, not union. All the sweetness of the visible world is stored in invisible hives.

Unembarrassed greatness is not to be expected from the poetry of such a world.* Yet Rilke is uniquely successful in evoking the traditional responses of the emotions to fundamentally new impacts. At his bidding the soul travels as though through familiar land; but on arrival it finds itself in a place where it never meant to be. It is not for nothing that the central position in the *Duino Elegies*—the fifth among the ten—is occupied by *Les Saltimbanques*. There is an

---

* Mr. Eliot, in discussing the question of whether a poet 'thinks', says: 'We talk as if thought was precise and emotion was vague. In reality there is precise emotion and there is vague emotion. To express precise emotion requires as great intellectual power as to express precise thought.' This is an important point admirably put, although it would be difficult to find a word other than 'thought' for the *intellectual* power required to express precise emotion. Yet the passage continues: 'But by "thinking" I mean something different from anything that I find in Shakespeare'—namely, as we saw, 'thinking to a purpose', etc. (*Selected Essays*, p. 135).

Asked for a definition of the 'unembarrassed greatness of poetry' I would accept Mr. Eliot's sentence and say that, among other things, it is 'the precise expression of precise emotion'. But I would add that precise emotion is a mode of response or even of comprehension, closely linked to thought. Their common medium is language. Indeed, precise emotion is the result of that sustained and refining interaction between thought and emotion to which we give the name of culture. The only measure for the precision of emotion is in its articulation. Inarticulate emotion is vague and thoughtless. And precise emotional articulation in language is possible only within a definite 'system of correspondences' between thought, feeling and external impacts. This, however, is hardly provided by the situation in which modern poetry finds itself involved. This situation is inimical to such precision partly because by 'thought' we have come to 'mean something different from anything' we may find in Shakespeare or Dante.

acrobatic element in Rilke's poetry itself which tinges its greatness
with the hue of the abstruse. For his most superb accomplishment
is the *salto mortale* of despair which lands the soul in a 'Raum der
Rühmung', a sphere of praise, where all the praise is sung in honour
of the singer while the voiceless world, deranged and dizzy, is left
behind to face the music.

'What was it that Zarathustra once told you? That poets lie too
much?—But Zarathustra too is a poet. . . . *We* lie too much.'[56]
These words of Nietzsche sound like an anticipated motto to Rilke's
letters. For the utter precariousness of Rilke's vision is exposed
most painfully in endless prose variations which form a large part
of his correspondence. Only a generation of recipients and
readers, benumbed and befogged by every conceivable spiritual
deprivation, and insensitive to the intimate relation between
language and authenticity, could accept as genuine spiritual guidance
pronouncements which more often than not show the unmistakable
stylistic imprint of untruth; of that most dangerous kind of untruth
which does not spring from fraudulent intent, but from a self-
deception so profound that nothing less powerful than a false
inflection, a hollow adjective or a synthetic noun can undeceive us
of its hypnotic persuasion. Rilke takes the unending curtain-calls
which acknowledge his poetic achievement, in the costume of his
inspiration. Then, and only then, the prophecy turns to performance, and the visionary glance seems produced by make-up. But
it was Nietzsche, the thinker, not Rilke, the poet, who was obsessed
with the problem of the actor-artist, as it was Nietzsche who wrote
the lines:

> *Daß ich verbannt sei*
> *von aller Wahrheit!*
> *Nur* Narr! *Nur* Dichter! . . . [57]

> [Oh, that I be banished
> from all Truth!
> Mere fool! Mere poet! . . .]

This fact brings to its paradoxical conclusion an argument that took
its bearings from a theory expounding that, while the poet merely
makes poetry, it is the thinker who is unequivocally committed to
his thought.

'My earliest serious concern was with the relationship between

Art and Truth,' wrote Nietzsche in 1888, right at the end of his conscious life, in a renewed attempt to understand the mind that in 1870 conceived *The Birth of Tragedy*. 'And even now,' the meditation continues, 'I am seized with holy terror in the face of that dilemma. The belief that informs *The Birth of Tragedy* is a belief in Art, against the background of yet another belief: that it is *impossible to live with Truth*. . . . The will to *illusion* . . . is profounder, more 'metaphysical', than the will to Truth, Reality and Being'.[58] And in *The Will to Power* we read: 'For a philosopher it is an abomination to say, "the Good and the Beautiful are one"; and if he dares to add, "also the True", then one ought to beat him. Truth is ugly. . . . We have *Art* in order *not to perish of Truth*.'[59] Thus the essential function of art is, according to Nietzsche, to think and feel existence to that conclusion which convinces us of its perfection, 'to create perfection and the fullness of life', to '*affirm, bless* and *deify* existence'.[60]

This is the perfect definition of Rilke's poetic project. It also marks the summit reached by art and poetry in its steep ascent to the heights of absolute creativeness. At this point the separation between art and reality appears to be complete. Reality is the death of the spirit and art its salvation. Where does truth reside? Is it in the deadly real world or in the saving vision of the artist? The question lingers on the all but imperceptible border-line between delusion and lunacy, between Nietzsche's madness and Rilke's prophetic pose, tenaciously maintained even beyond the confines of poetic inspiration. Nietzsche, believing that truth was insufferable and that poetry was an illusion, continually suspected that at least some of his thought was merely poetry. Rilke, on the other hand, succeeded most of the time in convincing himself that the thought behind his poetry was the mind of truth. Illusion or truth, Superman or Angel, Will to Power or the Will to Inwardness—in both Nietzsche and Rilke the human mind and imagination are engaged in the ultimate task of creating a world to take the place of the spiritually useless productions of God.

'Indeed, the whole book acknowledges only an artist's meaning behind everything that happens—a "god" if you like, but certainly only an artist-god . . . desirous of achieving his delight and sovereignty through making things and unmaking them . . . and who, in creating worlds, frees himself from the agony . . . of his inner conflicts. The world . . . seen as the successful salvation of god, as a vision . . . of one who suffers most, one who is the richest in conflicts and contradictions and can only save himself by creating illusion. . . .'⁶¹ The book in question is *The Birth of Tragedy*, thus described by Nietzsche himself in 1886, sixteen years after it was written. A critic could hardly do better in the case of *Duino Elegies* and *Sonnets to Orpheus*.

In January, 1889, Nietzsche, then in Turin, became clinically insane. On the fourth of that month the uncanniest of all calls to Orpheus was posted at the Turin railway station. The note was addressed to Nietzsche's friend, the composer Peter Gast. It ran: 'To my maestro Pietro. Sing a new song for me: the world is transfigured and all the heavens rejoice.' It was signed 'The Crucified'.

Sharing with each other the fruits of defeat, inflicted upon all besiegers of the Absolute in a world without Truth, thought ceases to be merely thought and poetry is no longer merely poetry. Song, trying to prove the glory, and thought, determined to dispel the illusion, are adventurers in the same heroic saga. It tells the story of one Tantalus who has deprived the gods of their seats at the banquet. Sitting all by himself at the divinely laid table, he yet cannot eat without letting them into his own secret: that he does not think well enough of himself to believe in the reality of his triumph. This is their curse which he cannot escape. Intoxicated with their wine, he glories in their absence; but with the sobriety of his thought returning, he sees the water of life receding before the hollow of his outstretched hand.

It is the redeeming achievement of Nietzsche and Rilke that they have raised, the one in the intensely felt plight of his thought, the other in his intensely meditated poetry, the abysmal contradictions of their age to a plane where doubt and confusion once more dissolve into the certainty of mystery.

VI

OSWALD SPENGLER AND THE PREDICAMENT OF THE HISTORICAL IMAGINATION

OSWALD SPENGLER AND THE PREDICAMENT
OF THE HISTORICAL IMAGINATION

OSWALD SPENGLER, who died in 1936, performed one of the most curious feats in the history of modern thought: in a remarkably short time he has achieved a kind of highly topical oblivion. The first volume of his great work *The Decline of the West* appeared in 1918, and the second followed in 1922.[1] It was passionately debated at the time. A special issue of the philosophical journal *Logos* was published in which the headmasters of all the schools of German philosophy launched critical campaigns for or against this surprisingly learned and alarmingly catastrophe-minded *Oberlehrer*. Furthermore, a book called *Der Streit um Spengler* assembled the numerous expert voices of critics into a confused chorus which left behind the effect of agitated historical embarrassment. And now, when the author of *The Decline of the West* would be only just over seventy, his work is by general consent utterly out of date.

Yet the 'utterly' carries a suspicious emphasis. It sounds a little like the comforting agreement of a party of grown-up empiricists who all saw the ghost of a very unpleasant uncle during the preceding night: 'But he has been utterly dead for the last fifteen years!' And so he has; yet his ill-tempered prophecies have unfortunately come true; the family was called together to discuss the impending auction of the family estate.

The uneasiness is not surprising. For the history of the West since 1917 looks like the work of children clumsily filling in with lurid colours a design drawn in outlines by Oswald Spengler. The spiritual exhaustion of the age has been the dominant theme of our most-discussed writers, of D. H. Lawrence, Franz Kafka, T. S. Eliot, not to mention the gloomily vigorous Americans; and when they indulge in prophetic visions of the future, in the manner of Aldous Huxley, George Orwell or even the dying Fabian H. G. Wells, the emerging picture is invariably an elaboration of themes from *The Decline of the West*. Spengler even predicted the disappointing behaviour of that god who has since so sadly failed many of our intellectuals. Some time before the Russian revolution he wrote: 'Socialism, only half-developed to-day, is indeed fighting against

143

Imperialism; yet one day it will become arch-expansionist itself with all the vehemence of Destiny'.[2]

Destiny—this brings us to the very centre of Spengler's vision of history. History is Destiny, unfolded through the life and death of cultured human societies. All these societies share a common rhythm of development, which Spengler sees in analogy with the life-and-death rhythm of living organisms. Cultures—this and not 'civilizations' is the proper term to use with Spengler—come into being, are young and full of vigorous metaphysical sap, flower like splendid vegetables on the herbaceous borders of an indifferent cosmos, and decay; or rather, are frozen into rigid forms by the metaphysical winter of their old age. It is this petrified stage of a culture which Spengler calls 'civilization'. With our Western culture the great chill finally descended in the course of the nineteenth century.

It is amazing how far Spengler is carried along by his precarious analogy. For according to him, when the freezing-point of a culture is reached, it expands and breaks whatever may try to contain it. Then, with its spiritual substance exhausted, outward expansion is the only gesture of life that is left. The age of Caesarism is upon us. A strict and rigid order of the molecules within, is the condition of successful raids on the outward world; or in terms of government and foreign policy: the totalitarian State becomes the instrument of inevitable Imperialist wars. Their outcome is, however, of little importance to the spiritual existence of the members of such a society. In victory or defeat their spirits will remain sterile—as barren, Spengler says, as the society of the Romans under their conquering Caesars. After some time, however, this powerful structure, spiritually dead as it is, is bound to fall to pieces, probably under the elusive but irresistible impact of new forces, alien and hostile to the existing order, and possessed of the stuff of which cultures are made: creative spontaneity and religious devotion.

In this struggle between the civilized engineers and barbaric, but God-inspired men, the barbarians will win. But before the time of a new culture comes, for Destiny's sake, Spengler proclaims, be an engineer! Don't waste your life in the futile agony of trying to realize what you may have left of a soul. This is no time for souls. If you become a painter, a poet, a composer, he says, you will find yourself in no time whatever frustrated, or else corrupted by those aesthetic cliques, which offer, in terms of power, influence, licentiousness, easy sales of bogus wares, some compensation for the pains of a spiritual vocation gone astray. For the *Zeitgeist* is inexorable; as inexorable now as it was in Roman times. Then, too, it would have been absurd for a young intelligent citizen to hatch out some irrelevant variation of post-Platonic philosophy, if he was clever enough to organize armies and provinces, and to plan new cities and roads.[3] Then as much as now, all spiritual, aesthetic, philosophical resources had been spent. Culture was, as it were, put into inverted commas and reduced to a museum, or a pleasure-garden, exhibiting the past together with its contemporary parodies. To-day, Spengler says, there is more intelligence, taste, character and ability in the technical staff of any first-rate engineering works than in the whole of contemporary music and painting.[4] His conclusion is: 'I can only hope that men of the new generation may be moved by my book to take up engineering instead of poetry, join the Navy rather than a School for Painting, become politicians rather than philosophers'.[5]

Yet *The Decline of the West* is by no means a pamphlet written for boys. It contains the results of an enormous amount of learning and intellectual labour. Its scope—all the major societies in traceable human history—is as fantastic as its claim: to give the philosophy of the West to end all Western philosophies. Thus its subject is not history in any conventional sense of the term, but what the author calls 'the world-as-history'.[6]

It is impossible to refute such a mighty enterprise by listing, as so many of its opponents did, factual inaccuracies. There will always be sufficient indisputable facts left to support the structure, if one allows such a structure to be supportable at all. The proper tools of empiricism can only deal with Spengler's brushwood, and inflict a few scratches on his landscape of peaks and valleys. The assertion, for instance, that Spengler's culture-organisms have no real historical existence, goes right outside the range of empiricism. It is impossible to destroy an analogy 'empirically', however much 'evidence' is assembled for the campaign. All historical generalizations are the defeat of the empiricist; and there is no history without them. Apply the strict empiricist test to the concept of 'nation', 'class', 'economic trend' or 'tradition', and the concept dissolves into a host of unmanageable *minutiae*. In every single case the question is merely how profound and subtle a generalization it is, or how much of the generalizing manoeuvre passes unnoticed; and it has every chance of not being recognized for what it is, if it is in keeping with the silent agreements and prejudices, the prevalent generalizing mood of society.

Professor Toynbee (whom Mr. E. H. Carr accuses of wanting to have Spengler metaphysically and eat him empirically) finds it disappointing that the author of *The Decline of the West* has nothing to say about the genesis of his cultures. It seems to him, so he says, a defect 'unworthy of Spengler's brilliant genius'.[7] But if one grants Spengler the power of genius, then it is as meaningless to blame him for his shortcoming as it would be to reproach Picasso for sometimes ignoring the rules of perspective. For what Toynbee finds disappointing is the very core of Spengler's method.

This method can best be illustrated by taking the following facts from Greek antiquity, a necessarily restricted and random collection. The figure of Alexander the Great merged even for his contemporaries with the myth of Dionysus. The Doric column was a prominent feature of a certain period of Greek architecture. Greek thinkers knew the strict chronology and calendar of the Babylonians and Egyptians, and yet their highly sophisticated way of measuring time never became integrated into Greek life. Neither Plato nor Aristotle had observatories. In the last years of Pericles the Athenians passed a decree by which all who propagated astronomical theories were made liable to impeachment. Thucydides states right at the beginning of his history that before his time (about 400 B.C.) no events of importance had occurred in the world.[8]

Let us assume that these facts are all soundly established. Let us further take it for granted that very many more such facts, useful for the purposes of a certain interpretation, can be added to the list. With these data before us, and with our historical imagination bent upon discovering some characteristics of the world of the mind which the ancient Greeks inhabited, a certain picture, however blurred at the beginning, is bound to emerge from the contemplation of the facts themselves. In other words, *the facts are the interpretation*, and facts from Greek antiquity, chosen by Spengler, are Spengler's interpretation of Greek antiquity.

This, however, ought not to be used too rashly as an argument against Spengler, for it applies to all written history that is more than an arbitrary list of data. Differences in quality between historians cannot solely be established by measuring the relative degrees of their selectivity or comprehensiveness, but mainly by appreciating the relative subtlety, accuracy, intelligence and sensitivity of the mind, reflected in the meaningful, and therefore selective, ordering of the facts. And Spengler's assembly of facts from Greek antiquity adds up to, briefly, the following picture. Greek consciousness differed from ours by the absence of any distinct historical or astronomical sense. It revolved around a centre of Pure Present. It interested itself not in the political or psychological biography of Alexander the Great, but in his kinship with a god, his mythological significance. The Greeks rejected instinctively the time-obsession of the Egyptians, and found it appropriate to burn their dead rather than mummify them for all time to come. They even went so far as to defend actively their particular vision of the world against astronomical encroachments, very much in the manner in which the Church once defended the central position of the earth against the Copernican attack. Compare the Doric architecture with, say, the Gothic and you will behold two fundamentally different visions of space; static and earth-bound the one, the other struggling with outstretched arms to grasp some glory above.

Professor Toynbee, when he first read Spengler, was afraid that his own inquiry 'had been disposed of . . . before even the questions, not to speak of the answers, had fully taken shape in my mind'; and it was only when he looked in Spengler's book for an answer to the question of *how* civilizations come into being, that he saw that there was still work for him to do.[9] One is tempted to imagine Darwin, on the point of throwing in his hand at the sight of Michelangelo's Creation of Man, and only regaining his self-assurance on discovering that the painter does not show us exactly how the job was done. For the question which Toynbee asks is indeed the question of empiricism, and the inability or unwillingness to answer it is not a flaw in Spengler's 'brilliant genius', but the secret of his ingenious brilliance. The empiricist would account for the prevalent use of, for instance, the Doric column at a certain time in terms, say, of building techniques, of available building materials, of economic conditions, perhaps even in terms of the psychology of the subconscious. Spengler, however, exposes himself to the ridicule of the empiricist by insisting that the Doric column, in whatever way one may describe the processes and causal connections involved in its manufacture, is the expression of the soul of a cultured community and a symbol of Pure Present. Now, it is no good believing that this can be *shown* to be wrong by saying: 'Nonsense; the Doric

L

column came into use because such and such a tribe at such and such
a time, prompted by certain economic and technical changes,
succeeded in converting into stone their original primitive buildings
made of tree-trunks; airy structures which had proved quite agree-
able and adequate for certain functions in this particular climate'.

This way of reasoning may be very illuminating and even completely satisfying to certain intellectual temperaments; yet it would
be quite useless as a tool for undermining Spengler's position. For
what a thing is, poses a question categorically different from the
question of *how* it came about; and the contention that the Doric
column is a symbolic creation of the Greek soul, is entirely un-
touched by the explanation that it is a petrified tree-trunk. The two
lines of interpretation never meet. Yet modern consciousness is
inclined to take for granted that they do meet and clash, and that
the symbol lies smashed under the weight of the tree-trunk. The
superstition is due to a squint; the same kind of squint which gazes
expectantly at the newest cosmologists for some information about
God, and to the psychologists for the forgiveness of sins. This state
of intellectual affairs may have been brought about by the enormous
birth-rate of modern science, which has overpopulated our minds
with most successful answers to questions of *How*, and left little
breathing-space for questions of *What* even to be asked without a
sense of embarrassment. But not to distinguish between the two is
a vulgar mental habit which has been unduly encouraged throughout a whole period of intellectual education; a period which has
been too exclusively fascinated by the virtues—indisputable in their
proper fields—of the empiricist and scientific discipline.

This, in turn, also accounts for the uncouthness of Spengler's
attempt to break the empiricist spell. But the very violence of his
attack exposes a genuine predicament of the historical imagination.
He wished to provide radical solutions for two cardinal problems
of historiography. The first of these problems concerns a hidden
conflict between facts and meaning, objectivity and pattern. For
the facts of history, as distinct from the facts of natural science, are
men, or groups of men, and the circumstances and events in which
they find themselves involved, or which they bring about. Even if
we limit our interest to the shortest period, the question of selection
arises. Clearly, the historian is not concerned with *all* men, circumstances and events; he has to pick and choose. And what is his
criterion of choice? However warily the answer is formulated, it

will trap the mind in a vicious circle. For it is the historian's view of what is historical that determines his selection. The 'historical' facts are singled out from the inarticulate mass of facts that constitute 'the past'. These selected facts must then be recorded in a coherent manner: in words, and with a view to plausible causal connections. Having been unavoidably biased in his selection of facts, either by the socially predominant or by his personal view of what is 'historical', now, at least, the good historian may hope to be 'objective' or 'purely technical'. But by describing in words men, human actions and human motives, he *implicitly* conveys and evokes emotions and passes moral judgments. If he is wise and subtle, the emotions evoked will be complex, the moral judgments fine and just. Yet they will be there, for they are in the words themselves and in our responses to human behaviour.

The goal of objectivity proves still more unattainable as soon as we are faced with the problem of establishing causal connections. For history is, of course, not concerned with physical pulls and pushes, or chemical reactions, which can be reproduced in the laboratory for experimental purposes. The stuff of history is made of unique situations, singular and complex because they are brought about, not by scientifically ascertainable causes but by human motives. And however many 'facts' the searching scholar may unearth to support his conclusions, these must finally be reached through the full exercise of his imaginative sympathy. Thus, in every single case, the historical picture is established by the historical imagination, not by scientific reason, and proved not by objective experiment, but by the persuasiveness of the historian's vision. This vision, to be persuasive, must have force; and its force lies in the quality of its order or pattern. In this last respect history is like a work of art, and what has happened in recent historiography, has happened time and again in the history of art: a nervous quest for a constant, or a centre, capable of imposing order and pattern on the confusing wealth of sensations and impressions. The crises in art as well as in thought—and therefore also in historiography—occur in periods when the centre of gravity ceases to be 'attractive', is rendered ineffectual by a new vision of reality and the ensuing perception by the human mind of new relevancies among the profusion of facts that surround him at all times. If, moreover, the remand for realistic accuracy in the minutest detail is met by increasingly prolific techniques to supply it, the old centre of gravity will fail completely, overwhelmed by the impossible task of holding together so many unexpected things. Such a time was the seventeenth century, and at its beginning stands John Donne's lamentation:

> And new Philosophy calls all in doubt,
> The Element of fire is quite put out;
> The Sun is lost, and th' earth, and no man's wit
> Can well direct him where to look for it.
>
> 'Tis all in peeces, all cohaerence gone;
> All just supply, and all Relation.

To-day, our historical consciousness teems with Relation and Function. Everything seems to depend on everything else, and we are unable to say precisely for what. Coherence can only be established within tiny fragments, and the general effect is one of oversubtlety, irrelevance and confusion. It is a situation similar to that in painting at the end of the Middle Ages when significance began to be attached to realistic detail and spatial perspective. If one compares the first fumbling attempts to make pictures from the unwieldy mass of accurately reproduced detail in accurately rendered space, with the assured and unrealistic order of medieval altar-paintings, one can scarcely help feeling that the new realism is but a triumph of mediocre pedantry. The whole mastery of the later Renaissance masters was needed in order to merge all the pieces into a new coherence, a new vision of pattern and order.

Oswald Spengler believed that he had found the new centre of gravity for history. Clearly, it cannot be supplied by a purely 'naturalistic' historiography, intent on disentangling the endless and chaotically complicated world of 'Relations', the events as they hang together by virtue of cause and effect. Spengler once said that the only difference between the opposed schools of historians, all labouring under the empiricist spell, lies in the conclusions which they reach after having observed for long enough the movements of a pair of scales. Some, seeing one side go up, find a perfectly satisfactory cause for the event in attributing it to the going-down of the other side. Some again would rather say that one side sinks because the other rises.[10] And had he had a chance of contemplating the opening sentence of the second chapter of Mr. E. H. Carr's *The New Society*, he might have added: 'And some even say it sinks because it sinks'. For Mr. Carr states: 'Experience shows that the structure of society at any given time and place, as well as the prevailing theories and beliefs about it, are largely governed by the way in which the material needs of the society are met'.[11] Experience seems to show very little indeed; for the ways in which the material needs of a society are met, do not 'largely govern', but largely *are* the structure of society. And, naturally, the theories and beliefs about the structure of a society largely depend on a large part of this structure, in the same way in which a theory about a house must be largely governed by what is a large part of the house. On the other hand, the 'structure of society' is, of course, a more elusive object of investigation than the structure of a building; for what *actually is* of structural significance is intimately bound up with the *consciousness and feeling* of this society regarding the question of what is important for the ordering of its collective existence. If, for instance, a society accepts as its foremost concern to make a success of its arrangements in the eyes of God, then its organized religion will form that prominent structural feature which economic affairs claim in our society. This is what Spengler means by his over-statement: 'It is possible to understand the Greeks without mentioning their economic relations; the Romans, on the other hand, can *only* be understood through these'.[12]

An ordered and at the same time objective vision of history, Spengler maintains, can only be achieved by cutting right through the cause-and-effect tangle. For no meaning or order can ever emerge unless we discover how *all* things in history are related, not merely one to the other, but to something else: to a constant, a crystallizing principle. And Spengler's constant is the Soul, or the Destiny, of a cultured society. Now at last all historical facts add up to a definite shape—*morphe*, in Greek—and Spengler's 'morpho-logical' history saves the perplexed historical mind from being led back and back along the dull thread of cause and effect. There is no clash between objectivity and pattern; on the contrary, only within their appropriate pattern can the facts be seen for what they really are: symbols of Destiny. Coin-currency, the nude statue, the city-state are all symbolic expressions of the Greek Soul; and a more modern Destiny and unified Culture-Personality will be seen at work in the discovery of perspective in painting, the invention of the printing-press, long-range weapons, the credit system and contrapuntal music.[13]

It is, I think, a perfectly legitimate problem which Spengler attacks with so much force, learning and imagination, and which he solves in so catastrophic a fashion. The problem was present right at the beginning of modern historical thought. Vico knew it, and, of course, Herder. Hegel tried to solve it in one way, Karl Marx in another. If, as a Marxist scholar said, Spengler has corrupted the 'concept of history', then Hegel or Karl Marx are his fellow-corrupters. For the purely empiricist concept of history is hopelessly spoilt as soon as the question of meaning or pattern is raised. It matters little whether the 'corrupting' is done in the name of the *Weltgeist*, or supplied by the goal of a classless society, dialectically driving history on towards its final scoring, or by Destiny presenting a cycle of dramas about a common theme, or by a court of divine justice passing judgment on a lot of original sinners. But, of course, the concept cannot really be corrupted. It is itself a corruption, the distorted shadow of the idea of a 'pure' natural science.

Spengler must be rejected on different grounds: not because his history is incorrect, but because it is untrue. And between the two reasons lies a world of difference. Spengler's history is untrue because the mind which has conceived it is, despite its learning and seeming subtlety, a crude and wicked mind. The image of man which lurks behind Spengler's vast historical canvas is perverted, and could only be accepted by a hopelessly perverted age. For Spengler has no idea of the true stature of the problem of human freedom. Therefore his historical vision is lacking in depth as well as in love, pity and pathos. It is a worthless and deeply untruthful sort of history which lacks these qualities, for they are the proper tools of human understanding.

If Spengler's men were real men, his Culture-Souls real souls, and his Destiny really destiny; if, in other words, Spengler had realized the full pathos of human freedom under the shadow of necessity, his historical plot would move us with the force of tragedy. As it is, there is no terror and no pity in his acceptance of Destiny, but merely a conscious decision for the false values; and this is the classical definition of sin and wickedness. Destiny, he says, has decreed that our spiritual values should be frustrated in this period of history; therefore let us join the enemies of the spirit. Thus Spengler is not a historian, but a false prophet. For whether a prophet is true or false does not depend on the correctness of his predictions. It depends on the purity and sincerity of his concern for the things threatened by human sin and divine anger. Indeed, his predictions are the more likely to be correct, the less he is a true prophet and the more affinities he has within himself to the destructive tendencies of his age, that is, to the very stuff that will determine the evil future. And Spengler appears merely concerned with lending Destiny a hand in the business of destruction.

Yet this deliberate choice of the wrong is again intimately linked with another very real perplexity of the historical imagination: the relativity of all values. History shows that men of different societies lived by different values; and all these different values, embodied in various religious beliefs, moral and legal codes, works of art, were effective in their own way and satisfactory within the limits of the general unsatisfactoriness of human affairs. From history itself no absolute values will ever emerge. For our historical consciousness differs profoundly from that of the Old Testament, or that of Thucydides. Our history is a variety-show of gods of every description, and as historians we could not care less if at least one of them is outraged by all the others; and Thucydides' opening statement that before his time nothing really important ever happened, is the denial of our sense of historical proportion.

If there is any valid philosophy of history, it is scepticism; and an age which is as historically minded as ours, is necessarily a sceptical age. But nothing is more difficult than to be a consistent sceptic, and nothing easier than to slip on the sceptical road and, in a crisis of balance, embrace the nearest absolute lamp-post. With the possible exception of Montaigne, there is no sceptical thinker who could not be caught out in some such embarrassing embrace. During the nineteenth century the broadest emergency exit from the embarrassment of historical relativity led into history itself as the progressive unfolding of the Absolute. Hegel flung it wide open, and Karl Marx guided a whole mass movement through the gate.

Spengler, however, radically renounced the idea of progress. He assumed the part of the long-awaited hero who freed the historical imagination from the last shackles of the Absolute, and boasted of his courage to face the Medusa of limitless historical relativism, calling himself the Copernicus of historiography. History, he says, does not revolve around our system of values or virtues. The real meaning of all religions, all thoughts, all works of art can only be experienced within the particular culture that has produced them. Nothing is universal. History does not write anything with capital letters. We must cease to speak of the forms of Thought, the principles of Tragedy, the truth of Religion, the function of the State.[14] Whenever we are tempted to believe in the universal validity of anything, we are merely lending our ears to the whispers of ghosts which may still haunt for a while this age of absolute historical scepticism.

What, then, according to Spengler, are the values left to us? Even if we feel they are there, must not this tempestuous insight rob them of their power to guide our actions? Luckily, says Spengler, we do not need them any longer. The new insight takes their place: the insight into our historical Destiny written with the only surviving capital letter. Questions about ultimate values must not be asked in the presence of the *Zeitgeist*. Ours is the business of 'civilization'. Let us build aeroplanes, no matter what they carry; roads, no matter where they lead; weapons, no matter what 'values' they defend or attack. For absolute scepticism is our intellectual fate, and absolute engineering our historical Destiny.

Again, as with Hegel and Marx, history itself arises as an Absolute from the vast bankruptcy of traditional values. This fact was still hidden behind clouds of idealism—of a metaphysical brand in the case of Hegel, of a messianic-social kind in the case of Marx. With Spengler, however, the mists have lifted: the spiritual bankruptcy itself is our history, our Absolute, our guiding principle. If Spengler is, after all, not quite out of date, this is because he has reduced to a wicked kind of absurdity a tendency of the mind which is certainly not unfashionable yet: the habit of applying to historical necessity for the marching orders of the spirit.

The late Munich comedian, Karl Vallentin—one of the greatest of the rare race of metaphysical clowns—once enacted the following scene: the curtain goes up and reveals darkness; and in this darkness is a solitary circle of light thrown by a street-lamp. Vallentin, with his long-drawn and deeply worried face, walks round and round this circle of light, desperately looking for something. 'What have you lost?' a policeman asks who has entered the scene. 'The key to my house.' Upon which the policeman joins him in his search; they find nothing; and after a while he inquires: 'Are you sure you lost it here?' 'No,' says Vallentin, and pointing to a dark corner of the stage: 'Over there'. 'Then why on earth are you looking for it here?' 'There is no light over there,' says Vallentin.

History, maybe, is the circle of light. But the key we are looking for is likely to be in a place unilluminated by the street-lamps.

THE WORLD OF FRANZ KAFKA

THE WORLD OF FRANZ KAFKA

Sometimes I feel I understand the Fall of Man better than anyone.—Franz Kafka.

I

THE relationship of Kafka's heroes to that truth for which they so desperately search can best be seen in the image through which Plato, in a famous passage of his *Republic*, expresses man's pitiable ignorance about the true nature of the *Ideas*. Chained to the ground of his cave, with his back towards the light, all he perceives of the fundamental reality of the world is a play of shadows thrown on to the wall of his prison. But for Kafka there is a further complication: perfectly aware of his wretched imprisonment and obsessed with a monomaniac desire to know, the prisoner has, by his unruly behaviour and his incessant entreaties, provoked the government of his prison to an act of malicious generosity. In order to satisfy his passion for knowledge they have covered the walls with mirrors which, owing to the curved surface of the cave, distort what they reflect. Now the prisoner sees lucid pictures, definite shapes, clearly recognizable faces, an inexhaustible wealth of detail. His gaze is fixed no longer on empty shades, but on a full reflection of ideal reality. Face to face with the images of Truth, he is yet doubly agonized by their hopeless distortion. With an unparalleled fury of pedantry he observes the curve of every line, the ever-changing countenance of every figure, drawing schemes of every possible aberration from reality which his mirror may cause, making now this angle and now that the basis of his endless calculations which, he passionately hopes, will finally yield the geometry of truth.

In a letter (December 16th, 1911) Kafka says: 'I am separated from all things by a hollow space, and I do not even reach to its boundaries'. In another (November 19th, 1913): 'Everything appears to me constructed . . . I am chasing after constructions. I enter a room, and I find them in a corner, a white tangle.' And as late as 1921: 'Everything is illusion: family, office, friends, the street, the woman, all illusion, drawing nearer and further away; but the nearest truth is merely that I push my head against the wall of a cell without doors or windows.'[1] And in one of his aphorisms

157

he says: 'Our art is dazzled blindness before the truth: the light on
the grotesquely distorted face is true, but nothing else.'[2]

Kafka's novels take place in infinity. Yet their atmosphere is as
oppressive as that of those unaired rooms in which so many of their
scenes are enacted. For infinity is incompletely defined as the ideal
point where two parallels meet. There is yet another place where
they come together: the distorting mirror. Thus they carry into the
prison-house of their violently distorted union the agony of infinite
separation.

It is a Tantalus situation, and in Kafka's work the ancient curse
has come to life once more. Kafka says of himself: 'He is thirsty,
and is cut off from a spring by a mere clump of bushes. But he is
divided against himself: one part overlooks the whole, sees that he
is standing here and that the spring is just beside him, but another
part notices nothing, has at most a divination that the first part sees
all. But as he notices nothing he cannot drink.'[3] Indeed, it was a
curse, and not a word of light which called the universe of Kafka's
novels into existence. The very clay from which it was made bore
the imprint of a malediction before the creator had touched it. He
builds to a splendid design, but the curse runs like a vein through
every stone. In one of his most revealing parables Kafka shows
himself completely aware of this: 'Everything seemed to fit the
design of his edifice magnificently. Foreign workmen brought the
marble, quarried for the purpose, each block fashioned for its proper
place. The stones lifted themselves up and moved along in obedience
to his measuring fingers. No edifice ever grew so smoothly as this
temple, or rather this temple grew truly in the way in which temples
ought to grow. Only that there were cut into every stone, obviously
with wonderfully sharpened instruments, clumsy scribblings from
the hands of senseless children, or perhaps inscriptions of barbaric
mountain-dwellers; mischievous texts, blasphemous, or totally
destructive, fixed there for an eternity which was to survive the
temple.'[4]

It is the reality of the curse that constitutes the ruthlessly compelling logic of Kafka's writings. They defy all attempts at rational
interpretation, for Kafka is the least problematic of modern writers.
He never thinks in disputable or refutable generalities. His thinking
is a reflex movement of his being and shares the irrefutability of all
that is. He thinks at an infinite number of removes from the Car-
tesian *Cogito ergo sum*. Indeed, it sometimes seems that an unknown

'It' does all the thinking that matters, the radius of its thought touching the circumference of his existence here and there, causing him infinite pain, bringing his life into question and promising salvation on one condition only: that he should expand his being to bring it within the orbit of that strange Intelligence. The formula has become: 'It thinks, and therefore I am not', with only the agony of despair providing overpowering proof that he is alive. He says of himself that he *is* the problem, and 'no scholar to be found far and wide'.[5]

There is, outside this agony, no reality about which he could entertain or communicate thoughts, nothing apart from the curse of his own separation from that Intelligence. Yet it is a complete world that is to be found within that pain, the exact pattern of creation once more, but this time made of the stuff of which curses are made. Like sorrow in the tenth of Rilke's *Duino Elegies*, despair is given a home of its own in Kafka's works, faithfully made in the image of customary life, but animated by the blast of the curse. This gives to Kafka's writings their unique quality. Never before has absolute darkness been represented with so much clarity, and the very madness of desperation with so much composure and sobriety. In his work an intolerable spiritual pride is expressed with the legitimate and convincing gesture of humility, disintegration finds its own level of integrity, and impenetrable complexity an all but *sancta simplicitas*. Kafka establishes the moral law of a boundlessly deceitful world, and performs in a totally incalculable domain, ruled by evil demons, the most precise mathematical measurements.

Small wonder at the pathetic plight of critics in the face of Kafka's novels. It was with incredulous amazement that I noticed extracts from reviews which appear as advertisements of the English translation of Kafka's *The Castle*: 'One reads it as if one were reading a fairy tale . . .', 'What a lovely, moving, memorable book !', 'A book of curious and original beauty'. All this, attributed by the publishers to critics of some repute, is, of course, perverse. A nightmare is not a lovely fairy-tale, and a torture-chamber of the spirit not full of original beauty. More serious, however, are the misinterpretations of Kafka by those who have undoubtedly made an honest effort to understand him. In the introduction to his own (and Willa Muir's) translation of *The Castle* Edwin Muir describes the subject-matter of this novel (very much in keeping with Max Brod's interpretation)

as 'human life wherever it is touched by the powers which all
religions have acknowledged, by divine law and divine grace', and
suggests that it should, with some reservations, be regarded 'as a sort
of modern *Pilgrim's Progress*', the reservation being that 'the "progress" of the pilgrim here will remain in question all the time'.
Acccording to him '*The Castle* is, like the *Pilgrim's Progress*, a
religious allegory'.[6]

From a great number of similar attempts to elucidate the darkness
of Kafka's world I am choosing these sentences as a starting-point
for a discussion of the work of this writer, and of *The Castle* in
particular, because they express most succinctly what seems to me
a disquieting misconception of its nature, the more disquieting
because it is harboured by men of letters who are seriously concerned
with literature and have, like Max Brod, Kafka's lifelong friend and
editor of his writings, and Edwin Muir, his English translator,
grasped the religious relevance of their author. Thus their misapprehension would seem to reflect a very profound religious confusion, so profound indeed that one can scarcely hold the individual
critic responsible for it. It is the very spiritual uprootedness of the
age which has deprived us of all sureness of religious discrimination.
To men, suffering from spiritual starvation, even a rotten fruit of the
spirit may taste like bread from Heaven, and the liquid from a
poisoned well like the water of life. If the critic is, moreover, steeped
in psychology and comparative religion (as we all unwittingly are)
the difference may appear negligible to him between Prometheus
clamped to the rock, and the martyrdom of a Christian saint;
between an ancient curse, and the grace that makes a new man.

The Castle is as much a religious allegory as a photographic
likeness of the devil could be said to be an allegory of Evil. Every
allegory has an opening into the rarified air of abstractions, and is
furnished with signposts pointing to an ideal construction beyond.
The Castle, however, is a terminus of soul and mind, a *non plus ultra*
of existence. In an allegory the author plays a kind of guessing
game with his reader, if he does not actually provide the dictionary
himself; but there is no key to *The Castle*. It is true that its reality
does not precisely correspond to what is commonly understood in
our positivist age as real, namely, neutral sense-perception of objects
and, neatly separated from them, feelings; hence our most authentic
and 'realistic' intellectual pursuits: natural sciences and psychology;
and our besetting sins: the ruthlessness of acquisitive techniques and

sentimentality. In Kafka's novels there is no such division between the external sphere and the domain of inwardness, and therefore no such reality.

Kafka's creations are at the opposite pole to the writings of that type of Romantic poet, the true poetical representative of the utilitarian age, who distils from a spiritually more and more sterile external reality those elements which are still of some use to the emotions, or else withdraws from its barren fields into the greenhouse vegetation of inwardness. The author of *The Castle* does not select for evocative purposes, nor does he project his inner experience into a carefully chosen timeless setting. He does not, after the manner of Joyce, give away, in the melodious flow of intermittent articulation, the secret bedroom conversations which self conducts with self. There are no private symbols in his work, such as would be found in symbolist writing, no crystallized fragments of inner sensations charged with mysterious significance; nor is there, after the fashion of the Expressionists, any rehearsing of new gestures of the soul, meant to be more in harmony with the 'new rhythm' of modern society. Instead of all this, the reader is faced with the shocking spectacle of a miraculously sensitive soul incapable of being either reasonable, or cynical, or resigned, or rebellious, about the prospect of eternal damnation. The world which this soul perceives is unmistakably like the reader's own; a castle that is a castle and 'symbolizes' merely what all castles symbolize: power and authority; a telephone exchange that produces more muddles than connections; a bureaucracy drowning in a deluge of forms and files; an obscure hierarchy of officialdom making it impossible ever to find the man authorized to deal with a particular case; officials who work overtime and yet get nowhere; numberless interviews which never are to the point; inns where the peasants meet, and barmaids who serve the officials. In fact, it is an excruciatingly familiar world, but reproduced by a creative intelligence which is endowed with the knowledge that it is a world damned for ever. Shakespeare once made one of his characters say: 'They say miracles are past, and we have our philosophical persons, to make modern and familiar things supernatural and causeless. Hence it is that we make trifles of terrors, ensconcing ourselves in seeming knowledge when we should submit ourselves to an unknown fear.' In Kafka we have the abdication of the philosophical persons.

In his work the terror recaptures the trifles, and the unknown fear invades all seeming knowledge—particularly that of psychology. Any criticism of the current religious interpretation of Kafka (which, at least, meets the religious aspect of his work on its own plane) is, I think, well advised to avoid the impression that it sides surreptitiously with other equally well-established dogmas about this writer. One of them, the psychological, is laid down by critics fascinated by Kafka's indubitably strained relationship with his father. But to interpret Kafka's novels in the perspective of the Oedipus complex is about as helpful to our understanding of his work as the statement that Kafka would have been a different person (and perhaps not a writer at all) if he had had another father; a penetrating thought, of which even psychologically less initiated ages might have been capable if they had deemed it worth thinking. This kind of psychology can contribute as much to the explanation of a work of art as ornithological anatomy to the fathoming of a nightingale's song. But so deeply engrained is positivism in the critics of this age that even when they are genuinely moved by the symbolic reality which the author has created, they will soon regain the balance of mind required for the translation of the symbol into what it 'really' means; and by that they mean precisely that meaningless experience which the artist has succeeded in transcending through his poetic creation. If, for instance, to the author the *meaning* of his senselessly tormenting feud with his father has been revealed through the discovery (which, in creating his work, he has made) that what he is *really* called upon to find is his place within a true spiritual order of divine authority, the interpreter will insist that what the author 'really' means by talking about God, is that the quarrels with his father should stop.

In Kafka we have before us the modern mind, seemingly self-sufficient, intelligent, sceptical, ironical, splendidly trained for the great game of pretending that the world it comprehends in sterilized sobriety is the only and ultimate reality there is —yet a mind living in sin with the soul of Abraham. Thus he knows two things at once, and both with equal assurance: that there *is* no God, and that there *must* be God. It is the perspective of the curse: the intellect dreaming its dream of absolute freedom, and the soul knowing of its terrible bondage. The conviction of damnation is all that is left of faith, standing out like a rock in a landscape the softer soil of which has been eroded by the critical intellect. Kafka once said: 'I ought to welcome eternity, but to find it makes me sad'.[7]

This is merely an exhausted echo of the fanfares of despair with which Nietzsche (in many respects a legitimate spiritual ancestor of Kafka) welcomed his vision of eternity. In one of the posthumously published notes on *Zarathustra* he says about his idea of the Eternal Recurrence: 'We have produced the hardest possible thought—now let us create the creature who will accept it lightheartedly and blissfully!'[8] He conceived the Eternal Recurrence as a kind of spiritualized Darwinian test to select for survival the spiritually fittest. This he formulated with the utmost precision: 'I perform the great experiment: who can bear the idea of Eternal Recurrence?'[9] And an ever deeper insight into the anatomy of despair we gain from his posthumous aphorisms and epigrams which were assembled by his editors in the two volumes of *The Will to Power*, many of which refer to the idea of Eternal Recurrence: 'Let us consider this idea in its most terrifying form: existence, as it is, without meaning or goal, but inescapably recurrent, without a finale into nothingness . . .'.[10] Nietzsche's Superman is the creature strong enough to live for ever a cursed existence, even to derive from it the Dionysian raptures of tragic acceptance. Nietzsche feels certain that only the Superman could be equal to the horror of a senseless eternity, and perform the great metamorphosis of turning 'this most terrifying knowledge' into the terror of superhuman delight. And Kafka? On most of the few occasions when, in his diary, he speaks of happiness he registers it as the result of a successful transformation of torture into bliss. This is one of his most horrible entries (November 21st, 1911): 'This morning, after a long time, I again took pleasure in imagining that a knife is turned in my heart'. And in 1921, in the account of a dream: 'There was bliss in my welcoming, with so deep a sense of freedom, conviction and joy, the punishment when it came'.[11] If Nietzsche's Superman is the aesthetic counterbalance to the weight of the curse, then Kafka is its chosen victim. What some of his critics interpret as signs of religious achievement in his later writings, is merely the all-engulfing weariness of a Nietzschean Prometheus, which Kafka expressed in the fourth of his Prometheus legends: 'Everyone grew weary of the meaningless affair. The gods grew weary, the eagles grew weary, the wound closed wearily.'[12]

Thus Kafka's work, as much as Nietzsche's, must remain a stumbling-block to the analysing interpreter to whom, in the enlightened atmosphere of modern Europe, the word 'curse' comes only as a faint memory of Greek tragedy, or as a figurative term for

M

a combination of ill-luck and psychological maladjustment. Yet the grey world of Kafka's novels is luminous with its fire. Perhaps one cannot expect from modern man that, when he sees light, he should be able to distinguish between burning sulphur and the radiance of Heaven. And although Mr. Muir is right in saying that Kafka's novels are about life in the grip of a power 'which all religions have acknowledged', this power is certainly not 'divine law and divine grace', but rather one which, having rebelled against the first and fallen from the second, has, in its own domain, successfully contrived the suspension of both. Undoubtedly, the land surveyor K., hero of *The Castle*, is religiously fascinated by its inscrutably horrid bureaucracy; but again it is a word from Nietzsche, and not from the Gospels, that sums up the situation: 'Wretched man, your god lies in the dust, broken to fragments, and serpents dwell around him. And now you love even the serpents for his sake.'

2

The Castle is not an allegorical, but a symbolic novel. A discussion of the difference could easily deteriorate into pedantry, the more so as, in common and literary usage, the terms are applied rather arbitrarily and have established themselves as meaning more or less the same thing. It will, however, help our understanding of Kafka's work if we distinguish, in using these two terms, two different modes of experience and expression. I shall therefore define my own—probably not less arbitrary—use of the terms.

The symbol *is* what it represents; the allegory represents what, in itself, it is *not*. The terms of reference of an allegory are abstractions; a symbol refers to something specific and concrete. The statue of a blindfolded woman, holding a pair of scales, is an *allegory* of Justice; bread and wine are, for the Christian communicant, *symbols* of the Body and Blood of Christ.* Thus an allegory must always be rationally translatable; whether a symbol is translatable or not depends on the fundamental agreement of society on the question of what kind of experience (out of the endless range of possible human experience) it regards as significant. The possibility of allegorizing will only vanish with the last man capable of *thinking in abstractions*, and of forming *images* of them; yet the validity of

---

* At this point I would like to beg the indulgence of the reader for disregarding the established theological terminology. The following discussion will, I hope, to some extent justify my apparent arbitrariness, which I do not wish to maintain outside the scope of this particular argument.

symbols depends not on rational operations, but on complex experiences in which thought and feeling merge in the act of spiritual comprehension. The sacramental symbols, for instance, would become incommunicable among a race of men who no longer regard the life, death, and resurrection of Christ as spiritually relevant *facts*. An allegory, being the imaginary representation of something abstract, is, as it were, doubly unreal; whereas the symbol, in being what it represents, possesses a double reality.

Goethe, summing up in one line at the end of *Faust II* the mature experience of his life, attributes whatever permanent reality there may be in a transient world, to its symbolic significance. What is, is only *real* in so far as it is symbolic. Earlier in his life he defined the 'true symbol' as 'the representation of the general through the particular, not, however, as a dream or shadow, but as the revelation of the unfathomable in a moment filled with life.'

The predicament of the symbol in our age is caused by a split between 'reality' and what it signifies. There is no more any commonly accepted symbolic or transcendent order of things. What the modern mind perceives as order is established through the tidy relationship between things themselves. In one word: the only conceivable order is positivist-scientific. If there still is a—no doubt, diminishing—demand for the fuller reality of the symbol, then it must be provided for by the unsolicited gifts of art. But in the sphere of art the symbolic substance, dismissed from its disciplined commitments to 'reality', dissolves into incoherence, ready to attach itself to any fragment of experience, invading it with irresistible power, so that a pair of boots, or a chair in the painter's attic, or a single tree on a slope which the poet passes, or an obscure inscription in a Venetian church, may suddenly become the precariously unstable centre of an otherwise unfocused universe. Since 'the great words from the time when what *really* happened was still visible, are no longer for us' (as Rilke once put it in a Requiem for a young poet), the 'little words' have to carry an excessive freight of symbolic significance. No wonder that they are slow in delivering it. They are all but incommunicable private symbols, established beyond any doubt as symbols by the quality and intensity of artistic experience behind them, but lacking in any representative properties. Such is the economy of human consciousness that the positivist impoverishment of the one region produces anarchy in the other. In the end, atomic lawlessness is bound to prevail in both.

The intellectual foundation of every human society is a generally accepted model of reality. One of the major intellectual difficulties of human existence is, I think, due to the fact that this model of reality is in every single case a mere *interpretation* of the world, and yet exerts, as long as it seems the valid interpretation, the subtly compelling claim to being accepted as the only true picture of the universe, indeed as truth itself. This difficulty, manifesting itself in the deeper strata of doubt, by which, at all times, certain intellectually sensitive men have been affected, develops easily into a mental epidemic in epochs in which a certain model of reality crumbles and collapses. It seems that we have lived in such an epoch for a long time.

One of its main characteristics was the uncertainty, steadily increasing in the minds and feelings of men, about the relation between mundane and transcendental reality; or, in other words, about the meaning of life and death, the destiny of the soul, the nature and sanction of moral laws, the relative domains of knowledge and faith. As far as Christianity was the representative religion of the Middle Ages, their model of reality was essentially sacramental. A definite correspondence prevailed between the mundane and transcendental spheres. Faith was not established in any distinct 'religious experience', nor, as a particular 'mode of comprehension', kept apart from 'knowledge'. It was an element in *all* experience, indeed its crystallizing principle. Only within a mould and pattern determined by faith did experiences make sense and impressions turn to knowledge. This correspondence between the two spheres was so close that at every important stage of a man's life they met and became one in the sacraments.

The sacramental model of reality, intermittently disputed and questioned throughout the whole development of Christian theological thought, was upset in an historically decisive fashion at the time of the Reformation. During that period an intellectual tension, inherent in Christian dogma, developed into a conflagration of vast historical consequences. It produced an articulate climax—which was, however, a mere symptom of a more inarticulate, yet more comprehensive process—at a particularly exposed point of dogmatic faction: the sacramental dispute between Luther and Zwingli. Luther, despite his divergent interpretation of the traditional dogma, represents in it the essentially medieval view, whereas Zwingli, disciple of the humanist Pico della Mirandola, is the spokesman of modernity. To Luther the sacrament of the Last Supper *is* Christ (the bread and the wine *are* what they represent), while Zwingli reduces it to the status of an allegory (as merely representing what, in itself, it is not). From then onwards the word 'merely' has been attaching itself ever more firmly to the word 'symbol', soon gaining sufficient strength to bring about a complete alienation between the two spheres. Finally a new order of things emerged. Within it the transcendental realm is allotted the highest honours of the spirit, but, at the same time, skilfully deprived of a considerable measure of reality; the mundane, on the other hand, is recompensed for its lowering in spiritual stature by the chance of absorbing all available reality and becoming more 'really' real than before.

The sudden efflorescence of physical science in the seventeenth century is the positive result of this severance. Its successes have further contributed to the 'lower realm' setting itself up as the only 'really' real one, and as the sole provider of relevant truth, order and lawfulness. Scientific and other positivist pursuits owe the unchallenged dominion which they have wielded ever since over the intellectual life of Europe, to the ever more exclusive fascination which the new model of reality has had for the European mind.

As an unavoidable corollary of this state of affairs, religion and art lost their unquestioned birthright in the homeland of human reality, and turned into strange messengers from the higher un-reality, admitted now and then as edifying or entertaining songsters at the positivist banquet. What had once been a matter-of-fact expression of life, became a 'problem', worthy of a great deal of intellectual fuss and a negligible assignment of reality. As far as the arts are concerned, it is most revealing that the only *distinctive* artistic achievement of Europe since the end of the seventeenth century was accomplished by the art with the least claim to 'reality': music; while the most 'real' of all arts, architecture, degenerated more and more until it gained new vitality as the unashamed functional servant of technology.

In Germany, a country which, for historical reasons too complex ever to be unravelled, suddenly rose in the eighteenth century to the heights of European consciousness and to the fulfilment of the most extravagant intellectual aspirations (without any gradual transition from the Middle Ages), the plight of the poet within the new model of reality is most conspicuous. The artist as an exile from reality—this is one of the most authentic themes of German literature, from

Goethe's *Tasso* and Grillparzer's *Sappho* to Thomas Mann's *Tonio Kröger*. Kleist, Hölderlin, Nietzsche are the greatest among the victims of a hopeless collision between the minority demand for a realization of the spirit and a spiritualization of reality on the one hand, and, on the other, the inexorable resistance of a safely established spirit-proof view of life. Hölderlin is the greatest poet among those involuntary desperadoes of the spirit. His work is one continuous attempt to recapture the lost reality of the symbol and the sacramental experience of life. And for Goethe, to preserve his life, exposed at every point to the revengeful blows of the banished spirit, was, from beginning to end, a terrible struggle, entailing the most precarious manoeuvres of compromise, irony and resignation. It was only—ironically enough—in his scientific activities that he gave vent to his unrestrained fury against the analytical-positivist view of the world and its scientific exposition through mathematics and Newtonian physics. How gloriously he blundered into physical science, determined to meet the enemy on his own ground, and how stubbornly convinced he was of being right! He once said to Eckermann (February 19th, 1829): 'Whatever I have achieved as a poet is nothing to be particularly proud of. Excellent poets are my contemporaries, still better poets lived before me, and others will come after me. But in my own century I am the only man who knows what is right in the difficult science of colours; and this is something that gives me real satisfaction and a feeling of superiority over many.' His own idea of science was, as we have seen, based on the *Urphänomen*, a striking assertion of the symbol as the final and irreducible truth of reality.

Goethe lost the battle for the symbol. In the century that stretches between his death and Kafka's writing, reality has been all but completely sealed off against any transcendental intrusion. But in Kafka's work the symbolic substance, forced back in every attempt to attack from above, invades reality from down below, carrying with it the stuff from hell. Or it need not even invade: Kafka writes at the point where the world, having become too heavy with spiritual emptiness, begins to sink into the unsuspected demon-ridden depths of unbelief. In this cataclysm, the more disastrous because it overtakes a world which has not even believed in its own unbelief, Kafka's heroes struggle in vain for spiritual survival. Thus his creations are symbolic, for they are infused with (and not merely allegorical of) negative transcendence.

Kafka knew the symbolic relevance of his work; he knew, too, of the complete alienation of modern man from the reality of the symbol. One of his profoundest meditations runs as follows:

Many complain that the words of the wise are always merely symbols and of no use in daily life, which is the only life we have. When the wise man says: 'Go over', he does not mean that we should cross to some actual place, which we could do anyhow if it were worth the effort; he means some miraculous beyond, something unknown to us, something that he too cannot define more precisely, and therefore cannot help us here in the least. All these symbols merely express that the incomprehensible is incomprehensible, and we have known that before. But the cares we have to struggle with every day: that is a different matter.

Concerning this a man once said: Why such reluctance? If you only followed the symbols you would become symbols yourselves, and thus rid of all your daily cares.

Another said: I bet this is also a symbol.

The first said: You have won.

The second said: But unfortunately only symbolically.

The first said: No, in reality; symbolically you have lost.[13]

3

There are, however, allegorical elements to be found in *The Castle*: for instance, the names of many of the characters. The hero himself, who is introduced to us with the bare initial K. (undoubtedly an autobiographical hint,* and at the same time, through its very incompleteness, suggesting an unrealized, almost anonymous personality) is a land-surveyor. Kafka's choice of this profession for his hero has clearly a meaning. The German for it is *Landvermesser*, and its verbal associations are significant. The first is, of course, the land-surveyor's professional activity, consisting precisely in what K. desperately desires and never achieves: to produce a workable order within clearly defined boundaries and limits of earthly life, and to find an acceptable compromise between conflicting claims of possession. But *Vermesser* also alludes to *Vermessenheit*, hubris; to the adjective *vermessen*, audacious; to the verb *sich vermessen*, commit an act of spiritual pride, *and* also, apply the wrong measure, make a

* The first draft of the novel was written in the first person.

mistake in measurement. The most powerful official of the castle (for K., the highest representative of authority) is called *Klamm*, a sound producing a sense of anxiety amounting almost to claustrophobia, suggesting straits, pincers, chains, clamps, but also a person's oppressive silence. The messenger of the castle (as it turns out later, self-appointed and officially never recognized) has the name of *Barnabas*, the same as that man of Cyprus who, though not one of the Twelve, came to rank as an apostle; 'Son of Consolation', or 'Son of Exhortation', is the biblical meaning of his name, and it is said of him that his exhortation was of the inspiring kind, and so built up faith. And the Barnabas of the novel is indeed a son of consolation, if only in the desperately ironical sense that his family, whom the curse of the castle has cast into the lowest depths of misery and wretchedness, in vain expects deliverance through his voluntary service for the authority. To K., however, his messages, in all their obscurity and pointlessness, seem the only real link with the castle, an elusive glimmer of hope, a will-o'-the-wisp of faith. Barnabas's counterpart is *Momus*, the village secretary of Klamm, and namesake of that depressing creature, the son of Night, whom the Greek gods had authorized to find fault with all things. In the novel it is he whose very existence seems the denial of any hope which Barnabas may have roused in K. *Frieda* (peace) is the girl through whose love K. seeks to reach the goal of his striving; *Bürgel* (diminutive of *Bürge*, guarantor), the name of the little official who offers the solution, without K. even noticing the chance; and the secretary through whom K. does expect to achieve something and achieves nothing, is called *Erlanger* (citizen of the town of Erlangen, but also suggestive of *erlangen*, attain, achieve).

This discussion of names provides an almost complete synopsis of the slender plot of *The Castle*. Someone, a man whose name begins with K., and of whom we know no more, neither whence he comes nor what his past life has been, arrives in a village which is ruled by a castle. He believes that he has been appointed land-surveyor by the authorities. The few indirect contacts that K. succeeds in establishing with the castle—a letter he receives, a telephone conversation he overhears, yet another letter, and above all the fact that he is joined by two assistants whom the rulers have assigned to him—*seem* to confirm his appointment. Yet he himself is never fully convinced, and never relaxes in his efforts to make quite sure of it. He feels he must penetrate to the very centre of authority and wring from it a kind of ultra-final evidence for his claim. Until then he yields, in paralysed despair, broken by only momentary outbursts of rebellious pride, to the inarticulate, yet absolutely self-assured refusal of the village to acknowledge him as their land-surveyor: 'You've been taken on as land-surveyor, as you say, but, unfortunately, we have no need of a land-surveyor. There wouldn't be the least use for one here. The frontiers of our little estates are marked out and all neatly registered.... So what would be the good of a land-surveyor?'[14] says the village representative to him.

K.'s belief appears, from the very outset, to be based both on truth and illusion. It is Kafka's all but unbelievable achievement to force, indeed to frighten, the reader into unquestioning acceptance of this paradox, presented with ruthless realism and irresistible logic. Truth and illusion are mingled in K.'s central belief in such a way that he is deprived of all order of reality. Truth is permanently on the point of taking off its mask and revealing itself as illusion, illusion in constant danger of being verified as truth. It is the predicament of a man who, endowed with an insatiable appetite for transcendental certainty, finds himself in a world robbed of all spiritual possessions. Thus he is caught in a vicious circle. He cannot accept the world—the village—without first attaining to absolute certainty, and he cannot be certain without first accepting the world. Yet every contact with the world makes a mockery of his search, and the continuance of his search turns the world into a mere encumbrance. After studying the first letter from the castle, K. contemplates his dilemma, 'whether he preferred to become a village worker with a distinctive but merely apparent connection with the castle, or an ostensible village worker whose real occupation was determined through the medium of Barnabas'.[15] From the angle of the village all K.'s contacts with the castle are figments of his imagination: 'You haven't once up till now come into real contact with our authorities. All those contacts are merely illusory, but owing to your ignorance of the circumstances you take them to be real.'[16] The castle, on the other hand, seems to take no notice whatever of the reality of K.'s miserable village existence. In the midst of his suffering the indignity of being employed as a kind of footman to the schoolmaster, he receives the following letter from Klamm: 'The surveying work which you have carried out thus far has my recognition.... Do not slacken in your efforts!

Bring your work to a successful conclusion. Any interruption
would displease me. . . . I shall not forget you.'[12] From all this
it would appear that it is, in fact, the village that disobeys the
will of the castle, while defeating K. with the powerful suggestion that he misunderstands the intentions of authority. And yet
the authority seems to give its blessing to the defiance of the village,
and to punish K. for his determination to act in accordance with
the letter of its orders. In his fanatical obedience it is really he who
rebels against the castle, whereas the village, in its matter-of-fact
refusal, lives the life of the law.

Kafka represents the absolute reversal of German idealism. If it
is Hegel's final belief that in the Absolute truth and existence are
one, for Kafka it is precisely through the Absolute that they are for
ever divided. Truth and existence are mutually exclusive. From
his early days onwards it was the keenest wish of Kafka the artist
to convey this in works of art; to write in such a way that life, in all
its deceptively convincing reality, would be seen as a dream and a
nothing before the Absolute: 'Somewhat as if one were to hammer
together a table with painful and methodical technical efficiency, and
simultaneously do nothing at all, and not in such a way that people
could say: "Hammering a table together is really nothing to him",
but rather "Hammering a table together is really hammering a table
together to him, but at the same time it is nothing", whereby certainly the hammering would have become still bolder, still surer,
still more real and, if you will, still more senseless'.[18] This is how
Kafka describes the vision of artistic accomplishment which hovered
before his mind's eye when, as a young man, he sat one day on the
slopes of the Laurenziberg in Prague. Has he, in his later works,
achieved this artistic justification of nonentity? Not quite; what was
meant to become the lifting of a curse through art, became the
artistically perfect realization of it, and what he dreamed of making
into something as light as a dream, fell from his hands with the
heaviness of a nightmare. Instead of a vindication of nothingness,
he achieved the portrayal of the most cunningly vindictive unreality.
He had good reason for decreeing that his writings should be burned.

It is hard to see how *The Castle* can possibly be called a religious
allegory with a pilgrim of the type of Bunyan's as its hero. Pilgrimage? On the contrary, the most oppressive quality of Kafka's work
is the unshakable stability of its central situation. It takes place in
a world that knows of no motion, no change, no metamorphosis.

Its caterpillars never turn into butterflies, and when the leaves of a tree tremble it is not due to the wind. It is the stirring of a serpent coiled round its branches. There is, in fact, no pilgrimage to be watched in *The Castle*, and the progress not merely 'remains in question all the time', but is not even possible, unless we agree to call progress what Kafka once described in his fable of the mouse: ' "Alas," said the mouse, "the world is growing smaller every day. At the beginning it was so big that I was afraid, I kept running and running, and I was glad when at last I saw walls far away to the right and left, but these long walls have narrowed so quickly that I am in the last chamber already, and there in the corner stands the trap that I must run into." "You only need to change your direction," said the cat, and ate it up.'[19] Of the two points on which Kafka and Bunyan, according to Edwin Muir's introduction, are agreed: 'that the goal and the road indubitably exist, and that the necessity to find them is urgent', only the second is correct, and, indeed, to find them is so urgent for Kafka that life is impossible unless they are found. But do they exist? 'There is a goal, but no way; what we call way is only wavering,'[20] is what Kafka says about it. And *is* there really a goal for him? This is Kafka's self-reply: 'He feels imprisoned on this earth, he feels constricted; the melancholy, the impotence, the sickness, the feverish fancies of the captive afflict him; no comfort can comfort him, since it is merely comfort, gentle, head-splitting comfort glozing the brutal fact of imprisonment. But if he is asked what he actually wants he cannot reply, for—that is one of his strongest proofs—he has no conception of freedom.'[21]

Kafka's hero is the man who *believes* in absolute freedom, but cannot have any conception of it because he *exists* in a world of slavery. Therefore it is not grace and salvation that he seeks, but either his right or—a bargain with the powers. 'I don't want any act of favour from the castle, but my rights,'[22] says K. in his interview with the village representative. But convinced of the futility of this expectation, his real hope is based on Frieda, his fiancée and former mistress of Klamm, whom he is obviously prepared to hand back to him 'for a price'.

In K.'s relationship to Frieda the European story of romantic love has found its epilogue. It is the solid residue left behind by the evaporated perfume of romance, revealing its darkest secret. In romantic love, as it has dominated a vast section of European literature ever since the later Middle Ages, individualism, emerging from the ruins of a communal order of the spirit, has found its most powerful means of transcendence. The spiritually more and more autonomous, and therefore more and more lonely individual worships Eros (and his twin deity within the romantic imagination: Death) as the only god capable of breaking down the barriers of his individualist isolation. Therefore love becomes tragedy: overcharged with unmanageable spiritual demands it must needs surge ahead of any human relationship. In its purest manifestations, romantic love is a glorious disaster of the soul, carrying frustration in its wake. For what the romantic lover seeks is not really the beloved. Intermixed with his erotic craving, inarticulate, diffuse, and yet dominating it, is the desire for spiritual salvation. Even a 'happy ending' spells profound disillusionment for the romantic expectation. Perhaps it is Strindberg who wrote the last chapter of its history. It is certainly Kafka who wrote its postscript.

For K. loves Frieda—if he loves her at all—entirely for Klamm's sake. This is not only implied in the whole story of K. and Frieda, but explicitly stated by Kafka in several—afterwards deleted— passages of the book. It is contained in the protocol about K.'s life in the village which Momus has drawn up, and in which K. is accused of having made up to Frieda merely because he believed that in her he would win a mistress of Klamm 'and so possess a hostage which could only be redeemed at the highest price'.[23] On the margin of the protocol there was also 'a childishly scrawled drawing of a man holding a girl in his arms; the girl's face was hidden in the man's breast, but he, being much taller, was looking over her shoulders at a paper in his hand on which he was gleefully entering some figures'.[24] But perhaps still more conclusive than Momus's clearly hostile interpretation is another deleted passage giving K.'s own reflections on his love for Frieda: '. . . And soon afterwards—and there was not even time to think—Frieda had entered his life, and with her the belief (a belief which he was quite unable to abandon completely even now) that through her there was established an almost physical connection with Klamm, intimate to the point of whispered communications; perhaps, for the time being, it was only K. who knew of it, but it needed a mere touch, a word, a raising of eyes, to reveal itself first to Klamm, but then to everybody, as something unbelievable but yet self-evident by virtue of the irrefutability of life itself, the irrefutability of the embrace of love.... What was he without Frieda? A nonentity, staggering after glittering will-o'-the-wisps....'*[25]

The desperate desire for spiritual certainty is all that is left of romantic love. K. *wills* his love for Frieda because he *wills* his salvation. He is a kind of Pelagius believing that he 'can if he ought', yet living in a relentlessly predestined world. This situation produces a theology very much after the model of Gnostic and Manichaean beliefs. The incarnation is implicitly denied in an unmitigated loathing of 'determined' matter, and the powers which rule are perpetually suspected of an alliance with the devil because they have consented to the creation of such a loathsome world. Heaven is at least at seven removes from the earth, and only begins where no more neighbourly relations are possible. There are no real points of contact between divinity and the earth, which is not even touched by divine emanation. Reality is the sovereign domain of strangely unangelic angels, made up of evil and hostility. The tedious task of the soul is, with much wisdom of initiation and often with cunning diplomacy, gradually to by-pass the armies of angels and the strong-points of evil, and finally to slip into the remote kingdom of light.

The castle of Kafka's novel is, as it were, the heavily fortified garrison of a company of Gnostic demons, successfully holding an advanced position against the manoeuvres of an impatient soul. I do not know of any conceivable idea of divinity which could justify those interpreters who see in the castle the residence of 'divine law and divine grace'. Its officers are totally indifferent to good if they are not positively wicked. Neither in their decrees nor in their activities is there discernible any trace of love, mercy, charity or majesty. In their icy detachment they inspire certainly no awe, but fear and revulsion. Their servants are a plague to the village, 'a wild, unmanageable lot, ruled by their insatiable instincts ... their shamelessness knows no limits',[26] an anticipation rather of the blackguards who were to become the footmen of European dictators than the office-boys of a divine ministry. Compared to the petty and apparently calculated torture of this tyranny, the gods of Shakespeare's indignation who 'kill us for their sport' are at least majestic in their wantonness.

* These, and the passages from the Pepi and Bürgel episodes which will be quoted later, have not yet appeared in English. Max Brod published them from Kafka's manuscripts only with the second and third editions of *Das Schloss*, volume IV of *Gesammelte Schriften*. All references to volume IV are to the third edition, New York, 1946.

From the very beginning there is an air of indecency, indeed of obscenity, about the inscrutable rule of the castle. A newcomer in the village, K. meets the teacher in the company of children. He asks him whether he knows the Count and is surprised at the negative answer: ' "What, you don't know the Count?" "Why should I?' replied the teacher in a low tone, and added aloud in French: "Please remember that there are innocent children present". '27 And, indeed, what an abhorrent rule it is! The souls of women seem to be allowed to enter the next realm if they surrender, as a sort of pass, their bodies to the officials. They are then married off to some nincompoop in the village, with their drab existence rewarded only by occasional flashes of voluptuously blissful memories of their sacrificial sins. Damnation is their lot if they refuse, as happened in the case of Amalia, Barnabas's sister, who brought degradation upon herself and her family by declining the invitation of the official Sortini.

The unfathomable depths of nonsense into which an interpretation can be lured by its own mistaken assumptions is revealed in Max Brod's critical dealings with that crucial point in the story of Barnabas's family. In his epilogue to *The Castle* Max Brod writes: 'The connection between the castle—that is divine guidance—and the women . . . may appear mysterious and even inexplicable in the Sortini episode, where the official (Heaven) requires the girl to do something obviously immoral and sordid; here a reference to Kierkegaard's *Fear and Trembling* may be of value. . . . The Sortini episode is literally a parallel to Kierkegaard's book, which starts from the fact that God required of Abraham what was really a crime, the sacrifice of his child; and which uses this paradox to establish triumphantly the conclusion that the categories of morality and religion are by no means identical.'28 This is, for the believer, downright blasphemy, and a critical insult to the intelligence of a reader able to read for himself the Bible, Kierkegaard and Kafka. The comparison between Kierkegaard and Kafka would indeed be relevant. It might bring home, even to a modern reader, the difference between Purgatory and Hell. For this is the precise relationship between Kierkegaard's *Fear and Trembling* and Kafka's *Castle*. The sacrifice of Isaac a parallel to Sortini's designs on Amalia? But this means, without any polemical exaggeration, to ascribe to the God of Abraham a personal interest in the boy Isaac, worthy rather of a Greek demi-god. Moreover, He, having tested Abraham's absolute obedience, did not accept the sacrifice. Yet Sortini (who conveys to Max Brod the idea of divine guidance and Heaven itself) can, to judge by the example of his colleagues, be relied upon not to have summoned Amalia to his bedroom merely to tell her that one does not do such a thing.

To return from the comic escapades of literary criticism to Franz Kafka's novel: the castle represents neither divine guidance nor Heaven. It is for K. something that is to be conquered, something that bars his way into a purer realm. K.'s antagonism to the castle becomes clear from the very first pages of the book. This is how he responds to the first telephone conversation about his appointment which, in his presence, is conducted between the village and the authorities: 'K. pricked up his ears. So the castle had recognized him as the land-surveyor. That was unpropitious for him, on the one hand, for it meant that the castle was well informed about him, had estimated all the probable chances and was taking up the challenge with a smile. On the other hand, however, it was quite propitious, for if his interpretation were right they had under-estimated his strength, and he would have more freedom of action than he had dared to hope.'[29]

The correspondence between the spiritual structure of *The Castle* and the view of the world systematized into Gnostic and Mani-chaean dogma is indeed striking. There is, however, no reason to assume that Kafka had any special knowledge of those ancient heresies. In their radical dualism they are merely the model systems of a deep-rooted spiritual disposition, asserting itself over and over again in individuals and whole movements. Gnostic and Mani-chaean is, above all, 'the face that is filled with loathing and hate' at the sight of physical reality. Kafka refrains from any dealings with nature. There is, apart from the mention of a starry sky, wind and snow, not one description of nature in *The Castle*. Within the human sphere everything that is of the flesh is treated with a sense of nausea and disgust. All the habitations of men are lightless, airless and dirty. The nuptial embrace between K. and Frieda takes place amidst puddles of beer on the floor of a public bar, the room still filled with the stale smells of an evening's business, while mass prostitution is carried on in the stable of the inn.

But Kafka has also found subtler means of conveying his revolt against the 'real'. One evening K. is waiting in the dark courtyard of the inn for Klamm to emerge from his village room and enter his

sledge. The coachman, noticing K., encourages him to wait inside
the sledge and have a drink from one of the bottles kept in the
side-pockets. K. opens the bottle and smells: 'Involuntarily he
smiled, the perfume was so sweet, so caressing, like praise and good
words from someone whom one loves very dearly, yet one does not
quite know what they are about and has no desire to know, and is
simply happy in the knowledge that it is he who is saying them.
Can this be brandy? K. asked himself doubtfully and tasted out of
curiosity. Yes, surprisingly enough, it was brandy, and it burned
and warmed. How strangely it transformed itself, as he drank, from
something which was hardly more than a medium of sweet perfume,
into a vulgar drink, fit for a coachman!'[30] Whether intentional or
not, this profanation of the perfume of a spirit in the process of being
'realized', is a wonderfully subtle symbol of a Manichaean perspective of the world. And the most telling formula of this Manichaean
disposition Kafka once found after finishing one of his stories: 'I can
still derive some temporary satisfaction from a work of this kind . . .
but happiness only if I ever succeed in lifting the world into a sphere
pure, true, unchangeable' (diary note of September 25th, 1917).[31]

Is his castle of that sphere? It is, no doubt, the highest realm K.
is capable of perceiving. This is what misled the critics, but not
Kafka himself, into equating it with God. But it is certainly not
quite irrelevant that in his personal confessions Kafka never, not
once, utters the belief that the incessant striving of his spirit was
directed towards God, or prompted by *amor Dei*. All the time his
soul is preoccupied with the power of Evil; a power so great that
God had to retreat before it into purest transcendence, for ever out
of reach of life. Life itself is the incarnation of Evil: 'Knowledge of
the diabolical there can be, but not belief in it, for there is nothing
more diabolical than what exists'.[32] And then again the reality of
life, still identified with Evil, is denied completely: 'There is only a
spiritual world; what we call the physical world is the evil in the
spiritual one . . .'.[33] Thus the idea of final authority, merely by
assuming the shape of physical reality in *The Castle*, falls, without
the author either willing it or being able to help it, under the spell
of Evil. It is the paradox of spiritual absolutism that the slightest
touch of concreteness will poison the purest substance of the spirit,
and one ray of darkness blot out a world of light.

Yet Kafka is neither a dogmatic follower of the Gnosis nor a
Manichee; he is an artist, and although the cursed rule of the castle

is the furthest point of the world to which his wakeful mind can reach, there dawns, at its extreme boundaries, a light, half suspectingly perceived, half stubbornly ignored, that comes from things outside the scope of Klamm's authority. K. knows only one thing: that he must come to grips with Klamm; yet at the same time he knows that his very obsession with this thought precludes him from reaching what he mistakenly believes only Klamm can give. He senses dimly that humility and humour would bring him the possession of which he deprives himself by his very striving for it. In Pepi who, for a short time, was promoted to the rank of barmaid in the local inn (and thus to the opportunity of serving beer to Klamm), now trembling at the prospect of losing her position again, K. meets the caricatured embodiment of his own ambition. In giving advice to her he shows a remarkable knowledge of his own disease: 'It is a job like any other, but for you it is the kingdom of Heaven. Therefore you set about your business with exaggerated zeal . . . you tremble for your position, feel constantly persecuted, try by overdoing your friendliness, to win over those who you believe could help you; but you merely annoy and repel them; for what they look for in a bar is peace, and not, on top of their own cares, the anxiety of a barmaid.'[34] And later: 'If I compare myself to you, I suspect that both of us have tried, in too noisy, too childish, too inexperienced a fashion, to get something which is to be had easily and simply through Frieda's matter-of-factness. We are crying and scratching and tossing about, like little children who tug at the tablecloth, but gain nothing, only cause all the nice things to tumble down, making them unobtainable for ever.'[35]

But it is in K.'s adventure with the castle official Bürgel that this insight finds its most striking parable. K., summoned in the middle of the night to an interview with the official Erlanger, has, in his weariness and exhaustion, forgotten the number of the right door, and enters (more in the hope of finding an empty bed there than an official of the castle) another room. There he encounters, lying in bed, the official Bürgel. The ensuing dialogue, or monologue rather, is one of Kafka's greatest feats in the art of melting the solid flesh of a grotesque reality and revealing behind it the anatomic structure of the miraculous. Bürgel promises K. to settle once and for all his affairs in the castle. K. is not in the least impressed by this offer. He waves it aside as the boast of a dilettante: 'Without knowing anything of the circumstances in which K.'s appointment had

N

been made, and nothing of the difficulties which it met in the village and in the castle, and of the complications which had either already arisen or were in the air; without knowing anything of all this, indeed without even showing—and might one not take that for granted with a secretary?—that he had at least a faint notion of it, he offered, by sleight of hand, and with the help of a little pad of notepaper, to settle the matter up there.'[36] It is the unbelief of a labyrinthine mind in the very existence of simplicity. And while K. grows ever more weary, Bürgel delivers, in a rapturous crescendo, the message of the miracle: if a man takes a secretary of the castle by surprise; if, in the middle of the night, the applicant, almost unconscious of what he does, slips, like a tiny grain through a perfect sieve, through the network of difficulties that is spread over all approaches to the centre of authority, then the castle, in the person of this one secretary, must yield to the intruder, indeed must almost force the granting of the request upon the unsuspecting subject: 'You believe it cannot happen? You are right, it cannot happen at all. But one night—who can vouch for everything?—it does happen after all.' It is an event so rare that it seems to occur merely by virtue of rumour, and even if it does occur, one can, 'as it were, render it innocuous by proving to it—and this proof is easy enough —that there is no room for it in this world'.[37] And Bürgel goes on with his rhapsody, describing the shattering delight with which a secretary responds to this situation. But when he ends, K. is sound asleep, and, with the conditions of the miracle fulfilled before his eyes, as oblivious of its possibility as he had been in his tortured wakeful pursuit of it.

Indeed, no comfort can be found *within* this world. Yet the power, not only to experience, but poetically to create this world, must have its source *outside*. Only a mind keeping alive in at least one of its recesses the memory of a place where the soul is truly at home, is able to contemplate with such creative vigour the struggles of a soul lost in a hostile land; and only an immensity of goodness can be so helplessly overcome by the vision of the worst of all possible worlds. This is the reason why we are not merely terrified by the despair of this book, but also moved by its sadness, the melancholy of spiritual failure carrying with it a subtle promise.

In one of his most Manichaean sayings Kafka speaks of the power of a single crow to destroy the heavens; but, he adds, this 'proves nothing against the heavens, for the heavens signify simply: the impossibility of crows'.³⁸ And although these birds swarm cease-lessly around *The Castle*, its builder built it from the impulse to render them impossible. Is it, one wonders, yet another phantom hope in a deluded world that prompts, in the book, a child, a simple girl and a wretched family to turn with a mysteriously messianic expectation to the land-surveyor K.? And makes, on a deleted page of the unfinished manuscript, a mother invite the homeless stranger to her house with the words: 'This man should not be allowed to perish'?³⁹ Or is it perhaps the reflection of a faith, maintained even in the grip of damnation, which Nietzsche once expressed: 'Whoso-ever has built a new heaven has found the strength for it only in his own hell'.*

* Long after this essay was written, I found the following passage in an as yet unpublished letter of Kafka's: 'No people sing with such pure voices as those who live in deepest hell; what we take for the song of angels is their song'.

VIII

KARL KRAUS: THE LAST DAYS OF MANKIND

KARL KRAUS: THE LAST DAYS OF MANKIND

I

ONE of the most important contributions to German literature during the last fifty years has remained almost unnoticed abroad: the work of the Austrian satirist and poet Karl Kraus, who was born in Bohemia in 1874, lived and wrote in Vienna and died there in 1936. To discuss the reasons for his obscurity is one way of speaking of his unique achievement.

His work is untranslatable. This seems the more surprising because most of it is written in prose: aphorisms, essays, satirical dramas. The majority of these appeared first in his journal *Die Fackel*, which he founded in 1899 in Vienna and to which he was, after a few years, the sole contributor. From time to time he collected his writings according to different themes and published them as books. His essays appeared in seven volumes with the titles: *Sittlichkeit und Kriminalität* (Morality and Court Justice) in 1908, *Die Chinesische Mauer* (The Wall of China) in 1910, *Weltgericht* (Day of Judgment) in 1919, *Untergang der Welt durch schwarze Magie* (The Destruction of the World by Black Magic) in 1922, *Literatur und Lüge* (Literature and Untruth) in 1929 and, posthumously published in 1937, *Die Sprache* (Language). Of his dramas the greatest is *Die letzten Tage der Menschheit* (The Last Days of Mankind), written during the Great War and published in 1919. His other dramatic works are: *Literatur* (1921), *Traumtheater* (Dream Theatre) (1922), *Traumstück* (Dreamplay) (1922), *Wolkenkuckucksheim* (Cloudcuckooland) (1923), and *Die Unüberwindlichen* (The Unconquerable) (1927). The rest of his work consists of verse, aphorisms, translations and adaptations. There are nine volumes of *Worte in Versen* (Words in Verse), published between 1916 and 1930, and one volume of *Epigrams* (1927). His aphorisms appeared in three volumes: *Sprüche und Widersprüche* (Dicta and Contradictions) (1909), *Pro Domo et Mundo* (1912), and *Nachts* (1919). He translated Shakespeare's *Sonnets* (1933), and adapted for his own stage and broadcast performances a number of Shakespeare's dramas, the most significant adaptation being that of *Timon of Athens*. In later years he gave more and more time to what may seem a strange anti-climax to his literary preoccupations, and yet was the necessary

counterpoise to his weightier themes: he recast the libretti of many
of the less-known operettas by Offenbach, which, accompanied
only on a piano, he performed, sitting behind a little table, with
incomparable artistry, musicality, wit and profound charm. A
volume of *Zeitstrophen*, topical stanzas added by him to Offenbach's songs, appeared as the offspring of this work in 1931. For
the purpose of his own performances he also adapted a number of
satirical comedies by Nestroy.

Bibliographies are a dull business.* Yet in the case of Karl Kraus
the very titles of his books suggest his range: *Day of Judgment*—and
Offenbach, The Last Days of Mankind—and *Language*. The historical
occasion of his apocalyptic themes is the fall of the Austrian Empire,
or rather the gradual corruption of its moral, intellectual and artistic
life. He foretold the end of Austria-Hungary. Yet this fact would
not in itself suffice to call him a prophet. He was a prophet in a
truer sense. Inspired by an ethical and religious conviction, he was
the servant not of any dogma, but of a living spiritual power. No
word is primitive and unspoiled enough to describe the almost
frightening directness, spontaneity and naïvety with which he himself experienced his calling. There seems to be no place for him in
a period of German literature which, on its highest level, was
characterized by the quest for a new lyrical idiom to express unheard-of novelties, subtleties and complexities of inner experience,
as in the case of Rilke; or by the gentle cultivation of the autumn
flowers of an over-ripe civilization, as with Hofmannsthal; or by
the self-conscious development of a new prophetic style, as with
Stefan George; or by the blending of pessimism, music, psychology
and irony, as with Thomas Mann; not to mention the many who,
in their more or less refined and respectable mediocrity, made
names for themselves more often than not by virtue of the provincial
inferiority and the increasing barbarism of the surrounding literary
world and the general incompetence and irresponsibility of its
critics.

In such a period of literature Karl Kraus arrived like an elemental
spiritual force in a beauty-parlour of the soul. Yet the word 'elemental' is misleading; for the elements, too, were a fashion in his

* This bibliography is offered in the place of detailed references. They would be rather
pointless. Outside one or two libraries and perhaps some second-hand bookstalls, the works
of Karl Kraus are at present unavailable. With a few exceptions, they are likely to remain
out of print until the City of Vienna fulfils its uniquely enlightened promise to republish
his complete works.

time, the *dernier cri* of nervous sophistication. Naturalists and expressionists alike appeared as advocates of the demons of the depth, and as rebels against the anaemic refinements of aestheticism. But with a few exceptions (among them Hauptmann, Wedekind and Barlach as the most remarkable) theirs was merely a rebellion of resentment and bad manners. Inarticulateness became the apogee of 'self-expression', intellectual asthma, uttering embryonic sentences, counted as a sure sign of intellectual passion, and crippled souls freed themselves of their inhibitions by noisily throwing about their crutches. In the case of Karl Kraus 'elemental' means something different. Through him and in him the spontaneous strength of a tradition and culture comes to life once more, and, finding itself in an environment of betrayal and decay, gains a highly differentiated consciousness of itself, without for a moment suffering the embarrassments of self-consciousness.

This rare fusion of spontaneity and subtlety, of ethical integrity and intellectual complexity, he shares—in different fields of creative activity—with Kierkegaard and, in modern German literature, only with Franz Kafka. In modern English literature something similar is to be found in the work of T. S. Eliot, with the *tertium comparationis* not, of course, residing in any external aspects of their writings, not in form and content, but in the spiritual and ethical situations from which their works spring.

Both Kierkegaard and Kafka have become known to the world through adequate translations. What is it then that makes the work of Karl Kraus untranslatable? It is due equally to its substance and its literary technique. Karl Kraus did not write 'in a language', but through him the beauty, profundity and accumulated moral experience of the German language assumed personal shape and became the crucial witness in the case this inspired prosecutor brought against his time. Thus he does not convey through the written word something which, if needs be, could be conveyed in another medium; he merely confronts with the true spirit of language the representative idiom of his society. And at the mere approach of his words the language-scene of the age is uncannily illuminated, revealing souls and minds corrupted by untruth and self-deception.

In 922 numbers of *Die Fackel* there is not one polemical essay which does not begin and end with an opposition of this kind. His campaigns are not aimed at hostile opinions or ideologies. In every single case his field of action is the ever-widening no-man's-land between appearance and reality, expression and substance, word-gesture and personality. The tirades of rhetoricians, the pamphlets of politicians, the feuilletons of renowned authors are passed through the filter of language, leaving behind mere dregs of folly and residues of false pretence.

In his satirical work the dead word is resurrected and comes back as a spirit of destruction. Men, having tried to live by insincere phrases, now die of their own clichés. The triumph of medical science is undone by the products of the printing-press, and the effect of the ink used by a generation of irresponsible journalists is shown to be as deadly as that of the Black Death.

For Karl Kraus the word has personal life. Language, passion and thought are one and the same for him. Language is the name of the activity of his passionate thinking; his passion and his thought are identical with their articulation. This is as much as to say that the objects of his thinking and writing are not concepts, but ideas; and not ideas which he 'holds', but ideas by which he is held. Poetry and passionate speech, said Goethe, are the sources of life of every language. In this sense every word which Karl Kraus wrote is alive with the life of language, every sentence the result not of construction, but of creation and growth. This was difficult to grasp for an age which betrayed on every level of intellectual activity a preference for constructed abstractions. A noble conspiracy of hard precision seemed at work everywhere to save us from the embarrassments of emotional vagueness and sentimental inexactitude. But inter-mingled with this brave renunciation of soul that struggled to express itself in this manner, was the terror of an age that had lost its soul and made an artistic and intellectual virtue of a terrible emergency. Karl Kraus did not simply accept the loss. He diagnosed sin where others submitted to fate. He attempted atonement where others resigned themselves to the curse. It is this that makes him a prophet. Others may tell their dreams, their nightmares (as Joyce, Kafka, Picasso do). He was wide awake and was seized by the word. It is a biblical happening in a modern setting: 'The prophet that hath a dream, let him tell a dream; and he that hath my word, let him speak my word faithfully. . . . For ye have perverted the words of the living God. . . .' The word for Karl Kraus was an event, as concrete as the word that 'the Lord sent . . . unto Jacob, and it hath lighted upon Israel'.

The work of Karl Kraus is rich in words. And every single word is of the greatest possible precision. It is precise through its infinite ambiguity. He intended it to be like that, in conscious protest against the rationalist superstition that a word could ever create— or convey—a clear-cut concept, and fix, as it were, a definite object in the void of the universe. For Karl Kraus all thoughts are in the world even before they are thought. They are dispersed among the elements of language. The artist gathers them together and welds them into his thought. He once said: 'Language is the divining-rod which discovers wells of thought'. Thus language, for him, is a means not so much of communicating what he knows, but of finding out what he does not yet know. Words are living organisms, not labels stuck to objects. They are at home in a cosmos of the spirit, not in a chance assembly of 'atoms of perception'. Each of them has a range of its own, and once struck, opens up numberless trains of thought. The greater the number of associations into which the word enters, the greater its value in a piece of writing. This again must come as a surprise to intellectuals whose sharpest weapon in dispute is the question: What do you mean by that? It is a double-edged weapon: useful in combating vagueness, it yet may defeat language itself if it will not rest until the linguistic emptiness of mathematical precision is reached. Applied excessively it destroys all the indefinable and imponderable agreements upon which any cultured community is based; and, indeed, much of modern philosophizing is merely the intellectual symptom of the loss of spiritual community.

Karl Kraus's answer to the stock question would be: 'I mean what I say; yet what I say means the opposite of what you understand it to mean. Therefore I mean what I say *and* its opposite. Nevertheless, I mean something more exact than your sense of exactitude is likely to grasp. For the world of the word is round, and language is Delphi.'

Textbooks would call Karl Kraus a master of language; but he is its master by being its slave. He has no 'command of words'; he is at their command, avenging their honour upon all who violate them. Thus this implacable enemy of all phrase-ridden traditionalism and nationalism is more deeply steeped in a national tradition than any other German writer of his time.

2

When in 1899 he founded *Die Fackel* his themes seemed trifling to a reading public which, through its press, had become accustomed to the daily excitements of world politics. Karl Kraus dealt with little themes: with the insolence of office, the corruption of language. He unmasked the sham morality of a society which punished as an offence the prostitution of women, but bestowed high honours on men who habitually prostituted their minds and talents to the interests of power and finance. As a literary critic he defended the autonomous rights of poetry against the erudite insensitivity and philological sterility which had monopolized literary judgment in the Universities, as well as against the conceited garrulousness and verbose pretence of the book-reviewers of the journals. As a critic of the theatre he fought against the increasing domination of the stage by 'realistic' actors and producers who sapped great drama of all its poetry and passion by performing it with the bored accents of the drawing-room, covering up the emptiness of the spirit with the thrills and glamours of elaborate stage effects. 'In the past,' Karl Kraus would say, 'we had actors who were real, and *décor* which was of cardboard; now the *décor* is real and the actor of cardboard.'

Soon he began to 'perform' himself. First he read his own writings in public. Then he included in his programmes the early works of Gerhard Hauptmann, and some of the satirical comedies of Raimund and Nestroy. He also read poetry: Claudius, Goethe, Liliencron. Finally he founded his Theatre of Poetry. The theatre of the time abounded with technical innovations, with an inexhaustible variety of styles of production and acting; painters, tailors, electricians, engineers ruled the stage, collectively conspiring to squeeze into insignificance the human individual and the word of the poet. Amidst these ornamental ruins of the stage Karl Kraus's Theatre of Poetry consisted of a platform, a few curtains and a table, and in it was heard the voice of one man. There was nothing of the claptrap virtuosity one usually associates with such one-man shows. The man who, night after night, alone at his writing-desk, was besieged by the spectres of the spiritual decomposition of his age, which he exorcised through his satirical work, lent his voice to the creations of dramatic and poetic genius. He read *Iphigenie auf Tauris* and *Pandora* by Goethe and, again and again, Shakespeare's tragedies and comedies.

What his spellbound audiences witnessed was not an impersonation of different characters. He neither moved about the stage, nor changed his voice in the manner of the ventriloquist. Yet the scene was alive with a multitude of voices, and full of genuine dramatic tension. It was as though the gulf had been bridged between the dramatic imagination of the poet and the inevitable inadequacies of the 'real life' of his figures on a real stage. Karl Kraus took his listeners to the very centre of poetic creation. The characters which he enacted were not meant to produce the illusion of reality; they had the reality of the poet's illusions. It was easy enough for the audience to distinguish between the many *dramatis personae*; yet they were all creatures of *one* impulse and *one* passion, and were not wearied by the long journey through the emptiness of space that stretches, in our society, from the subtle order of artistic creation to the crudity and disorder of public reception. His theatre bestowed upon dramatic poetry the privilege which any competently performed piece of music enjoys: the directness of communication, the freedom from interference by the unwieldiness of matter. The infinite variety of word-experience had found its authentic interpreter in Karl Kraus, on the highest level of poetic beauty as well as in the witches' cauldron of inferiority which took shape in his satirical work.

Even in the first years of *Die Fackel* when, to a superficial observer, it may have seemed that a brilliant polemical talent had launched out against what was merely a typically Austrian form of corruption, more perceptive minds already recognized that behind every dwarf that Karl Kraus attacked there loomed the shadow of a giant. Indeed, it was an Austrian *débâcle* of the spirit, the single incidents of which fill his first diatribes. Yet there was no need for him to change his satirical method when the domestic scene of discontent broadened into a European disaster. Into his language he had gathered the storm at a time when his age was still busy sowing wind. But even after the storm had broken over the whole world, his work still remained untranslatably Austrian in its idiom, untranslatably German in its diction.

Three elements from heterogeneous sources came together to form the character of this son of a wealthy Jewish family from Bohemia, and to make him one of the greatest literary personalities of his time: the ethical radicalism of an Old Testament prophet, the conservatism and the anti-plebeian idiosyncrasies of an Austrian

aristocrat of pre-1848, and that mystical relationship to language
which characterized some of the German Romantics and enabled
them to achieve one of the greatest feats in the history of translation—the rendering in German of Shakespeare's dramas. Of
these three ingredients it is the second which is the most puzzling
in a man who was regarded as a destructive revolutionary by the
majority of his conservative, liberal and social-democratic fellow-
citizens. And, indeed, his conservatism was different from what an
age that knew only of 'political' decisions meant by 'conservative'.
For him it was not an ideology. He hated all ideologies. He saw
them as what they were and are: the intellectual pretence of a
spiritually impoverished age, the inflated paper currency of the
bankruptcy of culture.

After 1848 ideologies spread in Austria like an infectious disease.
They emerged from the stagnant waters of discontent which the
unfinished revolution had left behind. Unrealized political desires
rationalized themselves into bogus systems of political thought, and
emotional frustration developed into mental hysteria. Go-getting
journalists stirred Austrian *Urgemütlichkeit* into paroxysms of dis-
comfort, and the lower strata of Alpine feeblemindedness worked
their way to the surface and became politically conscious. Hun-
garian pig-breeders and Viennese stockbrokers struggled for an
intellectual articulation of their demands for greater profits. From
the ethnical hotch-potch of the Sudeten Germans sprang the
doctrine of racial purity, and racially pure but cosmopolitan Jews
became ardent propagandists of the Teutonic mythology of Richard
Wagner. In a pandemonium of *Gemütlichkeit* and confused political
aspirations, where commercial travellers hobnobbed with *Geist*,
priests with corrupt journalists, bankers with saviours of the people
and advertising agents with artists, the last remnants of Austrian
culture dissolved. And this culture had proved particularly corruptible. Its very generosity and blissful lack of formulated moral
convictions, its baroque taste for untidiness, its sense of drama and
dramatic upheaval, and its childlike trust in its own everlastingness,
made it the more susceptible to the poison of industrialization and
commercialization. A people in whom faith had always had
preponderance over the intellect, enthusiastically embraced political
ideologies which offered a substitute for the evaporating convictions
of religion.

In Karl Kraus's satirical work this dissolute scene is confronted with the integrity of a tradition and culture which in him had preserved itself and retained an amazing vigour. The question may be asked: What precisely was this tradition, and in what accurate historical sense was Karl Kraus justified in denouncing its betrayal by the age in which he lived. This type of question seems to have become the touchstone of 'historical precision' and academic sophistication. But the question itself tolls the bell for something which, if ever it was alive in him, has died in the questioner. In the face of Karl Kraus's work it is as pathetically irrelevant as the question, What is truth? once was in the face of its embodiment.

One cannot arrive at a concept of culture or of tradition by adding up certain facts or achievements. One cannot define them by singling out certain values. Nor can one deny their existence by pointing out certain shortcomings of periods claimed as periods of culture, or by drawing attention to the ever-present risk and uncertainty, disunity and foolishness, wickedness and confusion of human nature. Culture and tradition are precisely what is alive in the work of Karl Kraus and dead in the society which he attacked. It is the accumulated religious, ethical and aesthetic experience of a community which, in spite of all its complexity, diversity and subtlety, expresses itself spontaneously and unmistakably in the conduct, judgments, beliefs and creations of its members. An age without any sense of religious, ethical and aesthetic order has no culture. This does not mean that an age of culture has no experience of disorder. On the contrary, it is only through the sense of order that disorder can be experienced. Ulysses in Shakespeare's *Troilus and Cressida* is the man of culture. He has that conservative sense of degree and order capable of perceiving chaos:

> Take but degree away, untune that string,
> And, hark, what discord follows! each thing meets
> In mere oppugnancy: the bounded waters
> Should lift their bosom higher than the shores
> And make a sop of all this solid globe:
> Strength should be lord of imbecility,
> And the rude son should strike his father dead:
> Force should be right; or rather, right and wrong,
> Between whose endless jar justice resides,
> Should lose their names, and so should justice too.

> Then everything includes itself in power,
> Power into will, will into appetite;
> And appetite, an universal wolf,
> So doubly seconded with will and power,
> Must make perforce an universal prey,
> And last eat up himself.

Any student of history may prove that Ulysses's sense of degree is merely a subjective illusion. He may demonstrate that, at all times, strength is the lord of imbecility, and that all sons, if only sufficiently rude, strike their fathers dead in one way or another. Yet by proving his case he would only show that in him right and wrong have lost their names and that, in some ages, imbecility of imagination can become the judge of strength of vision. There is hope in an age and for an age only so long as there exist in it some individuals who within themselves have retained that order of degree, and denounce its general loss. It was Kierkegaard who said (and Karl Kraus who quoted) that 'the individual cannot help his age; he can only express that it is doomed'. And this is the only way in which he can bring help to it. This paradox links the work of Karl Kraus with the prophecies of the Old Testament, makes *The Last Days of Mankind* the last Austrian document of European culture, and its author one of the last genuine conservative spirits in it.

3

The Last Days of Mankind is not a drama in any accepted sense of the word. Its book edition has eight hundred pages, and its list of characters thirteen. It has no hero, no unity of space, time or action. In time it stretches from 1914 to 1919. It takes place on the battle-fields of Europe, in stock exchanges and hospitals, in the offices of journals, the lecture-rooms of Universities, the headquarters of armies, and again and again in the streets of Vienna. The author says in the preface that the drama which, if performed on earth, would last for ten evenings, is meant to be enacted in a theatre on Mars. 'Audiences here would not be able to bear it. For it is blood of their blood, and its contents are those unreal, unthinkable years, out of reach for the wakefulness of mind, inaccessible to any memory and preserved only in nightmares—those years when characters from an operetta played the tragedy of mankind.' That is the all-pervading theme of this incommensurable satirical work: the discrepancy between the stature of the protagonists and the weight and significance of the play which they have succeeded in getting up.

In 1914 it seemed a typically and exclusively Austrian theme. Only in Vienna could it first have forced itself upon a satirical mind. With overpowering *vis comica* Karl Kraus's satires bring out the incongruity between the kindheartedness and nonchalance of the inhabitants of that country and the 'iron rule' of war and conquest, between the soft and sentimental ring of their dialects and the heroic accents of *Nibelungentreue*, between their excessive admiration for waltz-enchanted soubrettes and the worship of the god Mars. And with equal power this writer conveys the terror and pity of the creature helplessly caught in a tragedy and unable to recognize his own guilt.

This theme, it seems, has ceased to be a provincial one. I know of no other which throws so much light on the particular character of our time. We are imbued with the idea that it is greatness and strength of personalities which account for dramatic events, achievements and catastrophes alike, and that it is in mediocrity that safety lies. In that we are the involuntary heirs of the Renaissance and of Romanticism. We deplore that a man like Hitler ever came to power. But behind our regret may lurk a suspicion that he was a 'great man' after all; an evil genius, but a genius nevertheless. For we judge by the spectacular consequences of his dominion. We have not yet grasped the demonic possibilities of mediocrity. We believe that the only appropriate partner of Mephisto is a genius. It was Karl Kraus who discovered to what satanic heights inferiority may rise. He anticipated Hitler long before anyone knew his name.

Thus, through him, the theme of literature has undergone a radical change. In bygone days it was the business of the imagination to create within the world of the senses the image and symbol capable of expressing the wealth of inner experience. It was in art that man, dissatisfied with the triviality of everyday existence, found a reality more adequate to what he felt to be the truth of his life. To-day it is different: our task—and difficulty—is rather to find within ourselves something big enough to be charged with the responsibility for the monstrous dimensions of our external reality. In a better age the disaster of the world which we seem to have caused, and the still greater destruction which we face, would have been the doing of mythological creatures, enemies of mankind, hostile gods who tear open the mountains and burn the habitations

o

of men in the volcanic fire; of giants, cyclops and sinister magicians who have robbed Olympus of its secrets and with them threaten to extinguish life. In our uncanny and more enlightened epoch all this is merely the result of a conspiracy of sobriety, scientific planning, mediocrity and human insignificance. The demonstration of this terrifying incongruousness fills the pages of *The Last Days of Mankind*. Its heroes are troglodytes living in the skyscrapers of history, barbarians having at their disposal all the amenities and high explosives of technical progress, fishmongers acting the role of Nelsons, ammunition salesmen crossing Rubicons and hired scribblers tapping out on their machines the heroic phrases of the bards. And there are, on the more passive and pathetic side, their victims on active service: farm labourers with a few weeks of battle training, honest-to-goodness little people with pensionable salaries and paid holidays, decent folk whose imagination is unable to grasp even a microscopic fragment of the horror which they are commanded to inflict upon the world by faithfully serving machines, pulling levers and pressing buttons. And the effects are registered by men whose imagination is blunted and whose moral judgment is corrupted by the insidious poison of journalistic language which has emptied the word of all its reality and meaning.

This is Karl Kraus's thesis: If our imagination sufficed to visualize the reality behind the news column of one morning paper, this reality would not and could not exist. And if one man's imagination were inspired by it and gave expression to it, all the tragedies of ancient Greece would dwindle into idyllic sentimentalities before such a drama of human corruption and human agony. But such an imagination does not exist, and therefore there exists such a reality; there exists such a reality, and therefore no such imagination. This is the last wonder of the world, and compared to it all the others are children's playthings. Man has achieved a technical superiority over himself which threatens him with unavoidable disaster. The combined employment of technique and 'man-power' has got the better of the power of his humanity. Between his technical mastery (which would have terrified Prometheus) and his imagination (which not even pigmies could eke out to make from it fairy tales for their children), he has fixed a gulf spacious enough for Armageddon to take place.

There were in German literature men before, and contemporary with, Karl Kraus who had recognized the immense dangers, indeed the apocalyptic character, of their age and whose works were prompted by this sense of urgency; there were, for instance, Nietzsche and Stefan George. But with them the experience of their time inspired the attempt to transcend it in the dimension of time itself, and to redeem it in the vision of a future which would be greatness itself and purity of spirit. Karl Kraus, on the other hand, insisted upon the timeless significance of the contemporary scene. For him it was not a cacophonous overture, played in the dark, before the curtain rises on a stage of light; it was itself the drama, redeemable not through the expectation of future goodness, but only through the faithful realization of present evil. He spiritualized the raw material of experience which his time offered. His method was quotation. He took the material of experience as it was: the coffee-house conversation of the journalists, the stock exchange rendezvous of the racketeers, the fragments of talk which struck his ear in the streets of Vienna, the judgments of the law courts, the leading articles of the newspapers and the chatter of their readers— in fact, all that looks like the triviality of daily life—and endowed it with a soul: an anti-soul, as it were. This he achieved not by recasting, shaping, modifying the experience. He quoted verbatim. 'The most improbable deeds which are here reported,' he says in the preface to *The Last Days of Mankind*, 'really happened; I have registered only what was done. The most improbable conversations which are here conducted, took place; exaggerations and inventions are quotations. . . . Documents assume a living shape, reports come to life as persons, persons die as leading articles. The feuilleton is given a mouth to deliver itself as a monologue; phrases walk on two legs—men kept only one. Inflections of voices rush and rustle through our days and grow into the chorus of the unholy plot. People who have lived amidst mankind and have survived it, the executive organs and spokesmen of an age that has no flesh but blood, no blood but ink, are reduced to shadows and marionettes, that is, to the form befitting their busy sham-existences. Cyphers and lemurs, masks of the tragic carnival, have living names because this must be so, and because nothing is accidental in this time conditioned by chance. This gives nobody the right to regard it as a local affair. Even the noises of a Viennese rush-hour are directed from a cosmic point.' He achieves the effect of satire, drama, tragedy, not merely by effectively arranging the material of experience, but by taking it as it is and transferring it into another medium.

This procedure resembles an experiment usually performed for schoolboys by their physics masters. A little balloon, sealed, but not inflated, an inconspicuous shrivelled little object, is put under a bell-jar which is then emptied of its content of air. The minute quantity of air which had remained in the shrivelled balloon, now, in the new medium, suffices to make it into a full-blown globe. The material of the balloon has not changed, but its appearance and shape are decisively transformed.

In the work of Karl Kraus something similar takes place. He transfers his characters, all these leader-writers and leader-readers, shareholders and opinion-makers, war-reporters and truth-distorters, into a medium the laws of which issue 'from a cosmic point'. And there he shows, on a full-blown and transparent object, the diabolic structure of what before looked merely like innocuous mediocrity and banality. Thus his apocalypse has found its appointed executors. In the absence of an accepted mythology it is Tom, Dick and Harry who charge through the world as apocalyptic horsemen.

What then is that 'cosmic point' with its strange perspective which, seemingly distorting all things, yet makes them appear in their true significance? It is the point of intersection where nature and spirit meet, the crux of the universe and the focal point of the soul of a creature made in God's image. Karl Kraus's satirical work tells the story of the Fall once more in all its fearful actuality.

Through *The Last Days* go, as the chorus of the tragedy, two figures called *The Optimist* and *The Grumbler*. The Grumbler is the author himself, and by choosing this denigrating name he has made ironical use of a title bestowed upon him by some of his contemporaries. The Optimist is the reasonable man (and it is important that he is not satirically caricatured, but is throughout the Grumbler's intelligent partner), showing a great deal of common sense, psychological understanding and historical appreciation. He is balanced, while the Grumbler is desperate. The Optimist always sees both sides of a problem, whereas the Grumbler refuses to learn how to squint. The Grumbler speaks in eschatological terms, the Optimist in terms of history. 'I don't know what you are talking about,' the Optimist would say, 'our situation is far from being unique. Life has always been precarious; there has always been a crisis.' 'Profound, indeed,' the Grumbler would reply, 'if only I did not have the uneasy feeling that you use your knowledge as an excuse to behave as though there were no crisis at all.' 'We have lived in illusory and artificial safety up till now,' the Optimist would assert, 'and what we witness is a return to normal.' 'No,' would be the Grumbler's retort, '*you* have lived in illusory and artificial safety, and what *I* witness is a deadly complication of abnormality.'

The dialectic of these dialogues consists in the perpetual juxta-position of psychological understanding and moral experience. In a world abounding with psychological penetration and analytical literature, the work of Karl Kraus was of the greatest value for a generation lost in a welter of relativities. He who spent hours over the decision where to put a comma would yet be able to decide instantly on a moral issue. His moral word was 'Yes, yes', or 'No, no', but his sentences were complex organisms of the subtlest structure. In the moral sphere where most contemporary writers would lose their way in a tangle of problems he would see none; but he would prove to all of them that they had given too little thought to the sound of their words and to the rhythm and syntax of their sentences. And what, above all, he taught those who were able to hear him, was the meaning and extent of moral responsibility. His unfailing and instinctive response to what are 'strictly moral' questions was the result of his having pondered over them endlessly in 'strictly amoral' fields: in the sphere of aesthetics and language. *Language*—the collection of his essays on this subject—is probably the profoundest book that exists on style and the use of German. It is the work of an artist and moralist, not of a pedant and grammarian. There it becomes clear that the ruthlessness of his moral judgment springs from the delicate tact and care which he shows in his dealings with the 'crystallized tradition of the spirit of man'. To his impatience with the wrongdoers corresponds his infinite patience with language, and to his relentless ethical determination his compassion for the maltreated word. He knew what few critics of his time knew: that the aesthetic judgment is a moral judgment if it is to be more than the diffuse reaction of a vaguely refined sensitivity. For him *De gustibus non est disputandum* was an alarming advertisement of a *moral* bankruptcy. He saw the connection between maltreated words and the maltreatment of human souls and bodies, and he avenged lives by restoring words to their state of integrity, health and vigour in which, of their own accord, they could 'speak to the yet unknowing world how these things came about'. Through him it is language itself that opens its mouth and speaks to those who use it deceitfully: 'But ye are forgers of lies, ye are all physicians of no value'.

4

In one of the dialogues with the Optimist, the Grumbler asserts that Germany and Austria were more deeply affected by the corruption of the spirit than the West. The corruption of England, for instance, could not suffice to produce and maintain a satirist.

> THE GRUMBLER: There is no English satirist.
> THE OPTIMIST: Bernard Shaw.
> THE GRUMBLER: Precisely.

The kind of literary work commonly called 'satire' is rather vaguely defined. If, for instance, Heinrich Heine and Bernard Shaw are satirists, then one must find a different name for Karl Kraus. If, however, he is a satirist—and I believe he is the first European satirist since Swift—then Heine and Shaw are merely earnest jesters. The difference lies in the nature of their negative enthusiasm. Is its *positive* pole love, or sentimentality? Faith, or an expectation? An idea, or an intellectual concept? Is its creation therefore the other side of poetry, or of *belles-lettres* (though they may be rhymed as in the case of Heine, or concerned with social reforms as in the case of Shaw)? Is the writer of satires a wit thriving on the foolishness of society, or a genius whose soul is wounded by the sinfulness of his age?

Schiller, in his essay *Ueber naive und sentimentalische Dichtung*, says of the true satirist that he would have been a great poet had 'the moral perversity of his age not filled his heart with bitterness'. And Karl Kraus did write poetry, published in the nine volumes of *Worte in Versen*. If there could be any doubt left about the authenticity of his satire, it would be removed by his lyrical utterances. They set in relief the works of hate against a background of light. As the scope of his satirical work widened and the darkness of its world deepened, so his poetic genius gained in simplicity and spontaneity, his lyrical work in tenderness and affection. It shows his satire to be merely the imploring gesture of a lover who seeks to guard what he loves against the evil of the world closing in upon it. He is not a 'modern' poet. His subjects, images, rhymes and rhythms are traditional. His poems are about love and hatred, memories of childhood and visions of dreams, waterfalls, winter and spring, the green at a dusty roadside, the eyes of an old beggar-woman, the loyalty of a dog, *Le papillon est mort*, and *Ein toter Tag schlägt seine Augen auf.* . . . But they are made of brittler stuff than their traditional appearance would suggest. Their material seems purified in the purgatory of the satirist's experience, and hardened by the determination of one who was called to defend what is left of the innocence of the world.

Karl Kraus said of himself:

> Nicht Gott, nur alles leugn' ich, was ihn leugnet,
> Und wenn er will, ist alles wunderbar.

At the end of *The Last Days of Mankind* the voice of the Lord sounds through the silence of a horribly devastated scene. The voice speaks the words attributed to the old Emperor of Austria who died during the Great War: *Ich habe es nicht gewollt.* The *satirist* Karl Kraus brought to life a world whose every breath was a denial of God's designs, and was the chaos that decided that His will should not be done. The *poet* Karl Kraus praised the order of a universe in which all is well if only He wills it so. It was an Austrian theme with which Karl Kraus began. It was the theme of our world with which he ended: the faith that lies on the other side of despair.

REFERENCES

EXCEPT for quotations from Goethe and Nietzsche, all references are to individually specified works. Where no translator is mentioned, the translations are my own.

In the case of Nietzsche all references are to the *Musarion-Ausgabe* of his works, twenty-three volumes, Munich, 1922, abbreviated M.A.

With so many editions of Goethe in existence, I have tried to enable the reader to look up the context of the quoted passages in any edition available to him, by giving chapter, act, scene or numbered verse of the individual work. Where this method has proved impossible, references are to the *Jubiläums-Ausgabe* of Goethe's works, forty volumes, Stuttgart and Berlin, abbreviated J.A., or the large *Grossherzogin Sophie von Sachsen-Ausgabe*, four sections, Weimar, 1887, abbreviated W.A. Poems are quoted from Goethe's *Gedichte in zeitlicher Folge*, two volumes, Leipzig, 1920, abbreviated P. For the sake of the particular accuracy demanded by the context I have avoided English verse renderings of Goethe's poetry. Letters and conversations are specified, either in the text itself or in the following notes, only by their dates. The same applies to letters of Nietzsche and Burckhardt, and to letters or diary notes of Franz Kafka.

The biographical and critical literature on the subjects of these essays is so vast that even a selective bibliography would almost fill a volume of its own. Apologies are offered for the unavoidable omission.

I

GOETHE AND THE IDEA OF SCIENTIFIC TRUTH

[1] J.A., XXX, 18–31, 388–92.
[2] J.A., XXVI, 314–15.
[3] J.A., XXVII, 5.
[4] P., II, 224.
[5] *Goethes Schriften zur Naturwissenschaft*, Berlin, 1926, I, xxxviii–ix (Introduction by Richard Müller-Freienfeld).
[6] J.A., XXXIX, 294–5.
[7] *Goethes Schriften zur Naturwissenschaft*, I, xl.
[8] J.A., XXXIX, 312–13.
[9] Ibid., 251.
[10] Ibid., 249–50.
[11] Ibid., 131.
[12] Conversation with Kielmayer, September, 1797.
[13] P., II, 56.
[14] Ibid., 381.
[15] J.A., XXXIX, 374.

[16] Ibid., 81.
[17] Ibid., 64.
[18] Ibid., 64.
[19] J.A., XL, 61.
[20] Ibid., 63.
[21] J.A., XXXIX, 72.
[22] J.A., XL, 200.
[23] Ibid., 202.
[24] W.A., 3, VI, 59.
[25] J.A., XXXIX, 106.
[26] Ibid., 34.
[27] J.A., IV, 242.
[28] J.A., XXXIX, 58.
[29] Ibid., 72.
[30] Ibid., 72.
[31] J.A., XL, 71.
[32] J.A., XXXIX, 70.
[33] J.A., XXXV, 325.
[34] J.A., IV, 229.
[35] J.A., XXXIX, 35.
[36] Ibid., 68.
[37] Ibid., 76.
[38] *Wandlungen in den Grundlagen der Naturwissenschaft*, Zürich, 1947, 65.
[39] J.A., XXXIX, 374.
[40] J.A., XXXV, 305.

II

GOETHE AND THE AVOIDANCE OF TRAGEDY

[1] Karl Jaspers, *Unsere Zukunft und Goethe*, Zürich, 1948, 22.
[2] Letter to Schiller, December 9th, 1797.
[3] Act IV, scene 5.
[4] March 17th, 1832.
[5] *Sämtliche Werke*, in six volumes, Berlin, 1923, IV, 124. Translation, with a slight modification of my own in the last line, by J. B. Leishman, *Selected Poems of Friedrich Hölderlin*, London, 1944, 98.
[6] J.A., XXVIII, 251.
[7] Book II, chapter 2, J.A., XIX, 191, 192.
[8] *Faust II*, verses—in the numbering including both parts—11300-3.
[9] *Faust I*, verse 3217.
[10] Ibid., verses 1745-6.
[11] Ibid., verse 1700.
[12] Ibid., verses 3249-50.
[13] Ibid., verse 324.
[14] *Faust II*, verse 11585.

[15] Ibid., verse 11586.
[16] Ibid., verses 11936–7.
[17] To Karl Ernst Schubarth, November 3rd, 1820.
[18] *Faust II*, verses 11404–07.

III

BURCKHARDT AND NIETZSCHE

[1] *Jakob Burckhardt-Gesamtausgabe*, Stuttgart, Berlin und Leipzig, 1930, V, 21, 22.
[2] Burckhardt's letter to Riggenbach, August 28th, 1838.
[3] *Gesamtausgabe*, VIII, 3.
[4] Ibid., V, 215.
[5] Ibid., VII, 14.
[6] Ibid., VII, 15, 16.
[7] Ibid., VII, 15.
[8] *Maximen und Reflexionen*, J.A., XXXVIII, 261.
[9] Burckhardt's letter to Willibald Beyschlag, June 14th, 1842.
[10] *Gesamtausgabe*, VIII, 5.
[11] Ibid., VII, 52.
[12] Ibid., VII, 2.
[13] Ibid., VII, 1.
[14] Ibid.
[15] Ibid., VII, 2.
[16] Nietzsche's letter to Gersdorff, November 7th, 1870.
[17] Schopenhauer, *Sämmtliche Werke*, Grossherzog Wilhelm Ernst Ausgabe, Leipzig, II, 1217–19.
[18] *Gesamtausgabe*, VII, 3.
[19] Ibid.
[20] M.A., III, 138.
[21] Nietzsche's letter to Gersdorff, November 7th, 1870.
[22] Burckhardt's letter to Schauenburg, March 5th, 1846.
[23] *Gesamtausgabe*, VII, 28.
[24] M.A., VII, 369.
[25] M.A., XV, 245, 246.
[26] Nietzsche's letter to Burckhardt, January 6th, 1889, first published in Edgar Salin, *Jakob Burckhardt und Nietzsche*, Basle, 1938, 227.
[27] Ibid., 226.
[28] *Gesamtausgabe*, VII, 6, 7.
[29] Ibid., 202.
[30] Burckhardt's letter to Preen, June 16th, 1888.
[31] Burckhardt's letter to Alioth, November 19th, 1881.
[32] Burckhardt's letter to Riggenbach, December 12th, 1838.
[33] Burckhardt's letter to Brenner, March 16th, 1865.
[34] *Gesamtausgabe*, VII, 126.
[35] H. Gelzer, *Ausgewählte kleine Schriften*, Leipzig, 1907, 325.

IV

NIETZSCHE AND GOETHE

[1] J.A., XXXVII, 102–05.
[2] M.A., VII, 204.
[3] M.A., XVII, 364.
[4] *Wilhelm Meisters Wanderjahre*, Book I, chapter 6, J.A., XIX, 72.
[5] Ibid., chapter 10, J.A., XIX, 132.
[6] Ibid., 146.
[7] *Faust II*, verses 11127–42.
[8] March 17th, 1832.
[9] J.A., XXXVII, 104.
[10] J.A., V, 247, 248.
[11] M.A., XIX, 85.
[12] *Wilhelm Meisters Wanderjahre*, Book I, chapter 10, J.A., XIX, 138, 139.
[13] M.A., XVI, 235.
[14] M.A., XVII, 149, 150.
[15] J.A., XXXVIII, 266.
[16] Ibid.
[17] J.A., IV, 219.
[18] *Wilhelm Meisters Wanderjahre*, Book III, chapter 13, J.A., XX, 187.
[19] M.A., XVII, 48.
[20] M.A., VII, 207.
[21] Ibid., 349.
[22] J.A., XXVII, 175.
[23] P., II, 20.
[24] Ibid., 39.
[25] M.A., III, 365.
[26] M.A., XVI, 8.
[27] M.A., XVII, 150.
[28] *Faust II*, verses 11600–03.
[29] Ibid., verses 7438–9.
[30] Ibid., verses 11404–7.
[31] P., II, 66.
[32] M.A., XVII, 344.
[33] M.A., IX, 174, 175.
[34] M.A., XIV, 109.
[35] M.A., XXI, 73.
[36] M.A., IX, 55, 56.
[37] Ibid., 245.
[38] M.A., III, 247.
[39] M.A., IX, 448.
[40] Ibid., 252.
[41] M.A., XXI, 81.
[42] Ibid.
[43] M.A., XVIII, 65.
[44] M.A., XIV, 11.

[45] *Faust II*, verses 6222-7, 6246-8.
[46] M.A., XVII, 346.
[47] M.A., XIX, 352.

v

RILKE AND NIETZSCHE

WITH A DISCOURSE ON THOUGHT, BELIEF AND POETRY

[1] T. S. Eliot, *Selected Essays* (1917-32), London, 1948, 141.
[2] Ibid., 135.
[3] Ibid., 13.
[4] Ibid., 137.
[5] Ibid., 138.
[6] First published in a Berlin literary journal and reprinted in *Erzählungen und Skizzen aus der Frühzeit*, Leipzig, 1930, 347-56.
[7] *Ewald Tragy*, Munich, 1929-30.
[8] Unpublished, but partly quoted in Ruth Mövius, *Rainer Maria Rilkes Stundenbuch, Entstehung und Gehalt*, Leipzig, 1937, and in M. Sievers, *Die biblischen Motive in der Dichtung Rainer Maria Rilkes*, Berlin, 1938.
[9] Lou Andreas-Salomé, *Friedrich Nietzsche in seinen Werken*, Wien, 1894.
[10] *Das Florenzer Tagebuch*, published together with other diaries in *Tagebücher aus der Frühzeit*, Leipzig, 1942.
[11] *Ausgewählte Werke*, Leipzig, 1938, I, 14.
[12] Ibid., 17.
[13] M.A., XX, 158.
[14] Letter to Malwida von Meysenbug, January 14th, 1880.
[15] *Tagebücher aus der Frühzeit*, 92.
[16] M.A., XXI, 248.
[17] M.A., XIX, 359, 365. Cf. also Nietzsche on the Dionysian Goethe, M.A., XVII, 149, 150.
[18] Letter to Ellen Key, quoted in Paul Zech, *Rainer Maria Rilke: Der Mensch und das Werk*, Dresden, 1930, 118, 119.
[19] *Tagebücher aus der Frühzeit*, 38.
[20] Cf. Rilke, *Sonnets to Orpheus*, I, III, and Nietzsche, M.A., XII, 156, 157; XIX, 228.
[21] M.A., XIII, 237.
[22] *Tagebücher aus der Frühzeit*, 89.
[23] M.A., XX, 248.
[24] *Ausgewählte Werke*, I, 176.
[25] M.A., XX, 152.
[26] *Ausgewählte Werke*, I, 143.
[27] M.A., XXI, 251.
[28] *Briefe*, Wiesbaden, 1950, II, 308-11.
[29] Ibid., 382, 407.
[30] *Selected Essays*, 135.
[31] Ibid., 134.
[32] Ibid., 135 (my italics).

[33] Hegel, *Werke*, Berlin, 1835, X$_3$, 243, and X$_1$, 16.
[34] *Rainer Maria Rilke*, Cambridge, 1952.
[35] *Briefe*, II, 395.
[36] *Ausgewählte Werke*, II, 297.
[37] M.A., XIV, 80.
[38] M.A., XII, 157.
[39] *Briefe*, II, 480.
[40] M.A., XIV, 234.
[41] *Briefe*, II, 405.
[42] *Tagebücher aus der Frühzeit*, 71.
[43] M.A., XIV, 121, 125.
[44] M.A., XIV, 187.
[45] Ibid., 191, 180.
[46] Cf. J. F. Angelloz, *Rainer Maria Rilke*, Paris, 1936, 3.
[47] M.A., XIII, 97, 11.
[48] *Ausgewählte Werke*, I, 364, 365.
[49] *Briefwechsel in Gedichten mit Erika Mitterer*, Wiesbaden, 1950, 56.
[50] M.A., XIV, 119.
[51] *Briefe*, II, 481–3.
[52] M.A., XIV, 121.
[53] M.A., XI, 79.
[54] *Ideen* 13, Athenäum III, Berlin, 1800.
[55] *Werke*, ed. Kluckhohn, III, 357.
[56] M.A., XIII, 166.
[57] M.A., XX, 190.
[58] M.A., III, 362, 363.
[59] M.A., XIX, 229.
[60] Ibid., 228.
[61] M.A., III, 10.

VI

OSWALD SPENGLER AND THE PREDICAMENT OF THE HISTORICAL IMAGINATION

[1] First volume: *Der Untergang des Abendlandes—Gestalt und Wirklichkeit*, Munich, 1918. Second volume: *Der Untergang des Abendlandes—Welthistorische Perspektiven* Munich, 1922. Authorized English translation by Charles Francis Atkinson: *The Decline of the West*, London, first volume: *Form and Actuality*; second volume: *Perspectives of World-History*. My references are to the English edition to which I am also indebted for the—sometimes modified—translations.
[2] I, 37.
[3] I, 44.
[4] I, 293.
[5] I, 41.
[6] I, 25.
[7] Arnold Toynbee, *Civilization on Trial*, Oxford, 1948, 10.
[8] I, 8–10.

[9] *Civilization on Trial*, 9–10.
[10] I, 29.
[11] E. H. Carr, *The New Society*, London, 1951, 19.
[12] I, 35.
[13] I, 47.
[14] Cf. I, 23.

VII

THE WORLD OF FRANZ KAFKA

[1] Franz Kafka, *Gesammelte Schriften*, edited by Max Brod, Prague, 1937, VI, 108. The present, rather confused, state of Kafka editions is unavoidably reflected in my references. Whenever possible, I refer to English translations of his works. Frequently, however, I had to modify the English text, partly for the sake of greater accuracy and partly for the sake of the particular emphasis required in the context of my discussion. Where my references are to the original, the translations are my own.
[2] *The Great Wall of China*, translated by Willa and Edwin Muir, London, 1946, 151.
[3] Ibid., 140.
[4] *Gesammelte Schriften*, VI, 237.
[5] *The Great Wall of China*, 145.
[6] *The Castle*, translated by Willa and Edwin Muir, London, 1947, 6.
[7] *Gesammelte Schriften*, VI, 231.
[8] M.A., XIV, 179.
[9] Ibid., XIV, 187.
[10] Ibid., XVIII, 45.
[11] *Gesammelte Schriften*, VI, 108.
[12] *The Great Wall of China*, 129.
[13] Ibid., 132.
[14] *The Castle*, 79.
[15] Ibid., 38.
[16] Ibid., 95.
[17] Ibid., 150.
[18] *The Great Wall of China*, 136.
[19] Ibid., 133.
[20] Ibid., 145.
[21] Ibid., 135.
[22] *The Castle*, 98.
[23] Ibid., 316, in Max Brod's 'Additional Note'.
[24] Ibid., 317.
[25] *Gesammelte Schriften*, IV, 380, 381.
[26] *The Castle*, 269.
[27] Ibid., 21.
[28] Ibid., 317.
[29] Ibid., 15.
[30] Ibid., 132, 133.

[31] Quoted by Max Brod as motto to *Franz Kafka*, A Biography, translated by G. Humphreys Roberts, London, 1947.

[32] *The Great Wall of China*, 157.

[33] Ibid., 149.

[34] *Gesammelte Schriften*, IV, 353.

[35] Ibid., 355.

[36] Ibid., 300.

[37] Ibid., 308, 309.

[38] *The Great Wall of China*, 146.

[39] *Gesammelte Schriften*, IV, 428.